Mosaic Leadership

Mosaic Leadership

African, Asian, Middle Eastern and Indigenous Perspectives

Edited by

Prof. Jonathan Passmore

Dr. Badri Bajaj

Dr. Mongezi C Makhalima

WILEY

This edition first published 2026

Registered Offices
John Wiley & Sons, Inc., 111 River Street, Hoboken, NJ 07030, USA
John Wiley & Sons Ltd, The Atrium, Southern Gate, Chichester, West Sussex, PO22 8SQ, UK

For details of our global editorial offices, customer services, and more information about Wiley products visit us at www.wiley.com.

The manufacturer's authorized representative according to the EU General Product Safety Regulation is Wiley-VCH GmbH, Boschstr. 12, 69469 Weinheim, Germany, e-mail: Product_Safety@wiley.com.

Wiley also publishes its books in a variety of electronic formats and by print-on-demand. Some content that appears in standard print versions of this book may not be available in other formats.

Library of Congress Cataloging-in-Publication Data
Names: Passmore, Jonathan editor | Bajaj, Badri editor | Makhalima, Mongezi C editor
Title: Mosaic Leadership: African, Asian, Middle Eastern and Indigenous Perspectives / edited by Prof. Jonathan Passmore, Badri Bajaj, Dr. Mongezi C Makhalima.
Description: Hoboken, NJ : John Wiley & Sons, 2026. | Includes index.
Identifiers: LCCN 2025019873 (print) | LCCN 2025019874 (ebook) | ISBN 9781394365135 paperback | ISBN 9781394365159 adobe pdf | ISBN 9781394365142 epub
Subjects: LCSH: Leadership–Cross-cultural studies | Leadership–Developing counties | Multiculturalism–Developing countries
Classification: LCC HD57.7 .M675 2026 (print) | LCC HD57.7 (ebook) | DDC 658.4009172/4–dc23/eng/20250820
LC record available at https://lccn.loc.gov/2025019873
LC ebook record available at https://lccn.loc.gov/2025019874

Cover Design: Wiley
Cover Images: © TK

Set in 10/12pt Warnock Pro by Straive, Pondicherry, India

Contents

Foreword

Fons Trompenaars

Modern leadership needs personnel who can handle complexity, manage conflicts and show tolerance for diversity. Modern leadership requires new approaches because traditional Western leadership models are no longer suffice for today's global technological age and social transformation. This book represents an immediate reaction to this necessary condition. Through decoloniality, the book invites readers to explore new leadership possibilities by using leadership examples from African and Asian societies as well as Islamic communities and Indigenous peoples.

The Dilemma Reconciliation Process (DRP) stands as the central framework that guides us towards surpassing binary thinking. Through DRP, we integrate conflicting values into unified, advanced solutions instead of simply selecting between them. Today's interconnected global environment requires leaders to harmonise opposites, such as traditional frameworks and modern innovations as well as personal autonomy with collective progress, while preserving existing stability. Through its framework, leaders find ways to manage conflicting positions and develop solutions that respect multiple viewpoints.

The publication starts with a critical analysis of decoloniality, which encourages readers to confront the dominance of Eurocentric leadership theory. The book questions fundamental elements within standard leadership models, which originated from Western thought. The West African symbol Sankofa guides us to retrieve forgotten knowledge to build a brighter future that celebrates diverse human heritage.

The book continues with leaders and cultural insights from diverse regions. The book investigates leadership approaches through regional cultural lenses, while delivering deep understanding through cultural-based leadership practices. The African concept of Ubuntu establishes interconnectedness as its core principle while offering an alternative to Western leadership models that emphasise competitive individualism.

Through the study, we learn about Islamic perspectives, including the Rahmah mode, which develops compassionate leadership, and First Nations' 'Deep Listening' principle, which focuses on relationality. These approaches represent active living systems that have guided communities throughout numerous generations.

This book stands out by focusing on both analysis through critique and practical application. The publication goes beyond analysing Western-centric models because it delivers real-world leadership development frameworks that combine diverse perspectives. The DRP stands out as a key component of this initiative by providing practical steps that leaders can follow to handle difficult trade-offs and develop creative solutions. Through DRP, leaders gain the ability to accomplish reconciliation as a core value by treating all perspectives with respect.

The book's structure reflects its mission. The initial sections explore decoloniality alongside leadership development, followed by an analytical study of present leadership paradigms. Every chapter offers an extensive look at particular cultural approaches while providing both theoretical understanding and practical examples.

The Japanese philosophy of Kaizen leadership demonstrates how continuous improvement requires both small steps and team-based implementation. Mengzi's Five Virtues presents Confucian ethics as a framework for ethical leadership through moral principles. This book presents Ubuntu as well as Gacica leadership, which emphasises the African leadership approach while highlighting community reconciliation and healing as its main priorities.

The last chapter of the book creates a vision for the future direction of leadership development. The text pushes for genuine inclusion by rejecting superficial diversity integration in leadership development theory and practice. The author advocates for new leadership dynamics between collaborators, who will work together to treat all knowledge systems as equally valid and legitimate. The proposal does not reject Western models but instead plans to expand them for more inclusive and fair leadership approaches.

Throughout the upcoming chapters, you will encounter thoughts that will challenge your current beliefs while helping you see things from different perspectives and understand the complexity of our world. The text motivates readers to take action by applying these leadership insights to their own leadership roles, while building a fairer, more sustainable and peaceful future.

The publication presents itself as an advocacy text rather than a simple collection of academic work. Through this book, the authors invite readers to decolonise their thinking, while expanding their perspectives and leading others with wisdom, courage and compassion. This book calls for the resolution of current dilemmas by opposing fragmentation and instead unifying around commonalities between different entities.

With Sankofa, we are reminded to return and retrieve the forgotten things of our past so we can create a future that celebrates the diverse heritage of our human experience. With this book as your reference, you will learn how to achieve new leadership methods. We can build a fresh leadership model together that combines equity with universality and human-centeredness.

About the Editors

Jonathan Passmore

Jonathan is a chartered psychologist and holds five degrees plus qualifications in executive coaching, coaching supervision and team coaching. He is a professor of coaching at Henley Business School and has worked in a range of senior consulting and executive roles with PWC, IBM, OPM, CoachHub and EZRA-LHH. He is a past Chair of the BPS Division of Coaching Psychology. He has published widely, with over 250 scientific papers and book chapters, and 40 books on coaching, leadership, mindfulness and I/O psychology. He is listed in the Global Gurus and Coaching Thinkers 50 lists. He coaches leaders in business, politics and sport.

Badri Bajaj

Badri is a thought leader and practitioner in coaching and well-being. He is an Associate Professor at Jaypee Institute of Information Technology, Noida, India. He is the author of *Happiness A to Z: Evidence-Based Strategies for Achieving Well-being and Fulfilment*, and the co-editor of *The Health and Wellbeing Coaches' Handbook*. He has published highly cited articles in reputed journals, newspapers and magazines. He received the '100 Best Global Coaching Leaders Award' in 2017. He has conducted training for senior management and supervisors in IT organisations, the retail sector, the Indian Navy and professional associations. He has delivered presentations in the UK, India and the USA for different types of organisations. He has contributed immensely to promoting coaching in India. He has served as President of the Board of the International Coaching Federation (ICF) Delhi-NCR Chapter for two terms (2019–2021 and 2021–2023). During his stint as the president of ICF chapter, he curated two global coaching conferences in India and secured prestigious awards for the chapter.

Mongezi C Makhalima

Mongezi is Thinkers 50 Top 50 Global Coach, a Top 40 Organizational Culture Champion. He is an organization development specialist, organizational learning expert & Executive coach with over 30 years of working with organizations and leadership in corporates and NGO's. He has recently been named one of the Top 20 Global Gurus in Leadership & Coaching.He is currently the Chairperson of the Africa Board for Coaching, Consulting and Coaching Psychology (ABCCCP), and also sits as non-executive director on several boards in the NGO, film and music sectors.

Mongezi serves as adjunct faculty with the Gordon Institute of Business Sciences, working with MBAs as well as associate faculty with Duke CE, working with executives across the world. He has served as a faculty member in the Faculty of Commerce, Law and management of the University of the Witwatersrand as well as the Wits Business School, teaching Masters and advanced programmes in leadership and coaching. He holds several degrees including a PhD in Organisational Psychology and an MA in Coaching Psychology.

Mongezi has presented and written widely on the subject of coaching, mentoring and leadership and works with clients globally and locally in organisations that include: MTN, Sasol, CITI Bank, FNB, Rio Tinto, De Beers, Vodacom, Allan-Gray Orbis, Barclays PLC amongst others.

About the Contributors

Dina Khalid AlAlami
Dina is a Center for Public Leadership Fellow at Harvard Kennedy School, with extensive experience in the government education sector. Dina's expertise lies in designing inclusive and impactful educational programmes.

Raja'a Yousef Allaho
Allaho has over 20 years of experience in consultancy, training, coaching, and mentoring. She is the founder of a leading global accredited academy for coaching and Mentoring. She has supported leaders and executives by providing training, orientation, and coaching for Kuwait and the Gulf executives.

Mbithe Anzaya
Mbithe is an executive and leadership coach with over 25 years of experience in institutional development, providing coaching, mentorship and training across Sub-Saharan Africa.

Ekhoe Ame-Ogie
Ekhoe is an executive coach. She is the Founder and Lead Coach for Uthrive by Ameo Coaching Practice and the HR Leader for Deloitte West Africa.

Suzan Bou Naseredine
Suzan is a well-being consultant, mental health researcher, author and positive psychology practitioner. She uses solution-focused coaching in her leadership work.

Laura Brearley
Laura is a creative researcher, musician and Eco Arts facilitator who specialises in intercultural, interdisciplinary and intergenerational approaches to environmental arts and education.

Frans van der Colff
Frans is a South African based in Johannesburg, an Executive Fellow at Henley Business School Africa and has worked and done research in many African countries.

Terry L. Cross
Terry is a citizen of the Seneca Nation of Indians and the founder and senior advisor emeritus of the National Indian Child Welfare Association.

Dan Qin
Qin is Associate Professor at NUCB Business School, specialising in microeconomic theory and behavioural economics.

Rose Domnick
Rose Domnick is Yup'ik, originally from Saint Mary's, Alaska, a community of 600 on the Yukon River. She was Director of Preventative Services, Behavioral Health, at the Yukon Kuskokwim Health Corporation in Bethel, Alaska.

Ray Tak-yin Hui
Ray is a Senior Lecturer in the Faculty of Business and Law at the University of Roehampton and a Professor at the NUCB Business School, specialising in employee development, coaching, and HR technology applications.

Mamoru Itoh
Mamoru is the Founder of COACH A and established the first coach training program in Japan in 1997, a master coach and the author of several books on personal development.

Mavuto Kapyepye
Mavuto fosters leadership transformation by facilitating self-discovery through coaching, mentorship and training, empowering individuals and organisations across sectors.

Saraj J. Owusu
Sarah is an Organisation Development practitioner, Integral Coach, storyteller and innovation specialist. She is cofounder of the strategic innovation consultancy, InkDot, where her focus is making innovation practical and possible through culture transformation and leadership development processes, and crafting future-fit strategies for teams and organisations globally.

Rupinder Kaur
Rupinder is a dynamic leader, a military veteran, seasoned researcher, conference speaker and passionate storyteller. She is the Founder Director of Institute of Coaching and Mentoring with a vision to build transformative and bold leaders and coaches.

Ho C. Law
Ho is an internationally renowned professor and consultant with over 40 years' experience. Ho champions mental health and social prescribing and his work has been awarded the King's Award for Voluntary Service and Social Care Award.

Changrong Lu
Changrong is Associate Professor at NUCB Business School, specialising in Asian financial cooperation policy and currency internationalisation.

Dumisani Magadlela
Dumi loves working on anything to do with human connection. He is often referred to as a "people whisperer" for his work on rehumanizing shared spaces using Ubuntu and his practice of Ubuntu Intelligence.

Lisa Mantla
Lisa has a background in advocacy and now works as a trainer and facilitator using her advocacy skills to help organisations redesign their services.

Thulasi Mohanadas
Thulasi is an ABP award-winning Business Psychologist, EMCC Senior Accredited Executive Coach and Accredited Psychotherapist with the British Association of Behavioural and Cognitive Psychotherapies.

F. K. Tia Moin
Tia is a British-Bangladeshi Muslim woman, a Chartered Coaching Psychologist, PhD (Psychology) and a Consultant Organisational Psychologist with over 20 years of experience.

Haesun Moon
Dr. Haesun Moon is a Communication Scientist and educator passionate about human-centred learning and leadership. She is the author of Coaching A to Z and creator of the Dialogic Orientation Quadrant (DOQ). Haesun founded the Canadian Centre for Brief Coaching and the Human Learning Institute and teaches at the University of Toronto and Harvard's Institute of Coaching.

Ify Nonyelu
Ify is a psychologist with global expertise in coaching, organisational design and driving transformative change.

Jean Nyiramasuhuko
Jean is a coach working mainly with NGOs and women entrepreneurs in Rwanda.

Judith Okonkwo
Judith is a Business Psychologist and Ecosystem Developer. A global thought leader, over the last decade she has been a pioneer in the development of the African Extended Reality Ecosystem. She is also cofounder of We Will Lead Africa - a storytelling platform that gathers, curates and publishes stories of everyday African leadership; and the creator of the Oríkì Leadership Development Model.

Jummy Okoya
Jummy is an Associate Professor and Dean of Institutional Equity at the University of East London and also serves as an EDI advisor at Cambridge Judge Business School and London Business School.

Decimar Ogutu
Decimar is a certified coach and past president of the ICF Kenya Chapter.

Ugochi Ossai
UGOCHI is an ICF certified PCC coach. With an MBA and a degree in languages she is today a Leadership and Teams development coach, Mentor, Christian counsellor and Public speaker.

Lyra Puspa
Lyra Puspa is the President of Vanaya & Co. and Applied Neuroscientist, focusing on organisation transformation through brain-focused coaching and neurotechnology.

Mark Rose
Mark is Distinguished Professor and Deputy Vice Chancellor, Indigenous at Deakin University. He is an Adjunct Professor and Executive Director of the Emerging Indigenous Executive Leaders' Program at the Australian Graduate School of Management at the University of New South Wales.

Rajan Sinha
Rajan is the CEO of Mantrana Consulting Pvt. Ltd. and the Managing Partner of Asia Coaching Network, LLP. A leadership Coach, he has co-authored a book, Alchemy of Change-Managing Transition Through Value-Based Leadership.

Wen Tingting
Wen is Associate Professor and Full-Time Psychological Teacher at Shanghai Communications Polytechnic, and teaches courses including 'Mental Growth and Career Development, Theory and Practice of Psychological Counseling.'

Sok-Ho Trinh
Sok-Ho is a positive and business psychologist, integrative, evidence-based executive coach, and leadership, organisational behaviour, and psychology practitioner–scholar.

Dr. Qing Wang
Qing is an associate professor in Educational and Coaching Psychology at the School of Psychology and Cognitive Science, East China Normal University (ECNU). She established the Educational Coaching Research Group (ECRG) at ECNU.

Shigetsune Yamoto
Shigetsune is a professor at NUCB Business School, specialising in Entrepreneurship and Innovation Management.

Endorsement

"As someone who has spent a lifetime helping leaders grow across cultures and contexts, I'm deeply encouraged by the vision behind Mosaic. This book brings together vital leadership insights from so many international perspectives—broadening how we understand leadership in today's complex, multipolar world. It challenges familiar assumptions while offering new frameworks rooted in wisdom, relevance, and respect. Mosaic is a timely and important contribution to the global leadership conversation."

Dr. Marshall Goldsmith is the *Thinkers50* #1 Executive Coach and New York Times bestselling author of *The Earned Life, Triggers,* and *What Got You Here Won't Get You There.*

"Intelligent, alive, and full of global texture, Mosaic Leadership challenges the habit of looking West for wisdom. It celebrates leadership as a shared human story, local in detail, universal in truth, and proves that great ideas travel both ways. Essential reading for the next chapter of global leadership".

Jon Foster-Pedley, Dean, and Associate Pro Vice Chancellor, Sub-Saharan Africa, HenleySA and University of Reading.

"Mosaic Leadership" is an essential read, offering diverse leadership models that challenge the traditional, West-centric MBA approach. By embracing global perspectives, particularly China's evolving management philosophy, it emphasizes the value of inclusivity and diversity in leadership education. This book advocates for a richer, more inclusive global dialogue in management thinking."

Prof. Ning Hao, Vice Dean of School of Psychology and Cognitive Science, East China Normal University.

1

Moving Towards a Global Perspective on Leadership

Jonathan Passmore[1], Badri Bajaj[2], & Mongezi C Makhalima[3]

[1]*Henley Business School, University of Reading, UK*
[2]*Department of Humanities & Social Sciences, Jaypee Institute of Information Technology, Noida, India*
[3]*Africa Board for Coaching, Consulting & Coaching Psychology, South Africa*
[3]*Africa Centre for Work-Based Learning, South Africa*

Introduction

This book invites readers to lift their eyes from the modern-day management textbooks, especially from the Western-centric models and the traditional business school teachings, to consider a world beyond. We start this chapter with a brief overview of the history of leadership thought from Great Man Theories, which have their roots in classical societies, with the journeys of Odysseus and the battles of Achilles, Timor and Alexander the Great.

We note how these classical ideas have created a boundary, effectively defining leadership and its implications for both business schools and organisations. We argue that while these classical ideas have value, they should not become a citadel. Instead in a global society, they should instead be seen simply as outcrops on a plain which includes a multiplicity of ideas, models and frameworks. Over recent decades, these ideas from Western business schools have multiplied, from Great Man Theories to an increasing array of frameworks and models that now inform our understanding and application of leadership.

As we move forward towards the 2030s, to a new world order, one where the Western, rules-based consensus, anchored around the USA, has changed, we ask whether a Western-driven perspective is still appropriate. Or whether these dominant models represent just variations on a linear paradigm, situated within a 20th-century

Mosaic Leadership: African, Asian, Middle Eastern and Indigenous Perspectives,
First Edition. Edited by Jonathan Passmore, Badri Bajaj, and Mongezi C Makhalima.

Published 2026 by John Wiley & Sons Ltd.

Western capitalist economy. Such an economic model is however just one way of organising people, teams and organisations. Over tens of thousands of years, humankind has drawn on different ways of organising, some of which are still reflected in Indigenous, Asian and African societies. What insights can be gained by exploring these approaches more deeply, while also looking beyond the USA and Europe to consider Southern Hemisphere, Middle Eastern and Eastern perspectives?

The remainder of this book seeks to offer two ways to think about leadership: first, by examining leadership through four different lenses: African, Asian, Middle Eastern and Indigenous and, second, by offering 30 different models, ideas and frameworks drawn from traditions which have typically received less attention in the field of leadership. Finally, we close by exploring what the future of leadership learning might look like from a globally inclusive perspective.

We hope that in doing so, university programs and organisational leadership will broaden their approaches, offering students and learners the opportunity to look beyond 20th-century Western texts to enhance and deepen their understanding of the variety, complexity and dynamic nature of leadership in a new world order, which requires an understanding of difference to achieve one's own objectives.

A History of Leadership Thought

The evolution of modern leadership thought reflects a journey through various paradigms, each contributing unique insights to our understanding of effective leadership. From early 'Great Man' Theories to emotional intelligence and leader–follower exchange, these frameworks show how leadership is becoming increasingly complex and attuned to psychological dynamics and relationships within organisations.

The Great Man Theories

One of the earliest ideas in leadership studies, the Great Man Theory, posits that leadership traits are inherent and largely unteachable. Developed in the 19th century, it was widely popularised by Scottish philosopher Thomas Carlyle, who believed that great leaders are born with qualities like charisma, courage and wisdom that predispose them to lead (Carlyle, 1841). This perspective viewed leadership as a product of specific individuals who, by their nature, rose to prominence due to these exceptional traits. While influential, the Great Man Theory's inherent limitation is its exclusionary view: it assumes that leadership is reserved for a select few, rather than a skill set that can be developed by many.

Trait Theory

By the early 20th century, the Trait Theory extended the Great Man approach by seeking to identify specific personality traits that define effective leaders. Rather than attributing leadership to fate or birthright, psychologists and researchers aimed to identify the innate characteristics—such as confidence, determination and integrity—that effective leaders commonly share. While the Trait Theory represented progress by focusing on identifiable qualities, it faced challenges. Researchers found it difficult to pinpoint a definitive set of traits that apply universally across all leadership contexts, leading to criticisms that traits alone are insufficient to explain effective leadership (Stogdill, 1948).

Behavioural and Situational Leadership

Moving beyond fixed traits, the mid-20th century saw a focus on Behavioural Theory, emphasising that leadership is based on specific behaviours that can be learned and developed. Studies by Kurt Lewin and his colleagues identified democratic, autocratic and laissez-faire leadership styles, showing that different behaviours can be effective depending on the context (Lewin et al., 1939). This represented a more democratic view, suggesting that anyone could learn to lead by adopting appropriate behaviours. However, the limitation of this theory became evident as it failed to account for the adaptability required by varying organisational situations.

This limitation was addressed by Situational Leadership Theory, developed by Paul Hersey and Kenneth Blanchard in the 1960s. This model suggests that effective leadership varies depending on the task and the readiness of followers. It emphasised that leaders must adapt their approach according to these situational variables. The Situational Leadership Theory marked a critical step forward by recognising that leadership is a dynamic process, responsive to both the needs of the team and the environment (Hersey & Blanchard, 1969).

Intelligence in Leadership: Cognitive and Emotional

As leadership research evolved, so did the understanding of intelligence as a critical component of effective leadership. Beyond cognitive intelligence, which allows leaders to solve complex problems and make informed decisions, psychologists Daniel Goleman (1995) and Howard Gardner extended the concept, recognising the existence of multiple intelligences (Gardner and Laskin, 2011). Goleman (1995) argued that emotional intelligence was more important in the workplace for leaders than the traditional intelligence quotient (IQ). EI involves the ability to recognise, understand and manage one's own emotions, as well as to recognise and influence the emotions of others. Goleman identified five key components of emotional intelligence relevant to leadership: self-awareness, self-regulation, motivation, empathy and social skills.

Emotional intelligence shifted leadership thought by recognising that leaders who connect emotionally with their followers can inspire greater loyalty, productivity and engagement. High emotional intelligence enables leaders to navigate interpersonal dynamics effectively, manage stress and adapt to changing team needs. This model was groundbreaking because it demonstrated that leadership success is not solely based on intelligence quotient (IQ) or technical skills but also on the ability to foster positive, productive relationships within the organisation.

Leader–Member Exchange Theory

Furthering the interpersonal aspect of leadership, Leader–Member Exchange (LMX) Theory emerged in the 1970s to focus on the relationships between leaders and their followers. Developed by George Graen and his colleagues, LMX theory posits that leaders form unique relationships with each team member, which can affect job satisfaction, performance and organisational loyalty (Graen & Uhl-Bien, 1995). According to LMX Theory, high-quality exchanges, characterised by mutual respect, trust and support, lead to more engaged and committed employees, whereas low-quality exchanges can foster disengagement and lower productivity.

LMX theory's emphasis on individual relationships represents a significant departure from one-size-fits-all leadership models. It highlights the importance of inclusivity, recognising that leaders must cultivate trust-based, individualised relationships to effectively motivate and support their teams. This approach has been instrumental in advancing leadership practices that value personal connections and adapt to the diverse needs of each team member.

Transformational and Servant Leadership

Building on the idea of strong interpersonal connections, Transformational Leadership theory, popularised by James MacGregor Burns and later Bernard Bass, highlights the role of inspiration, motivation and visionary thinking in leadership. Transformational leaders aim to elevate their followers' goals and inspire them to achieve more than they thought possible. By fostering an environment where innovation, trust and personal growth are prioritised, transformational leaders can drive profound organisational change (Alimo-Metcalfe & Alban-Metcalfe, 2001; Bass, 1985; Burns, 1978). Transformational leadership emphasises moral values and prioritises the well-being and development of followers, leading to stronger and more resilient organisations.

Parallel to Transformational Leadership, Servant Leadership theory, introduced by Robert Greenleaf, stresses the leader's role as a servant first and foremost. This model argues that leaders should put the needs of their followers ahead of their own, focusing on personal development, community and ethical responsibility. Servant leadership has become increasingly influential, particularly in fields that prioritise social responsibility and community building, as it encourages leaders to act with empathy, humility and a commitment to the greater good (Greenleaf, 1977).

Inclusive and Adaptive Leadership

In recent years, leadership theory has moved towards inclusive and adaptive leadership models. Inclusive leadership emphasises the importance of diversity, equity and inclusion within organisations, advocating for leaders who recognise and leverage diverse perspectives to foster a collaborative and supportive environment. This approach is particularly relevant in today's globalised workforce, where diverse backgrounds and experiences can enhance creativity and innovation.

Adaptive leadership, popularised by Ronald Heifetz, encourages leaders to be flexible, innovative and responsive to change. This model emphasises the need for leaders to navigate uncertainty, engage in constant learning and challenge established norms to solve complex problems. Adaptive leadership is especially valuable in today's fast-changing world, where leaders are often required to pivot quickly and find creative solutions to new challenges (Heifetz, 1994).

In the next section, we will explore how these models, derived mainly from Western-centric approaches, impact the development of leadership in both business schools and wider management training.

Business Schools and Management Training

Today's business schools and management training programmes draw heavily on the extensive history of leadership theories, integrating past frameworks with contemporary concepts to build leaders who can succeed in complex, modern organisations. However, this knowledge base is situated within a specific cultural context, reflecting patterns of knowledge exchange, such as peer-reviewed journal articles and New York Times Best Seller list books. But there is a world of knowledge beyond these publications that is less frequently accessed.

The predominance of Western leadership theories in business schools and management training programmes can be traced back to the institutionalisation of these models within academia and corporate practice.

Henley Business School led this changed as a centre for managemnet education followibg the Second World War, developing the first MBA program (Remenyi, 2015) and continually innovating business education. Other institutions across the Global North, followed this pattern and established business education as a distinct discipline in the later half of the 20th century, while drawing on scientific management, psychological profiling and leadership typologies that aligned with dominant socio-economic structures. As a result, Great Man Theories, Trait Theories, Behavioural Leadership and Servant Leadership have become not only the foundational pillars of leadership education but also the implicit standards against which all leadership is assessed.

Business schools, particularly those in North America and Europe, have played a central role in codifying these ideas. Institutions such as Harvard Business School, the Wharton School and INSEAD have historically shaped the curricula of business education worldwide. The case study method, pioneered at Harvard, frequently presents leadership through the lens of Western corporate executives, reinforcing a paradigm that values command, control and strategic decision-making based on hierarchical structures. Similarly, MBA programmes globally have drawn from the same corpus of leadership literature, perpetuating the dominance of these models, even in contexts where alternative leadership paradigms might be more relevant.

This process of standardisation has had profound implications. As business schools expanded their reach through partnerships, satellite campuses and online learning, they effectively exported these leadership models to diverse regions of the world. Universities in Asia, Africa and Latin America frequently adopt textbooks, frameworks and accreditation standards that originate from Western institutions, leading to a replication of these theories without critical engagement with local or indigenous leadership traditions. Accreditation bodies that oversee business education, such as the Association to Advance Collegiate Schools of Business (AACSB) and the European Foundation for Management Development (EFMD), further reinforce these dominant models through their criteria for faculty qualifications, research outputs and programme design.

Beyond academia, these traditional leadership theories have deeply influenced corporate management training and executive development. Large multinational corporations have adopted leadership development frameworks that reflect these business school teachings, reinforcing their relevance in global business culture. Leadership competency models used in talent development, for example, often stem from trait-based or behavioural leadership theories, prescribing an ideal leader archetype that aligns with Western corporate ideals. Even the language of leadership assessments—terms like 'charismatic leader', 'transformational leader' or 'servant leader'—reflects the conceptual boundaries set by these traditional frameworks.

Consulting firms, professional development institutions and leadership coaching programmes further amplify the dominance of these ideas. Firms such as McKinsey & Company, Boston Consulting Group and Deloitte frequently base their leadership development solutions on the same traditional theories taught in business schools. The result is a self-reinforcing cycle where what is taught in academia shapes corporate leadership development, and corporate leaders, in turn, validate and demand these same models in management education.

In sum, the globalisation of business education and management training has cemented traditional Western leadership models as the gold standard. This dominance has meant that alternative ways of understanding leadership—whether rooted in indigenous knowledge systems, collectivist traditions or context-specific leadership practices—are often marginalised or excluded entirely. The implications of this hegemony will be examined in the following section, where we explore the limitations and challenges of these dominant frameworks in a world that requires a broader, more inclusive understanding of leadership.

Why Is This a Problem in a Globally Connected, Diverse World?

In a Western hegemony world view, all ideas originated from Europe or 'the New World', read the USA. This meant that leadership, as it emerged as an idea in the 1900s and was then popularised by business schools from the 1950s, was dominated by a Western perspective. What might be termed McDonaldisation of leadership thought. While there are different models, like 'Chicken Burger', 'Big Mac' and 'Filet o-Fish', they share a similar world view. By stepping beyond this, an alternative narrative of what constitutes leadership and how it can be developed can emerge.

The dominance of Western leadership theories in business education and corporate training is problematic in a world that is increasingly interconnected, diverse and complex. Leadership does not operate within a vacuum but is deeply embedded in cultural, social and historical contexts. The assumption that leadership models developed in one part of the world can be universally applied not only marginalises non-Western perspectives but also diminishes the effectiveness of leadership practices in diverse environments.

One key issue is cultural misalignment. Leadership, as understood in many non-Western societies, often emphasises communal decision-making, relational accountability and contextual wisdom—qualities that are often overlooked or undervalued in dominant Western theories. For example, Ubuntu leadership in African contexts prioritises collective well-being and interconnectedness, whereas Confucian leadership in East Asia places emphasis on harmony, respect and moral duty. By centring on Western frameworks, business schools and corporate leadership programmes risk imposing models that do not align with local values and organisational dynamics, leading to ineffective leadership practices in non-Western settings.

Another challenge is the reinforcement of hierarchical and individualistic leadership paradigms. Many traditional Western leadership theories, particularly Great Man and Trait Theories, focus on the individual leader's qualities, vision and decision-making abilities. While this may be effective in some contexts, it disregards more distributed, collaborative or servant-oriented leadership models that exist in many cultures. This narrow definition of leadership discourages alternative approaches that may be more sustainable, equitable and community-driven.

Moreover, the one-size-fits-all approach to leadership development fails to acknowledge the diverse challenges that leaders face in different regions. Leadership in a multinational corporation navigating regulatory complexities across jurisdictions is fundamentally different from leadership in a grassroots organisation working to empower marginalised communities. The assumption that a single framework can address all these scenarios reduces the adaptability and responsiveness of leaders, making them ill-equipped to tackle real-world complexities.

The lack of inclusivity in leadership education also has implications for representation and equity. As business schools continue to promote and reward research that aligns with dominant Western paradigms, scholars and practitioners from under-represented backgrounds often struggle to have their work recognised. This exclusion not only limits the breadth of leadership scholarship but also perpetuates a cycle in which Western-centric ideas are continuously reinforced, while alternative viewpoints remain on the margins.

The corporate implications of this hegemony are profound. Organisations operating in diverse markets require leadership approaches that reflect the lived experiences and values of their employees, customers and stakeholders. The imposition of rigid Western leadership models can create disconnects between leadership expectations and actual organisational culture, leading to disengagement, inefficiency and even conflict. In contrast, organisations that embrace a broader range of leadership perspectives tend to foster more inclusive, innovative and adaptive cultures.

In a globally connected world, the ability to integrate multiple leadership paradigms is not just a moral imperative but also a strategic necessity. The challenges of climate change, economic inequality and political instability require leadership that is contextually aware, ethically grounded and culturally responsive. The continued dominance of Western leadership theories limits the potential for more holistic, inclusive and effective leadership solutions.

In the next section, we will explore how leadership education and corporate training can be decolonised to better reflect the diverse realities of leadership across the world.

Alternative Thinking

Decolonising the syllabus will, to many, sound like a threat. Threats often lead to reactive responses and, in extreme cases, individuals, organisations and governments criticise, censor or ban words, books or ideas. This is predicated on the belief that if we don't mention it, if we ban it, if we burn it, it does not exist.

We can see this in multiple societies both over history and in our present world, where groups and governments have sought to eradicate an idea, whether that was Christianity in the 1st-century Roman world, homosexuality in the 20th century or 'diversity' in 2025. Such approaches are beautifully captured in Ray Bradbury's novel *Fahrenheit 451*.

Our intent in this book is not to remove Western models; they have much to offer, and for the Western mind, trained in academic discourse and which looks to science as the mode for sense-making, they work. But our intent is to add to these models, to recognise that there are different modes of sense-making and that through these different lenses, different worlds and different ways of leading can make sense. Modern leaders, in a multi-polar world, need to understand both.

Our Aims for This Book

We hope this book is a resource both for individual leaders and, more fundamentally, for those seeking to critically explore leadership in their own journeys—to both understand the nature of leading others and become better global leaders.

References

Alimo-Metcalfe, B., & Alban-Metcalfe, R. J. (2001). The development of a new transformational leadership questionnaire. *Journal of Occupational and Organizational Psychology, 74*, 1–27. https://doi.org/10.1348/096317901167208

Bass, B. M. (1985). *Leadership and performance beyond expectations.* Collier Macmillan: Free Press.

Burns, J. M. (1978). *Leadership.* New York: Harper & Row.

Carlyle, T. (1841). *On heroes, hero-worship, & the heroic in history.* London: James Fraser.

Gardner, H., & Laskin, E. (2011). *Leading minds: An anatomy of leadership.* New York: Basic Books.

Goleman, D. (1995). *Emotional intelligence.* Bantam Books, Inc.

Graen, G. B., & Uhl-Bien, M. (1995). Relationship-based approach to leadership: Development of leader-member exchange (LMX) theory of leadership over 25 years: Applying a multi-level multi-domain perspective. *The Leadership Quarterly, 6*(2), 219–247. https://doi.org/10.1016/1048-9843(95)90036-5

Greenleaf, R. K. (1977). *Servant leadership: A journey into the nature of legitimate power and greatness.* New York: Paulist Press.

Heifetz, R. A. (1994). *Leadership without easy answers.* Cambridge, MA: Harvard University Press.

Hersey, P., & Blanchard, K. H. (1969). Life cycle theory of leadership. *Training & Development Journal, 23*(5), 26–34.

Lewin, K., Lippit, R., & White, R. K. (1939). Patterns of aggressive behaviour in experimentally created social climates. *Journal of Social Psychology, 10*, 271–301. https://doi.org/10.1080/00224545.1939.9713366

Remenyi, D. (2015). *Henley Management College: A world class pioneer in management education.* Acpil.

Stogdill, R. (1948). Personal factors associated with leadership a survey of the literature. *Journal of Psychology, 25*, 35–71.

Section 1

Perspectives

2

Decoloniality and Leadership Development

Sarah J. Owusu[1] *& Judith Okonkwo*[2]

[1] *InkDot - Strategic Innovation Consultancy, Maputo, Mozambique*
[2] *Extended Reality Development Initiative, Lagos, Nigeria*

Introduction - Se wo were fi na wosankofa a yenkyi

The theory and practice of leadership must continuously evolve to remain relevant, and leaders must be equipped to navigate contemporary challenges. This book is about the need for a decolonial approach to leadership development that enables us to meaningfully meet the moment. We are living through significant complexity, with technological prowess and globalisation accelerating that complexity and humanity facing interconnected environmental, social and spiritual crises (Akomolafe, 2021). Our 'life-support systems' are being threatened, and this calls for a shift in our thinking (Maathai, 2004).

This predicament has emerged from an era of industrialisation—a quarter of a century moving from mechanisation to mass production, to computing and automation, and to a digital techno-capitalist era dominated by the internet, 'social' networks and artificial intelligence that we now inhabit. This chapter focuses on another historical phenomenon: colonialism and the power, dominance and violence of colonial systems that have resulted in the prevalence of the Western and Euro-centric worldview that persists in the fabric of society to this day. We will argue that this worldview also persists in our concepts of leadership and the way we develop leaders, whether in academic or organisational settings. This narrow paradigm is no longer

Mosaic Leadership: African, Asian, Middle Eastern and Indigenous Perspectives, First Edition. Edited by Jonathan Passmore, Badri Bajaj, and Mongezi C Makhalima.

Published 2026 by John Wiley & Sons Ltd.

sufficient. A more expansive, heterogeneous and inclusive body of leadership knowledge is needed to match the complex and interconnected nature of today's challenges.

In the next section, we begin by invoking the West African visual symbol of Sankofa. The section is dedicated to remembering and recovering what has been lost through the violence of the dominant paradigm, and to do so in a way that interrupts our usual patterns of learning, inquiry and knowledge production. We invite the reader to *experience* the wisdom of Sankofa before delving into the more theoretical aspects of decoloniality in leadership development.

The following section unpacks the terms coloniality and decoloniality, and is followed by a section that journeys through mainstream leadership development theories in order to reveal the dominant paradigm of leadership, one that we argue is highly individualistic, mechanistic and hierarchical.

The last core section provides some early sketches of what has served us in the process of writing this chapter in ways that reflect and model a decolonial approach. For us, decolonial leadership development is a living practice, and everything that we have committed to paper here should be seen as a living, breathing and evolving body of knowledge.

It is our view that a decolonial approach to leadership and leadership development is necessary if we are to meaningfully address the many challenges we face within organisations and in society at large. Leaders at all levels and from all types of backgrounds, organisations and institutions are influenced by the dominant paradigm we are steeped in; they also, however, have the ability to influence the paradigm and make space for a more fit-for-purpose approach. This book represents a start at decolonising the canon and syllabus of leadership development, but it is our hope that it does more than tell and theorise. It must become a spark for change, encouraging leaders to look beyond the traditional Western model, expanding their perspective to include perspectives from other spheres, from African, Asian, the Middle Eastern and First Nation peoples.

Sankofa—Remembering and Recovering

Allow your imagination to take centre stage. Yes, you have opened up an academic text, and you might expect to read what follows only using your intellect. We invite you to put those assumptions to one side for a moment and instead open up to a fuller experience—after all, you are more than a cognitive being.

Take three slow, deep breaths. Deeper than usual. In through the nose, out through the mouth. On the breath in, allow your stomach to relax and fill like a balloon, your rib cage expanding. As you breathe out, open your mouth and sigh out your breath completely and fully. Put the book down, and do this now.

Now place your attention on the adinkra symbol (Figure 2.1)—it is called: *Sankofa.*

Figure 2.1 Sankofa Symbol—Version 1.

Opening yourself up to the following perspectives:

1. **Perspective one:** observe the symbol, follow the curving lines with your gaze, and let the shape and lines enter your eyes—notice what it evokes in you.
2. **Perspective two:** get a pen and paper, and draw the symbol several times (or trace the lines with your fingers)—notice how the symbol feels as it is expressed through your hands.
3. **Perspective three:** say the word 'Sankofa' out loud or silently in your mind a few times—notice the way it sounds and the way it feels in your mouth.

Sankofa is an *adinkra symbol*—a visual conveyor of complex concepts, proverbs, philosophies, moral lessons, history, cosmology and spiritual beliefs. They codify knowledge, and as cultural artefacts they support 'the transmission of a complex and nuanced body of practice and belief' (Appiah, 1993). Adinkra symbols transcend words and offer imagery to invoke ideas and values.

Historically, they are linked back to the early 19th century and to the Gyaman and Asante (both subgroups of the Akan ethnolinguistic group of people from the pre-colonial West African regions that are today known as Ghana and Côte d'Ivoire). It is said that they were first used by Nana Kwadwo Agyemang Adinkra, a Gyaman king who was defeated by the Asante Empire that became a dominant power in the region (Willis, 1998). The Asante adopted and built on the tradition of the adinkra and integrated them into their own cultural, spiritual and ceremonial purposes through the centuries. In the present day, they remain a significant part of West African art, architecture and fashion and are recognised as rich holders of knowledge. Today, there are more than 100 documented symbols, each carrying a unique meaning. In the context of discussing decoloniality, it is worth reflecting on how this archive might have been different today had it not been subject to the dominance of one Empire over another.

Sankofa.

Se wo were fi na wosankofa a yenkyi.

Figure 2.2 Sankofa Symbol—Version 1.

Sankofa and its short description in Twi roughly translates to: it is not taboo to go back for that which you have forgotten. It invites us to return and gather what is at risk of being subsumed, lost or left behind. One version (Figure 2.2) shows a bird, with its head turned to face backwards, gently capturing or placing something on its back—perhaps an egg, a seed, some potentiality. There is a sense of care in the bird's gesture, as if the item must be protected—held safely and softly on the feathers of its arched back. The wisdom of Sankofa is to forge your future, but to do so embracing what came before (ancestry, heritage, history, lineage, experience and lessons). Sankofa is recovering and remembering.

By invoking Sankofa, our intention is to interrupt the usual patterns and expectations the reader might have in picking up a book on leadership development—a title that isn't immediately understood or accessible to the English speaker; imagery that doesn't follow the usual 'rules' of an academic manuscript; drawing on wisdom practices and technologies from our own cultural heritage and from beyond the mainstream. In the remainder of this chapter, we build on this, implicitly exploring questions such as: What if we de-centred the white-washed canon that is taught in most business schools? What if we resisted a homogenous view of what leadership is and created space for leadership lessons from beyond that narrow frame? What of ourselves has been lost, and what are the implications for our own leadership if we do not recover it? As Sankofa says, 'perhaps we should go back...perhaps we should return to ourselves' (Coates, 2015).

We invite the reader into an epistemological frame that seeks to organise knowledge differently and to support new ways of knowing. This chapter digs into ideas of coloniality and decoloniality in the context of leadership development in an attempt to shake free from colonial shackles. We nurture an alternative seed that may take root if we are willing to expand outside of what has become the dominant norm. It is a call to remember what leadership might have been and can still be.

Coloniality and Decoloniality

It is useful to clarify the terms we are using to discuss decolonisation in the context of leadership development, starting with the distinction between colonialism and coloniality. The former refers to periods of political and economic control by colonial powers and the latter to the patterns of power that persist beyond the end of colonial rule. As Maldonado-Torres (2007) puts it, 'coloniality survives colonialism'. In the case of leadership development, coloniality encompasses the theory, knowledge production, mindsets and structures that still determine how leadership is defined and practised. In the academy, it is codified and sustained in the teachings made available to students, in who gets to do the teaching and what standards we set for successful performance. Perhaps most insidious is how these notions become mainstreamed in our self-image, aspirations and relationships with the world (Fanon, 1952).

Both colonialism and coloniality have an embedded assumption of supremacy that leads to (and justifies) the exclusion, control and subjugation of ways of knowing and being that don't align with the normative standards. In this context, despite formal colonisation being over, our current reality is still shaped by colonisation, specifically the violent control that the United States (US) and European countries have exerted over much of the world. Given this, it should be no surprise that the structures we live within privilege a US–European worldview. This has implications for leadership development which we address in the next section.

To return to our definitions, decolonisation is the withdrawal from a colony to restore independence, sovereignty and self-determination. But if the effects of colonialism are longer lasting, and embedded in our knowledge and systems of meaning (Said, 1979), then decoloniality requires intentionally challenging the paradigms that we are steeped in. Decoloniality in leadership development will include the work of interrupting, disrupting, dismantling and uprooting the ways that the dominant paradigm shows up in our ideas of leadership, our ways of leading, and crucially the ways we develop leaders. It will also include making space for what has been erased or excluded through colonialism. When we refer to decolonising leadership development, and decolonial leadership, it is this deeper effort that we invoke.

Laying Bare the Dominant Narrative

Leadership development theory and practice, as it is widely known, accepted and taught today, is dominated by a Western paradigm of leadership. For much of the last century, this paradigm has formed the narrow knowledge base in the majority of the world's business schools, and today's business and management training programs draw on leadership theories that are fundamentally homogenous. This narrow cultural grounding is perpetuated through peer-reviewed journals, business school curricula and New York Times Best Seller list books that favour more of the same.

Let us lay out the evolution of the Western view of leadership, starting with the 19th-century Great Man Theories. Widely popularised by Scottish philosopher Thomas Carlyle, this theory posits that great leaders are born with qualities like charisma, courage and wisdom that predispose them to lead (Carlyle, 1841). Leaders were those who rose to prominence due to a set of inherent and largely unteachable, exceptional traits. By the early 20th century, Trait Theory extended the Great Man approach by seeking to identify the innate characteristics that effective leaders commonly share. Rather than attributing leadership to fate or birthright, it focused on identifiable qualities. Critiques of this theory point to the lack of a definitive set of traits that apply universally across leadership contexts, leading to conclusions that traits alone are insufficient to explain effective leadership (Stogdill, 1948). The mid-20th century saw a shift to Behavioural and Situational leadership, theorising that leadership behaviours could be learned and developed and that different leadership styles from democratic to autocratic and laissez-faire could be effective depending on the context (Lewin et al., 1939). Situational Leadership Theory marked a critical step forward by recognising that leadership is a dynamic process, requiring responsiveness to both the needs of the team and the environment (Hersey & Blanchard, 1969).

More recently, we see the rise of both cognitive and emotional intelligence as a critical component of effective leadership. Goleman (1995) argued that emotional intelligence (the ability to recognise, understand and manage emotions in self and others) was more important in the workplace for leaders than cognitive intelligence. Emotional intelligence recognises that leaders who connect relationally with their followers can inspire greater loyalty, productivity and engagement. Over time, this and other theories paved the way for Transformational Leadership, popularised by James MacGregor Burns (1978) and later Bernard Bass (1985), highlighting the role of inspiration, motivation and visionary thinking in leadership. Transformational leadership emphasises moral values, prioritises the well-being and development of followers to drive organisational change and leads to more resilient organisations.

Parallel to transformational leadership, Servant Leadership theory emerged, arguing that leaders should put the needs of their followers ahead of their own, focusing on personal development, community and ethical responsibility. Servant leadership has become increasingly influential, particularly in fields that prioritise social responsibility and community building, as it encourages leaders to act with empathy, humility and a commitment to the greater good (Greenleaf, 1977). In recent years, leadership theory has moved towards inclusive and adaptive leadership models.

Inclusive leadership emphasises the importance of diversity, equity and inclusion within organisations, and leaders who leverage diverse perspectives to foster a collaborative and supportive environment (Bourke & Dillon, 2016). Adaptive leadership, popularised by Ronald Heifetz (1994), encourages leaders to be flexible, innovative and responsive to change. This model emphasises the need for leaders to navigate uncertainty in today's fast-changing world, engage in constant learning and challenge established norms to solve complex problems.

At first glance, this account provides a seemingly diverse body of knowledge, theories evolving in response to a shifting world and the continuous redefinition of leadership. Scratch the surface and we see that these theories ultimately share a common worldview. While the above is not an exhaustive account, it does provide an overview of the key ideas that make up what Mbigi (2007) identifies as the European North Cultural Paradigm. That this paradigm has emerged should be no surprise if we look at the wider societal context that predates them; the theories emerge from, are reinforced by and perpetuate the Cartesian and Newtonian worldviews that had a stronghold in the 1600s and profoundly influenced the fabric of Western society with rationalism, the scientific method and the idea of the universe viewed as a predictable machine. Perhaps most pertinent is that the time period we explore above (from the Great Man theories to the current day) also saw the influence of Taylorism starting in the early 1900s and the industrial management method focused on efficiency, control, productivity and extraction. Finally, while the period of European colonisation and domination across the globe pre-date this timeframe, as we have seen, the effects of colonisation linger on.

A decolonial approach to leadership development must make explicit what values and principles are woven through our cultural and societal contexts, and therefore that are embedded in our theories. If we look across the leadership development theories laid out here, we see a number of (interconnected) themes:

1. **Individualistic:** A strong focus on the individual leader as the central unit of focus for leadership development, even as the role of the leader becomes more relational or 'in service'. The hyperfocus on the individual (Buffkins & Owusu, 2024) is at the expense of seeing leadership as a collective and interdependent

practice. Leadership is anchored in the Hero's Journey narrative (Owusu & Wilde, 2021) that perpetuates the view that leadership is a solo pursuit, with leaders modelling themselves on the celebrity leaders of the past century or two (an internet search for the greatest business leaders of 20th and 21st century and witness the queue the monochrome North American palette of Rockefeller, Ford, Disney, Buffet, Gates and Jobs).

2. **Mechanistic:** Viewing organisations as machines that are predictable, controllable and made up of interchangeable parts. The implication for leadership is that—alongside other dispensable human resources—the role of the leader is to run the organisation with a focus on efficiency and productivity above all and manage people and other resources as inputs in linear processes to achieve narrowly defined metrics. It prioritises the transactional and is concerned with 'perfecting...technological know-how' while losing the spiritual and relational (Biko, 1987).
3. **Hierarchical:** Hierarchical structures emphasise centralisation and control. While hierarchies have long been an organising mechanism for groups of people (including in both military and religious institutions), the particular brand of hierarchy we refer to became particularly prevalent through industrialisation where top-down control was used to manage large numbers of workers and factory machinery and production processes, and where power is centralised in the few. The reader may also draw similarities here with the colonial systems discussed above, where hierarchy enables the supremacy of the few and the dehumanisation of the many (Fanon, 1963).

While these themes may not be inherently negative or negative under all circumstances, they become problematic when they are imposed at the cost of any and all theories beyond this narrow frame and when their universality is assumed. While leadership theories come, go and evolve, we argue that the individualistic, mechanistic and hierarchical paradigm is sustained. These themes play out at the level of the individual leader (both in their inner and outer spheres), the team, the organisation and society at large, which in turn reinforces the characteristics back down the chain (see Table 2.1). The real-life consequences for leadership theory and practice: leadership theories and philosophies outside this

Table 2.1 Implications of the Key Themes Embedded in the Current Dominant Leadership Paradigm.

Theme	Inside 'I'	Outside 'I'	Team	Organisation	Society
Individualistic	Me as the centre of the universe	Prioritising own needs only, lack of connection and support	Individual performance metrics and incentives, lack of collaboration and support	Race to the bottom, zero-sum dynamics, short-term thinking	Nationalism, pandemic of loneliness and depression, othering
Mechanistic	Cognitive, reasoning and linear thinking above all	Productivity at all costs, Burnout, disregard for the relational/emotional	Separation/ fragmentation, narrow metrics, transactional, output focus and task-oriented	Extractive, People and planet as resources, profit above all, externalising harms	Environmental degradation, overshoot of planetary boundaries, fragility
Hierarchical	I am my role	Comparison, ideas of supremacy	Competitive, ranking, power over, winning at all costs	Control, top-down power dynamics, dehumanise	Oppression, resources and influence concentrated in a few

paradigm are not recognised; business schools and courses purport that all worthy ideas originate from Europe or the US; leaders who exhibit these characteristics are uplifted as examples of success (and those who don't are invisibilised and marginalised). This is the impact of the colonial imprint, and the power, dominance and violence that is sustained if we do not take decoloniality seriously.

We have shown that the field of leadership development remains narrowly dominated by a paradigm that is both harmful and unsuitable for the globally connected, diverse world that leaders must now be equipped for. So what are the decolonial approaches and alternatives that can get us out of this predicament? The next section begins the work of broadening and expanding our worldview by laying out leadership and leadership development theories, grounded in cultures and philosophies from the African continent.

Sketches of a Decolonial Approach

We have journeyed through the paradigm of leadership development that emerged over a time period where US–European colonialism exerted power, dominance and violence over much of the rest of the world—a dynamic that continues to linger in the fabric of society. We have characterised this leadership development paradigm as individualistic, mechanistic and hierarchical. While this paradigm has led to much technological progress, we have indicated that this has borne a significant cost. This narrow and singular worldview has problematic implications for the individual leader, teams, organisations and society as a whole (with each of these levels having a compounding effect on the others). Through the power-dominance-wealth trifecta, these theories have spread around the world and taken root as a forced ideal. While it might have sufficed in the 19th century, in the 21st we have the opportunity to broaden our perspectives.

Several cultures provide gifts of being and knowing that have and will advance the human race. In this section, we explore a number of these from the African continent that specifically speak to leadership and organisational practice. A growing movement of African thought leaders are challenging the singular view; from Mbigi's

(1997) African management philosophy to Okonkwo's (2010) Oriki leadership coaching model, they share African practices as additions and alternatives to the modern canon. We can consider practices of the Igbo of south-eastern Nigeria whose apprenticeship system, Imu Ahia (Ekwekwe, 2021), is built on the principles of symbiosis, mutual aid and shared prosperity. We can draw from Sophie Oluwole's (1997) insights into African and Western paradigms, shedding light on the origins of the current leadership crisis that has captured us in the individualistic, dominating and reductionist frame. We can take inspiration from Ncube's (2010) Ubuntu Leadership Framework which provides practical lessons for leadership that challenge the dominant narrative.

In its embodiment of the essence of interconnectedness and mutual respect (Mbigi & Maree, 1995), Ubuntu provides a deep remembering that anchors many leadership approaches of the African Cultural paradigm. The philosophy places its emphasis on connection and inclusivity, and makes space for leadership theory to be informed from a broader palette. Image 3 shows how a philosophical grounding in power, dominance and violence leads to upholding coloniality, while a grounding in Ubuntu has the positive recursive effects that move us in the direction of decoloniality. The remainder of this book covers such wisdom from African people and cultures in depth, alongside a multitude of insights from Asian, Middle Eastern and Indigenous peoples (Figure 2.3).

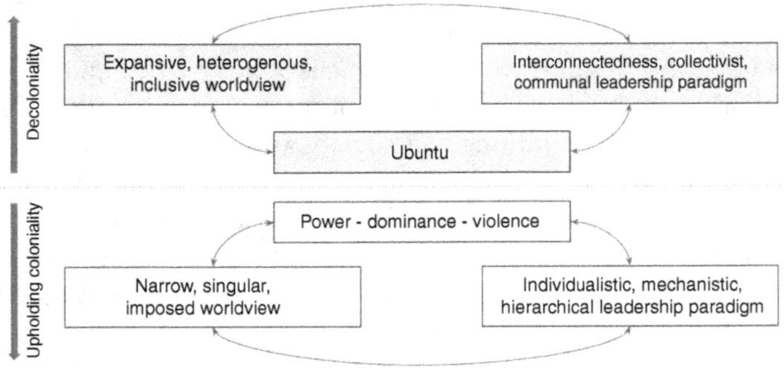

Figure 2.3 The Recursiveness of Coloniality and Decoloniality.

Some may find the description of the Western paradigm as upholding coloniality reductive; does decoloniality require us to give up the type of leadership that has led to immense scientific and technological progress and that has given us the quality of life and surplus that is the aspiration of many across the globe? The authors are proponents of keeping the best of what is and the aspects of any approach that are life-affirming. We are critical of what we see as a naïve and incomplete progress narrative (The Consilience Project, 2024) that excludes the many negative side effects of progress and invisibilised harms for the many while uplifting the benefits to the few: a world where in 2024, the top 1% of the world's population control more wealth than the bottom 95% (Oxfam, 2024). We are also wary of the tendency to continue amplifying problems by developing solutions from the same paradigm that caused the problems in the first place.

If the reader agrees that we find ourselves in a time of complexity, existential risk and far-reaching crises of civilisation and planet being pushed to its limits, then a detachment from the leadership paradigms that led us here is necessary. Decoloniality in leadership should provide us with the knowledge and practices that develop leaders who are willing to work through the 'mess that has been hidden, ignored, neglected through a narrative of progress, consumption, linearity, categorisation, control, prosperity, rationality' (Hogarth & Hankin, 2024). Our encouragement is that no matter where you are starting from, you expand your worldview (one inch at a time) beyond the dominant leadership paradigm. The interconnected and complex world that leaders now navigate requires it.

In writing this chapter, we have had to wrestle with the ways in which the dominant paradigm lives in us, even as leaders exposed to a diversity of perspectives and who are actively in pursuit of a decolonial leadership practice. It has been our attempt to model decoloniality in our research, inquiry and writing—from this, we can uncover some of what has worked for us:

- **Remembering:** This includes allowing for feelings of grief and yearning, for this is at the root of understanding what is missing. There is cultural memory embodied in artefacts such as texts, libraries and universities (Iyamah, 2024), as well as in our practices. To reverse the ways in which these have been demolished, concealed, censored, overwritten and appropriated we have to re/uncover and document for ourselves (Okonkwo & Owusu, 2016).

- **Deconstructing:** In writing this chapter, we have questioned what it means to lead, what makes a leader and who gets to lead (or define leadership). For this, perspective-taking is key as alternative perspectives provide fuel to counter what has become so normative that it is almost invisible. In this chapter, we have attempted to challenge and question, and where necessary to release, while acknowledging that much can be composted (Akomolafe, 2021).
- **Imagining:** We are attempting to establish a knowledge base—one that isn't dependent on colonial narratives—on which to build a new way of being for leaders everywhere. This requires a continuous commitment to dreaming, visioning and imagining. Accessing this means letting go of linear structures at times and instead drawing from symbols (as with the adinkra), story and narrative (Welch et al., 2020).
- **Collaborating and co-constructing:** In the spirit of collectivism, this chapter is a truly collaborative effort that requires being together in the exploration and development of viewpoints that neither author could have built alone. Of course, it has also been a collaboration with all of the work we have referenced, and it is a joy to us that this chapter will sit alongside the work of many others who are committed to decoloniality in leadership development.

This list is not exhaustive nor conclusive. It is an attempt to reveal our own process and learning. It is our hope with this chapter and this book, that the reader moves beyond the written word to apply insights encountered in their own lives. This list is a call to action to practice decoloniality in your own leadership, today.

Conclusion

We acknowledge that leadership is both a personal and collective pursuit, and that it is influenced by the worldview of the leader themselves. As such, we close this chapter by acknowledging our own positionality – the current, but continuously evolving, positions from which we write this chapter.

We have juxtaposed the current, dominant paradigm of leadership development with leadership theory and practices from the margins of the mainstream. We have drawn from our own cultural heritage but emphasise that a core principle of decoloniality is that it leaves space for a diversity of perspectives, so this chapter is an invitation to the readers to continue expanding their worldviews. The remainder of this book will contribute to this, and beyond these pages, we hope to see leadership-in-action emerging that helps us address the most critical challenges of our times.

References

Akomolafe, B. (2021). *These wilds beyond our fences: Letters to my Daughter on humanity's search for home.* Berkeley, CA: North Atlantic Books.

Appiah, K. A. (1993). *In my Father's house: Africa in the philosophy of culture* (1st paperback ed.). New York: Oxford University Press.

Bass, B. M. (1985). *Leadership and performance beyond expectations.* Glencoe, Il: Free Press.

Biko, S. (1987). *I write what I like.* London: Pearson.

Bourke, J. & Dillon, B. (2016). The six signature traits of inclusive leadership: Thriving in a diverse new world. Deloitte Insights Retrieved on 29th January 2025 from: https://www2.deloitte.com/us/en/insights/topics/talent/six-signature-traits-of-inclusive-leadership.html

Buffkins, Z., & Owusu, S. J. (2024). Power of pause: Lessons for a fundamental reorientation in DEIB. *Organzation Development Review, 56*(4), 25–31.

Burns, J. M. (1978). *Leadership.* New York: Harper & Row.

Carlyle, T. (1841). *On heroes, hero-worship, & the heroic in history.* London: James Fraser.

Coates, T.-N. (2015). *Between the world and I.* New York: Spiegel & Grau.

Fanon, F (1986). Black Skin, White Masks. Translated by Charles Lam Markmann, Pluto Press. (Originally published in French as *Peau Noire, Masques Blancs,* Éditions du Seuil, 1952)

Fanon, F. (1963). *The wretched of the earth.* Translated by Constance Farrington. New York: Grove Press.

Goleman, D. (1995). *Emotional intelligence: why it can matter more than IQ.* New York: Bantam Books.

Greenleaf, R. K. (1977). *Servant leadership: A journey into the nature of legitimate power and greatness.* New York: Paulist Press.

Heifetz, R. A. (1994). *Leadership Without Easy Answers*. Harvard University Press. https://doi.org/10.2307/j.ctv1pncrt0

Hersey, P., & Blanchard, K. H. (1969). Life cycle theory of leadership. *Training & Development Journal, 23*(5), 26–34.

Hogarth, H., & Hankin, C. (2024). Mess-making as a force for resistance: Reimagining environmental educational research for multispecies flourishing. *Australian Journal of Environmental Education., 40*, 340–358. https://doi.org/10.1017/aee.2024.28

Iyamah, J. O. (2024). Remembering is Resistance: Archival Practices to disrupt memoricide. Retrieved on 29th January 2025 from: https://gidajournal.com/remembering-is-resistance/

Lewin, K., Lippit, R., & White, R. K. (1939). Patterns of aggressive behaviour in experimentally created social climates. *Journal of Social Psychology, 10*, 271–301. https://doi.org/10.1080/00224545.1939.9713366

Maathai, W. (2004). Nobel Prize speech. Retrieved on 28th January 2025 from: https://www.nobelprize.org/prizes/peace/2004/maathai/lecture/

Maldonado-Torres, N. (2007). On the coloniality of being: Contributions to the development of a concept. *Cultural Studies, 21*(2–3), 240–270. https://doi.org/10.1080/09502380601162548

Mbigi, L. (2007). Spirit of African leadership: A comparative African perspective. In K. A. April & M. L. Shockley (Eds.), *Diversity*. London: Palgrave Macmillan. https://doi.org/10.1057/9780230627529_19

Okonkwo, J., & Owusu, S. J. (2016). Remembering—The gift of OD. *OD Practitioner, 48*(3), 57–63.

Owusu, S. J., & Wilde, J. (2021). Transformative narrative technology and identities: Unknotting the heroic myth in organization development. *Organization Development Review, 53*(3), 65–72.

Oxfam (2024). Multilateralism in an era of global oligarchy. Retrieved on 29th January 2025 from https://www.oxfam.org/en/press-releases/worlds-top-1-own-more-wealth-95-humanity-shadow-global-oligarchy-hangs-over-un

Said, E. W. (1979). *Orientalism*. New York: Knopf Doubleday Publishing Group.

Stogdill, R. (1948). Personal factors associated with leadership a survey of the literature. *Journal of Psychology, 25*, 35–71.

The Consilience Project (2024). Development in progress, July 16. https://consilienceproject.org/development-in-progress/

Welch, M. A., Saunders, A. A. P., Buergelt, P. T., Gilpin-Jackson, Y., Ferguson, J., & Marsick, V. J. (2020). Your story, our story: The transformative power of life narratives. *Reflective Practice, 21*(6), 861–876. https://doi.org/10.1080/14623943.2020.1821633

Willis, W. B. (1998). *The Adinkra Dictionary: A visual primer on the language of Adinkra*. Pyramid Complex.

3

Asian Approaches to Leadership

Rajan Sinha

Asia Coaching Network LLP with Mantrana Consulting Pvt. Ltd., Noida, Uttar Pradesh, India

Introduction

This chapter explores the evolution and characteristics of Asian leadership models, examining how deeply rooted cultural, religious and philosophical traditions have shaped leadership practices across Asia. Unlike Western leadership models, which are often systematic and individualistic, Asian leadership models prioritise community, long-term thinking and a holistic approach to problem-solving. These qualities have been critical to the success of Asian leaders in both regional and global contexts.

The chapter is structured into five sections, beginning with a history of Asian leadership models that emphasises their organic development through cultural texts and practices. We then address the impact of imperialism, where the European colonial rule disrupted traditional practices, and examine how Asian leadership reemerged in the post-war era under the influence of Western management theories. The discussion shifts to how cultural traits, such as hierarchy and collectivism, differentiate Asian leadership styles. Finally, we explore how contemporary leaders in Asia are blending tradition with modernity to address the challenges of the 21st century. By understanding these models, we gain insights into the strengths that Asian leaders bring to global business, particularly their ability to balance adaptability with cultural integrity.

Mosaic Leadership: African, Asian, Middle Eastern and Indigenous Perspectives,
First Edition. Edited by Jonathan Passmore, Badri Bajaj, and Mongezi C Makhalima.

Published 2026 by John Wiley & Sons Ltd.

A Brief History of Asian Leadership

Leadership in Asia has often been intertwined with cultural values, spiritual teachings and philosophical traditions, making it unique in its approach to governance and organisation. Unlike Western traditions that often seek to systematise leadership theories into academic frameworks, Asian leadership principles are frequently derived from moral and ethical guidance provided by religious texts, epics and historical teachings.

Chinese Leadership Models: Confucianism, Taoism and *The Art of War*

Confucianism has been a cornerstone of Chinese leadership philosophy for centuries. Developed by Confucius (551–479 BCE) (Chen & An, 2009; King & Zhang, 2014). This system emphasises the importance of hierarchical social structures and moral behaviour. A leader, according to Confucian thought, should embody *ren* (benevolence) and act with *li* (proper conduct). The ideal leader is a *junzi* (gentleman) who earns respect through virtue and wisdom rather than through coercion. This emphasis on moral integrity and role modelling has deeply influenced Chinese leadership across generations, emphasising the leader's role as a steward of societal harmony.

Taoism, another influential philosophy, offers a contrasting yet complementary approach to leadership. Rooted in the teachings of Laozi (Fu et al., 2008; King & Zhang, 2014), Taoism emphasises the concept of *wu wei* (effortless action) and adaptability. Leaders are encouraged to align themselves with the natural order and to avoid forceful control, instead allowing things to flow in their own course. This philosophy encourages leaders to be flexible, respond to changes with minimal intervention and lead by example—qualities that resonate with modern ideas of situational leadership.

The Art of War by Sun Tzu written in the 5th century BCE has had a lasting influence on leadership thinking in China and globally (Chen & An, 2009; Rowley et al., 2020). Its strategic principles, such as the importance of knowing oneself and one's enemy, understanding the dynamics of timing and positioning and achieving victory without conflict, have been adapted to business and organisational leadership. Unlike rigid management models, Sun Tzu's approach is highly situational, encouraging leaders to adapt their strategies to the unique challenges they face.

These principles continue to shape contemporary Chinese leadership. For instance, the emphasis on long-term strategic thinking is evident in the way Chinese companies (and Chinese political leadership) plan for sustained growth and market expansion. The focus on harmony and collective well-being underpins corporate cultures that value employee loyalty and community ties, helping Chinese firms navigate global markets while maintaining a cohesive internal culture.

Indian Leadership Models: Dharma, the *Mahabharata*, the *Ramayana* and Insights from Chanakya and Thiruvalluvar

In India, leadership models are deeply rooted in the concept of *dharma*, which means duty, ethics and moral responsibility. The concept emphasises the importance of doing what is right according to one's role in society, and it has guided leaders for millennia. *The Mahabharata* (Kaipa, 2014; Ramachandran, 2016), one of India's great epics, provides profound lessons in leadership through its characters and their struggles. Lord Krishna, a central figure in the epic, serves as a mentor and strategist, guiding Arjuna through dilemmas with wisdom that balances pragmatism and idealism. His counsel in the Bhagavad Gita (Deb, 2017; Sharma & Shilpa, 2013), a part of the *Mahabharata*, teaches leaders about the importance of detachment, purpose and selfless action.

The *Ramayana (*Gosling et al., 2013), another foundational text, offers a model of leadership through the character of Rama, who embodies virtues such as truthfulness, self-sacrifice and a commitment to *dharma*. Rama's leadership is characterised by his willingness to prioritise the well-being of his subjects, even at a great personal cost. This story has shaped the cultural expectation in India that leaders should be selfless and dedicated to serving the community. Rama was also to emerge as a role model in South-East Asian countries for leadership and governance. In fact, even today, Thai kings take on their official name after Rama.

Chanakya, also known as Kautilya, was a renowned philosopher, economist and political strategist in ancient India, most famously associated with the *Arthashastra*, a treatise on statecraft, economic policy and military strategy (Boesche, 2003). Chanakya's leadership principles are marked by pragmatism, strategic thinking and a keen understanding of human behaviour. He believed that a leader should be shrewd, adaptable and capable of navigating the complexities of power dynamics.

One of Chanakya's core tenets is that a leader must prioritise the welfare of the state, above all else. He emphasised the need for decisive action and the importance of maintaining order and discipline within the realm. Chanakya's famous saying, 'Before you start some work, always ask yourself three questions – Why am I doing it? What the results might be? And Will I be successful?' (Pillai, 2016). Such questions encapsulate his strategic mindset. This approach encourages leaders to think critically and act thoughtfully, qualities that are vital for effective leadership in any context.

Chanakya also advocated for the importance of building alliances and fostering loyalty among followers. His insights into human psychology and governance provide a framework for understanding power dynamics, making his teachings relevant not only in ancient times but also in contemporary leadership practices. In modern India, Chanakya's principles resonate with leaders who navigate complex political and business environments, emphasising the importance of strategy, loyalty and ethical conduct.

Thiruvalluvar, the author of the *Tirukkural,* is another key figure in the Indian leadership discourse (Sharma, 2016). His work, composed of 1,330 couplets, addresses ethics, politics, love and virtue. Thiruvalluvar's philosophy emphasises moral leadership, integrity and the importance of virtue in governance. His teachings advocate for leaders to possess qualities such as wisdom, humility and compassion.

One of Thiruvalluvar's key messages is that a leader should be guided by ethical principles and act in the best interest of their people. His aphorisms advocate for fairness and justice, emphasising that leadership is not merely about power but about responsibility towards the community. He famously stated, 'The true measure of a leader is how they respond to adversity', highlighting the importance of resilience and moral courage in leadership.

Thiruvalluvar also underscores the significance of communication and dialogue in leadership. He believed that effective leaders should engage with their followers, listen to their concerns and be approachable. This participative approach resonates with modern leadership practices that prioritise collaboration and open communication.

The *Panchatantra* and Hitopadesha (Rao, 2011; Sharma, 2017) and *Katha Saritsagara* (Chatterjee, 2015) are classical Indian texts that use storytelling to impart moral lessons and practical wisdom, which include insights on leadership. Here's a brief overview of the leadership models from them:

- § **Strategic Thinking**: Leaders should anticipate challenges and plan accordingly, much like in the story of 'The Crows and the Serpent', where the crows use strategy to outsmart a snake.
- § **Diplomacy and Negotiation**: Many tales emphasise the value of diplomatic skills in resolving conflicts, like in the story of 'The Lion and the Clever Rabbit'.
- § **Adaptability**: The ability to adjust to changing circumstances is seen as a key leadership trait, as highlighted in the story 'The Monkey and the Crocodile'.
- § **Wisdom and Prudence**: Leaders are often portrayed as needing to balance ambition with caution, like in the story of 'King Vikramaditya', where wise decisions and foresight lead to success.
- § **Moral Integrity**: Many stories stress the value of ethical behaviour and the long-term benefits of integrity in leadership.
- § **Resilience**: Stories highlight the importance of enduring hardships and bouncing back, a key quality in leadership.
- § **Networking and Alliances**: It emphasises the need for leaders to build alliances, as seen in stories where animals survive through cooperation.
- § **Understanding Human Nature**: It teaches that effective leaders should have a deep understanding of human behaviour and motivations, often portrayed through stories that show the consequences of misunderstanding or misjudging others.
- § **Decisiveness**: A leader's ability to make quick and effective decisions is often highlighted, ensuring success in complex situations.

Each of these texts uses allegory to explore aspects of leadership, such as the balance between power and wisdom, the importance of ethical decision-making and the value of strategic alliances.

In the modern context, Indian business leaders like Ratan Tata and Azim Premji have drawn upon these principles, emphasising integrity, social responsibility and a sense of duty towards employees and society. The Indian leadership model's emphasis on service to others, combined with a strategic mindset, has enabled Indian leaders to navigate complex challenges and thrive in global markets. By integrating the insights of Chanakya and

Thiruvalluvar, contemporary leaders can harness a rich legacy of wisdom that continues to inform ethical and effective leadership practices.

Japanese Leadership Models: Bushido, Zen Philosophy and Modern Business Practices

The influence of *Bushido,* or the way of the warrior, is central to Japanese leadership philosophy (Shibata, 2017). Rooted in the samurai traditions of the feudal period, *Bushido* emphasises virtues such as loyalty, honour, courage and self-discipline. Leaders in Japan have historically been expected to demonstrate commitment to their organisations and maintain a sense of duty and honour in their actions. Even in modern corporate environments, this has translated into a leadership style that prioritises loyalty to the company and a deep sense of responsibility towards employees and stakeholders.

Zen Buddhism has also played a role in shaping Japanese leadership, promoting mindfulness, simplicity and a focus on inner balance. The Zen approach encourages leaders to maintain calmness and clarity, even in the face of uncertainty, which is particularly valuable in the high-pressure world of business. This focus on mental discipline and awareness has made Japanese leaders effective in managing long-term projects and complex negotiations.

Modern Japanese business practices such as *Kaizen* (continuous improvement) and *Nemawashi* (consensus-building) reflect the blend of these traditional values with contemporary needs. *Kaizen* encourages incremental improvements and collective responsibility for quality, fostering a culture of collaboration and long-term thinking. *Nemawashi* involves laying the groundwork for decisions through informal discussions, ensuring that consensus is achieved before formal decisions are made. This approach contrasts with more direct decision-making styles seen in Western companies, highlighting the importance of harmony and collective agreement in Japanese leadership.

Leaders like Akio Morita, the co-founder of Sony, and Masayoshi Son of SoftBank have demonstrated how these principles can be adapted to global business environments. Morita's focus on innovation and long-term vision helped Sony become a global brand, while Son's investment strategies reflect a balance of risk-taking and strategic foresight, grounded in a deeply Japanese approach to leadership.

Leadership Models in South Asia: Balancing Tradition, Religion and Modernity

Leadership in South Asia, which includes countries like Pakistan, Bangladesh, Sri Lanka and Nepal, is shaped by a mix of Islamic, Buddhist and Hindu influences, alongside the legacy of colonial rule. In Islamic teachings, the concept of *Shura* (consultation) is central to leadership, emphasising that leaders should consult with their followers and make decisions that reflect the collective interest. This consultative style aligns with the region's emphasis on community cohesion and collective decision-making.

In Sri Lanka and Nepal, Buddhist teachings influence leadership with a focus on compassion, ethical conduct and mindfulness. Leaders are expected to act with compassion and maintain an awareness of the interconnectedness of life. This influences how leaders interact with their teams, emphasising empathy and the moral implications of their decisions.

The region's history of colonialism has also played a role in shaping contemporary leadership models. Leaders have often had to balance respect for traditional values with the adoption of Western business practices. For example, in Pakistan, leaders have drawn on the idea of *Ijtihad* (independent reasoning) to address modern challenges while adhering to Islamic principles, creating a unique blend of tradition and innovation.

South Asian leaders who operate in the global market, such as Indra Nooyi, former CEO of PepsiCo, have demonstrated the ability to bridge cultural divides by leveraging this blend of consultative decision-making, empathy and strategic vision. Their success in diverse markets highlights the adaptability and resilience of leadership models from this region.

Leadership in West Asia: Islamic Principles and Tribal Traditions

Leadership in West Asia, including the Middle East, is heavily influenced by Islamic teachings and traditional tribal customs. The *Quran* and *Hadiths* emphasise the importance of justice, fairness and accountability, guiding leaders to prioritise ethical behaviour and community welfare. The idea of *Ummah* (community) places the leader in a position of responsibility for the collective wellbeing, reinforcing a servant leadership model.

Traditional tribal values also play a role, emphasising loyalty, respect for elders and the importance of maintaining social harmony. Tribal leaders have historically acted as mediators and protectors of their communities, a role that has extended into modern business leadership in the region. This has fostered a leadership style that combines authority with a strong sense of duty towards the community.

In the contemporary era, leaders in West Asia have sought to integrate these traditional values with modern management practices, especially in rapidly developing economies like the United Arab Emirates and Saudi Arabia. Leaders like Sultan Ahmed bin Sulayem of DP World and Lubna Olayan of the Olayan Group have balanced their commitment to cultural values with an openness to global innovation, driving their companies to international success.

Imperialism and Empire

The influence of imperialism and colonial rule throughout Asia during the 19th and 20th centuries had a profound impact on the region's leadership models. European colonial powers imposed their administrative systems, often disregarding or undermining indigenous forms of governance and leadership that had evolved over centuries. This period saw a disruption of traditional leadership structures and the imposition of Western models of authority, which were often rigid, hierarchical and bureaucratic.

In India, the British colonial administration introduced Western education systems and business practices, replacing traditional village leadership and local governance structures. While this led to the decline of some indigenous leadership practices, it also sparked a response among Indian leaders who sought to reclaim their cultural heritage. The Indian independence movement, led by figures like Mahatma Gandhi, became a reassertion of Indian leadership values such as *satyagraha* (truth-force) and non-violent resistance, challenging the moral and ethical basis of British rule. However, it may not be out of place to mention that one of the leading Indian leaders during the freedom struggle, Subhash Chandra Bose, was infused with revolutionary fervour and idealism and strove for an alternative approach to freedom. Even though he died a premature death, his ideals continue to inspire many Indians.

Similarly, in China, the imposition of Western trade laws and territorial concessions during the Opium Wars and the subsequent weakening of the Qing Dynasty disrupted the Confucian-based governance that had held sway for centuries. The humiliation of colonial rule galvanised nationalist movements, culminating in the formation of the Republic of China in 1912 and later the People's Republic of China in 1949. These events reshaped Chinese leadership models, merging Marxist-Leninist principles with a revived sense of Chinese cultural identity.

In Southeast Asia, colonial rule by the British, Dutch, French and Spanish powers led to a fragmentation of local governance structures and a deepening of economic dependency. The imposition of Western bureaucratic systems changed traditional forms of leadership, with colonial administrators often dismissing local rulers as subservient agents. However, the struggle for independence in countries like Indonesia, Vietnam and the Philippines saw a resurgence of indigenous leadership principles adapted to modern revolutionary contexts.

The Middle East experienced a similar transformation as European powers like the British and French redrew boundaries and imposed mandates after the decline of the Ottoman Empire. Traditional tribal leadership was often marginalised in favour of Western-trained elites, leading to tension between modernist and traditionalist forces in the region. This tension is still evident today, as many Middle Eastern leaders navigate the challenges of modernisation while maintaining cultural authenticity (Ali, 2009).

The colonial period left a complex legacy in Asia, with traditional leadership models being both suppressed and transformed. The imposition of Western models of governance created a rift between indigenous practices and the modern state, a tension that many Asian countries have had to reconcile in the post-colonial era. However, the rise of nationalist movements across Asia also sparked a revival of traditional leadership values, laying the foundation for the emergence of uniquely Asian leadership styles that blend indigenous wisdom with the realities of a globalised world.

Asian Leadership—1950–2000

The aftermath of World War II brought significant changes to Asia, as countries across the continent gained independence from colonial rule and began the process of nation-building. The influence of Western management theories remained strong during this period, as newly independent nations sought to modernise their economies and integrate into the global system. However, the post-war era also saw the gradual reassertion of Asian cultural values in leadership, as countries sought to forge their own paths to development.

In Japan, the post-war period was characterised by a deep engagement with Western management practices, especially in the context of rebuilding the economy. American influences such as Total Quality Management and Lean Manufacturing were adopted by Japanese companies, leading to the rise of *Kaizen* and *Just-In-Time* manufacturing (Deming, 1986). Japanese leaders like Soichiro Honda and Akio Morita embraced a blend of Western efficiency with Japanese cultural values such as teamwork, loyalty and long-term thinking. This approach not only transformed Japan into a global economic powerhouse but also established a distinct model of leadership that valued continuous improvement and collective responsibility.

In India, the post-independence period saw the adoption of Western-style democratic governance, but traditional leadership concepts continued to play a role. Leaders navigated the challenges of building a modern nation-state while emphasising the importance of social justice and inclusivity, themes that resonated with India's cultural emphasis on *dharma*. The rise of family-run conglomerates such as Tata, Birla and Reliance reflected the blend of entrepreneurial spirit with a sense of duty towards society, a model that has remained influential in the Indian business landscape.

In China, the leadership of Mao Zedong initially rejected Western influence, instead drawing on Marxist-Leninist ideology blended with a distinctly Chinese interpretation of socialism. Mao's approach to leadership emphasised mass mobilisation and the importance of collective struggle, which aligned with traditional Chinese values of communal harmony and shared responsibility. However, after the reforms of Deng Xiaoping in the 1980s, China began to incorporate elements of Western capitalism while maintaining a strong centralised leadership structure. This hybrid model has continued to evolve, with Chinese leaders balancing market reforms with a focus on state control and long-term planning.

The Southeast Asian region took a pragmatic approach in the post-war period, with leaders like Lee Kuan Yew in Singapore emphasising the importance of stability, meritocracy and economic growth (Williams, 2014). His leadership style blended various elements that helped transform Singapore from a struggling post-colonial state into a global economic hub. He focused on long-term thinking, pragmatism over ideology, strong governance, strict law and order, balancing firmness with care, cultural sensitivity, strategic alliances, human capital development based on meritocracy, economic liberalisation, and so on. He also navigated East–West political dynamics; Lee drew on both Confucian values and Western principles of governance, creating a model that emphasised efficiency and social cohesion. This approach has been influential in other Southeast Asian nations, where leaders have sought to balance economic modernisation with respect for cultural traditions.

Ho Chi Minh, the founding father of modern Vietnam and a key figure in the Vietnamese struggle for independence, is remembered not only for his political acumen but also for his distinctive leadership principles (Bain, 1973). He was committed to liberating Vietnam from colonial rule, first from the French and later from the American influence. Some of the distinctive pillars of his leadership style were national identity, preservation of cultural pride, collective leadership, moral leadership and integrity, adaptability, education and long-term vision. His ability to inspire and mobilise the masses, combined with his pragmatic approach to politics, allowed him to effectively lead Vietnam through one of its most tumultuous periods. Today, his legacy continues to influence leaders and movements around the world, serving as a testament to the power of principled leadership in the quest for social justice and national liberation.

Golda Meir, Israel's fourth Prime Minister and one of the first women in the world to hold such a position, demonstrated a leadership style marked by resilience, pragmatism and a deep commitment to her nationalist cause. She was known for her strong will and tough decision-making, personal sacrifices, pragmatic diplomacy, accessible leadership style, motherly image, etc. Her legacy remains influential, particularly in how she balanced the ideals of Zionism with the practical realities of leading a nation in a region marked by conflict.

The post-war era was a time of negotiation between Western influences and traditional Asian values, with leaders across the continent working to create models that were both modern and culturally resonant. This blending of old and new has remained a defining feature of Asian leadership, as the region has emerged as a critical player in the global economy.

What's Different About Asian Cultures?

Asian cultures are diverse, encompassing a wide range of beliefs, traditions and social norms. However, certain broad cultural characteristics differentiate Asian leadership styles from their Western counterparts. These include a preference for hierarchy, collectivism, a focus on long-term relationships and a high-context communication style. The Dutch social psychologist Geert Hofstede's cultural dimensions theory provides a useful framework for understanding these differences (Hofstede, 1984).

One of the most notable features of Asian leadership is the emphasis on hierarchy and respect for authority. In many Asian cultures, social structures are hierarchical, with clear distinctions between different levels of status. This is reflected in leadership practices, where deference to seniority and respect for elders play an important role. For example, in Japanese organisations, the seniority-based *nenko* system has traditionally structured career progression, emphasising respect for experience and age.

Collectivism is another key characteristic of Asian cultures, where the interests of the group often take precedence over individual ambitions. This contrasts with the individualism that is more common in Western cultures. In collectivist societies, leaders are expected to act as guardians of the collective good, making decisions that benefit the community as a whole. This cultural orientation is evident in Chinese and Indian leadership styles, where leaders often emphasise the importance of family, community and social harmony.

Asian cultures also tend to have a long-term orientation, placing value on perseverance and strategic foresight. This contrasts with the more short-term focus seen in some Western business practices. Chinese businesses, for instance, often take a long-term view of investments and relationships, prioritising stability and sustainable growth over immediate gains. This perspective allows Asian leaders to build deep, trusting relationships with stakeholders and to navigate complex market dynamics with patience.

The communication style in many Asian cultures is high context, meaning that messages are often conveyed through non-verbal cues and indirect language rather than through explicit statements. This can make leadership interactions more nuanced, as understanding the context and reading between the lines becomes critical. Japanese business meetings, for example, often involve implicit communication and subtle cues, requiring leaders to be sensitive to the underlying dynamics of the group.

These cultural characteristics shape leadership styles that prioritise harmony, loyalty and collective success. While they can present challenges in fast-paced global business environments, they also offer unique strengths, such as the ability to build resilient organisations and to navigate complex social relationships. As Asian leaders have taken on more prominent roles in global companies, their ability to integrate these cultural strengths with the demands of international business has become a defining feature of their leadership success.

New Leadership Approaches in Asia

The last decades of the 20th century and this century have brought about a new era of leadership in Asia, characterised by an increasing willingness to blend traditional values with the demands of modern, digital-first economies. This new generation of leaders is shaping industries from technology to manufacturing while also addressing critical social and environmental challenges.

In India, technology leaders like Sundar Pichai (Google) and Satya Nadella (Microsoft) represent a shift towards innovation-driven leadership that is grounded in empathy and cultural awareness. They bring a deep understanding of both Indian cultural values and the expectations of a global audience, positioning them as effective leaders in diverse, multicultural environments. This approach has helped companies like Google and Microsoft expand their reach in emerging markets while maintaining their commitment to innovation and social responsibility. Ratan Tata, the former chairman of Tata Sons, was known for his compassionate, visionary and value-driven leadership, which has significantly influenced the growth and reputation of the Tata Group. His leadership style emphasised ethical business practices, social responsibility with empathy, humility and a global vision. He transformed the Tata Group from a largely India-focused conglomerate to a global powerhouse with acquisitions like Jaguar Land Rover, Tetley Tea and Corus Steel. In the political sphere, current Prime Minister Modi is navigating changes in social values, cultural pride, massive infra development, a fastest growing economy and a rising global influence.

In China, the rise of digital giants like Alibaba and Tencent has reshaped the landscape of leadership. Leaders such as Jack Ma have combined the strategic thinking of Chinese tradition with the agility required in the fast-paced tech sector. As China continues to evolve as a global technology hub, Chinese leaders are focusing on driving innovation while maintaining a strong emphasis on community welfare and national interests.

Japanese leaders are also adapting to the challenges of a globalised economy. While traditional values such as loyalty and *Kaizen* remain important, there is a growing recognition of the need for greater diversity and flexibility in leadership.

In the Middle East, Mohammed bin Salman (MBS) of Saudi Arabia (Abadi, 2023) and the Crown Prince of the UAE Sheikh Mohammed bin Zayed Al Nahyan (MBZ) (Litsas, 2023) are exhibiting distinct leadership models rooted in their vision for modernisation, economic diversification and regional influence. MBS's leadership is heavily defined by Vision 2030, a strategic plan aimed at diversifying Saudi Arabia's economy beyond oil. It focuses on developing sectors like tourism, entertainment and technology and positioning Saudi Arabia as a regional power. He has also pioneered massive social/cultural reforms, especially with regard to women's rights. Likewise, MBZ is working on UAE's global positioning and influence, developing it into a hub for business, tourism, and innovation, promoting sectors like renewable energy, space exploration and technology. He is also promoting a narrative of tolerance and openness in the UAE, supporting religious diversity and moderate Islam. This approach is intended to attract global investment and talent.

Conclusion

Asian leadership models have evolved significantly over centuries, from being shaped by philosophical and religious traditions to adapting to the demands of the modern, globalised world. Despite the disruptive impact of imperialism and the subsequent dominance of Western management theories, Asian leaders have rediscovered and revitalised their cultural values, integrating them into contemporary leadership practices.

Today, Asian leaders bring unique perspectives to global companies, balancing adaptability, long-term thinking and a focus on community well-being. These qualities have not only enabled them to thrive in diverse markets but also to redefine what effective leadership looks like in the 21st century. As the world becomes increasingly interconnected, the lessons from Asian leadership models offer valuable insights into leading with empathy, sustainability and strategic vision.

The rise of Asian leaders in global companies reflects a broader shift towards recognising the value of diverse leadership perspectives. By understanding and appreciating these models, businesses can foster more inclusive, effective and culturally sensitive leadership practices that resonate with a global audience.

References

Abadi, M. (2023). Role of culture on leadership and governance in Saudi Arabia. *International Journal of Leadership and Governance, 3*(1), 24–35.

Ali, A. J. (2009). Islamic perspectives on leadership: a model. *International Journal of Islamic and Middle Eastern Finance and Management, 2*(2), 160–180.

Bain, C. A. (1973). Calculation and charisma: The leadership style of Ho Chi Minh. *The Virginia Quarterly Review, 49*(3), 346–356.

Boesche, R. (2003). *The first great political realist: Kautilya and His Arthashastra.* Lexington Books.

Chatterjee, A. (2015). Tales of strategy and diplomacy: Lessons from the Katha Saritsagara. *Indian Journal of Leadership Studies, 8*(1), 92–105.

Chen, G. M., & An, R. (2009). A Chinese model of intercultural leadership competence. In D. Deardorff (Ed.), *The SAGE handbook of intercultural competence* (pp. 196–208).

Deb, S. (2017). The Bhagavad Gita and contemporary leadership lessons. *Indian Journal of Management Studies, 8*(2), 44–59.

Deming, W. E. (1986). *Out of the Crisis.* MIT Press.

Fu, P. P., Wu, R., Yang, Y., & Ye, J. (2008). Chinese culture and leadership. In J. S. Chhokar, F. C. Brodbeck, & R. J. House (Eds.), *Culture and leadership across the world: The GLOBE book of in-depth studies of 25 societies* (pp. 877–907). Lawrence Erlbaum Associates Publishers.

Gosling, J., Villiers, P., & Verma, H. (2013). Leadership and dharma: The Indian epics Ramayana and Mahabharata and their significance for leadership today. In J. Gosling & P. Villiers (Eds.), *Fictional leaders: heroes, villains and absent friends* (pp. 182–201). Palgrave Macmillan.

Hofstede, G. (1984). *Culture's consequences: International differences in work-Related values.* SAGE Publications.

Kaipa, P. (2014). Making wise decisions: Leadership lessons from Mahabharata. *Journal of Management Development, 33*(8/9), 835–846.

King, P., & Zhang, W. (2014). Chinese and western leadership models: A literature review. *Journal of Management Research, 6*(2), 1.

Litsas, S. N. (2023). Smart leadership: The cases of Mohamed bin Zayed Al Nahyan and Hamdan bin Mohammed Al Maktoum. In S. N. Litsas (Ed.), *Smart instead of small in international relations theory: The case of the United Arab Emirates*. Springer Nature: Cham.

Pillai, R. (2016). *Corporate Chanakya: Successful management the Chanakya way*. Jaico Publishing House.

Ramachandran, P. (2016). The multifaceted leadership model from Ramayana. *IBA Journal of Management & Leadership, 8*(1), 5.

Rao, V. (2011). Moral leadership lessons from Panchatantra and Hitopadesha. *Journal of Human Values, 17*(1), 15–24.

Rowley, C., Oh, I., & Jang, W. (2020). New perspectives on East Asian leadership in the age of globalization: Local grounding and historical comparisons in the Asia Pacific region. In *Leadership in East Asia*. Routledge.

Sharma, A. (2016). Ancient Indian texts and the ethics of leadership: Lessons from the Tirukkural. *Journal of Indian Philosophy, 34*(2), 129–145.

Sharma, A. (2017). Ethics, wisdom, and values in the Panchatantra and Hitopadesha: An Indian perspective on leadership. *International Journal of Indian Culture and Business Management, 14*(1), 65–80.

Sharma, S. K., & Shilpa, J. (2013). The Bhagavad Gita as a source of leadership and management. *Journal of Human Values, 19*(2), 173–182.

Shibata, H. (2017). Bushido and the Japanese way of leadership. *Asian Journal of Business Ethics, 6*(1), 12–29.

Williams, D. (2014). *The leadership of Singapore's Lee Kuan Yew and the implications for leadership development. Center for Public Leadership, Kennedy School of Government.* Harvard University. Available at: www.globalleadership. net/uploads/the_leadership_of_singapores_lee_kuan_yew__the_implications_for_leadership_development. pdf (accessed 3 June 2015).

4

African Approaches to Leadership Development

Mongezi C Makhalima[1,2]

[1] *Africa Board for Coaching, Consulting & Coaching Psychology, South Africa*
[2] *Africa Centre for Work-Based Learning, South Africa*

Introduction

This chapter explores some of the perspectives and approaches to leadership and leadership development from Africa. It highlights the complexities and challenges of this topic, given the history of Africa across the last 500 years and how these experiences have informed modern perspectives on the African continent. I hope the chapter provides both a deeper understanding of African approaches and useful lenses for Northern and Western researchers and practitioners.

A Complex Continent

In exploring perspectives on leadership in Africa, it is tempting to jump into research portals and consult universities to see what research has been published. While this may give one some information, it is likely to give one a skewed perspective about African leadership practices. For example, Abebe et al. (2020) have reviewed studies from across Africa. They highlight that from 1980 to 2019, there were 37 studies that focused primarily on organisational behaviour/human resources, 26 on entrepreneurship and 21 at the macro (strategy) level during the review period. Overall, the trend

Mosaic Leadership: African, Asian, Middle Eastern and Indigenous Perspectives, First Edition. Edited by Jonathan Passmore, Badri Bajaj, and Mongezi C Makhalima.

Published 2026 by John Wiley & Sons Ltd.

indicates a steady growth of African leadership studies with most of the publications occurring after 2000.

The challenge with these and many other modern research works is that they are generally focused on a narrow sphere of leadership (e.g. power and authority, motivation, etc.)—and, mostly due to the influence of university policies, are viewing African events through a Western lens or framework.

Before outlining some of the approaches to leadership, it is important to consider that a lot about leadership development in Africa is impacted by wider socio-political factors that remain to this day.

As simple as it sounds, embedded in the phrase 'African Leadership Development Practice' is deep complexity. In trying to unpick this phrase, let's consider some of these terms:

'Africa' is a construct and a complex one. A continent with 54 countries whose cultures are markedly different. The Northern parts of Africa like Morocco, Algeria and Libya do not see themselves as Africans. The south of Africa is a collection of very different economies and indigenous variations, while Central, West, and East Africa are widely different due to the linguistic and historical influences of previous colonisers.

'Leadership' as a construct has been evolving for the last 100 years. It is not a neat construct that fits into a box tied in a pretty ribbon. Whether one is looking at Process approaches or Trait approaches, or as any of the emerging contingency approaches that emerge in the modern study of leadership. Leadership itself has proved difficult to conceptualise.

'Development' can refer to a process of growth that involves evolution of approaches; however, it may also be referring to the approaches used to train and develop leaders, informed by these approaches.

Therefore a conversation about African leadership development should take into consideration these factors and a careful analysis of intersections of these constructs. Over and above these, it is important to consider several other factors that make this conversation a lot more complex, but they remain necessary for a more nuanced treatment of the conversation about leadership in Africa. These are as follows:

- Religion
- The Impact of Colonialism

- Era/Period of Analysis
- Praxis
- Education.

For example, a good majority of practitioners on the continent value more highly Western approaches to leadership, not necessarily because they are better but because that is also what is being taught in many of the business schools across Africa. Many African leaders go to Insead, Oxford and Harvard and learn the works of Warren Bennis, John Kotter and Peter Drucker, and these approaches pervade the content taught at most business schools in most parts of the continent.

The Rise of Ubuntu Leadership

Beyond that, when one looks at much of the research exploring the indigenous practices that have spilled over into corporate from traditional practices, Ubuntu leadership as outlined by people like Magadlela, Mbigi, Khoza and Bhengu has become ubiquitous.

Ubuntu leadership stems from a philosophy of the Bantu people who occupied most of South-East Africa from modern-day Uganda, Tanzania, Zimbabwe, Zambia and South Africa, among others. It emphasises the connectedness of all humans and how many leaders are in service to the human agenda. Ubuntu as an orientation to life is opposed to individualism and insensitive competitiveness. Neither is it comfortable with collectivism, where collectivism stresses the importance of the social unit to the point of depersonalising the individual. At the same time, it places great importance on working for the common good, as captured by the expression: 'Umuntu ngumuntu ngabantu' (Literally translated: A person is a person through other people), or 'I am because you are, you are because we are' (Khoza, 1994).

Many leaders are working on implementing principles of community leadership, as proposed by Khoza in place of or together with more Western frameworks. Khoza describes community leadership as one that 'perceives the business organisation as a community to which the individual belongs, not just one with a fixed legal contract but as a member by choice. This community is built on close interpersonal relationships and group interactions held together by a feeling of security and harmony on the part of all its members. The members submit themselves and their hopes and plans to this community' (Khoza, 2014).

> 'Compared with western management theory and practice, African management is characterised by flatter structures which stress inclusion, interdependence, democracy and broad stakeholder participation. Rather than formal, uniform policies, African managers call for an emphasis on flexibility in relation to policies, which can be easily initiated, changed and transformed through a broad-based collective, mass-scale consensus and participation of many stakeholders. Instead of the tendency towards impersonal relationships in western management theory within an organisational context, African culture calls for highly personalised relationships. In African organisations, harnessing spiritual and social capital is an important management challenge. While there is hierarchy in African organisations, respect for hierarchy is emphasised in ceremonies. What drives organisations, more than official roles within a hierarchy, is the informal power that derives from natural social clusters, and consultation and negotiation depend largely on who owns the issue. Representation of all stakeholders and inclusion of all groups are given emphasis so that African management is more about allowing multiple leadership roles and greater flexibility. Finally African management tends to prefer a web of interdependence of roles, relationships and competencies and is less concerned with structure and function than western management'. (Mbigi, 2006, p. 23)

Lekgotla Principle: A Device of Traditional African Leadership

The word 'Lekgotla' is a Sesotho/Setswana word that could be translated loosely into English as 'Court'—but it could connotatively be used to refer to a meeting, a gathering or even a conference. The lekgotla is a device of traditional leadership in many of the Southern African leadership practices, although it can be encountered across the different parts of the continent in different forms.

The lekgotla was (still is, in some rural contexts) the centre of daily administration of leadership, akin to a boardroom, where critical decisions were made about matters of the community or families. However, in the case of families, there would typically be other approaches of leadership behaviour given the intimate context of the family meeting.

However, observing the Lekgotla processes, when done right, gives the observer a great appreciation of the principles that underpin Ubuntu/Botho leadership, specifically around decision-making, listening, authority and power as well as cultural artifacts of time, wealth, team roles, etc.

My observations of my first lekgotla challenged a number of ideas I had about the power and authority of the chief. Young as I was, I was convinced that chiefs yield total power and a lekgotla meeting is essentially the authoritarian process, where the word of the chief was final. After all, I grew up with the often-mentioned proverb: 'Lefoko la kgosi le agelwa mosako'—A Setswana proverb that implies the chief or king has the last word. I appreciated better what this means after observing a few of these.

First of all, it was striking how much time is devoted to the ceremonies around the position of the king or chief. The attention to protocol, sitting arrangements and time of arrival (which many times could be delayed until everyone is settled or has 'fully arrived') can take a long time—and only then the chief arrives and sits. While there are variations, in many ways, there are no expectations for people to stand up when the chief arrives; however, there is a differential silence or at least lowered tones in recognition of his/her presence.

It is important at this point to highlight that while there are plenty of examples of female chiefs and regents in many African traditions, for example, Queen Mantathisi of the Batlokwa, Queen Ndzinga of the Donga and Queen Modjadji of the Balobedu, a lot of the misperception about traditional leadership in Africa is that it was male-dominated. This could not be further from the truth. Saidi (2010) states that in the early 1950s, over a quarter of the chiefs in Katanga Province in the then Belgian Congo were women, and this was after 50 years of colonisation. Another example from British colonial records shows that officials in Northern Rhodesia (today's Zambia) engaged in a battle for male labour with mothers-in-law and as a result sought to bring an end to bride service, the principal means through which women controlled young male and female labour and young men's access to marriage with their daughters and maintained their pivotal position in village social relations. All this to say, for brevity and convenience in the rest of the chapter, the use of the male pronoun is also referring to a female form of the role and the use of the female pronoun refers to the male form as well, except where specifically indicated.

Once the chief has taken their place, they might say a few words after the chief's first lieutenant has said something, and depending on the nature and size of the event, there might be more preambles before the actual subject of the meeting is embarked upon. The point of this particular section is to emphasise the time orientation of the community in this instance, where matters are not rushed, and it would appear that there is also something in the ceremony of the process and the preambles that establishes the atmosphere of the lekgotla, as well as establish the authority of the different roles.

After this initial protocol, the chief is largely silent throughout the lekgotla, perhaps nodding but very present in the meeting. Sometimes, the lieutenants of the chief, who are doing most of the talking and the running of the meeting, might pause to confer with the chief in whispers and nods. But it is pretty obvious most of the time that the role of the chief is not passive but an active participant that is listening but does not unduly interfere with the proceedings.

Depending yet again on the importance, depth and complexity of the matter, the lekgotla may take the whole day or a few hours—and yes, sometimes a few days. What is significant is the conclusion of the process where, again contrary to my perceptions of the authority of the chief, they literally speak last, and after the lieutenants have summarised the matter and agreements have been received, they would hand over to the chief for his observation and last word on the matter—and where necessary, tasks may be allocated back to his lieutenants; after which the lekgotla may adjourn, usually with the chief leaving first and then everyone else.

The most impressive element of this process, which is different from what was initially expected, is that in many of these meetings, the chief practices listening—and tempers his authority by delegating it to the lieutenants, but most importantly, listening to a number of issues in these proceedings, there's also a level of nuance that the chief applies to the final decisions and degrees. Most of the time, this nuance is tempered with compassion for the situation—and balancing perspectives for the benefit of the community (constituency), the parties involved in the matter as well as recognition of his authority and what's required of his role. Of course, this is entirely my interpretation as an observer.

The practice of this compassion would generally earn the chief more respect as a wise arbiter—in Setswana, the phrase used would be 'Ke motho' (they are a person—implying that s/he is humane).

Max Du Preez (2010) highlights this principle and its extant aetiology in his book, *Of Warriors, Lovers and Prophets,* where he describes Chief Mohlomi, one of the early Basotho kings, who in doing things as described above was fulfilling the instructions of his ancestors, who had instructed him 'You will grow to be chief, you will rule over men...go and rule your people well. Always temper your actions with justice and sympathy. Care for the needy, especially the children...' . This is the principle he continued to teach and demonstrate as a king and has been exemplified in some of the behaviours of subsequent kings like King Moshoeshoe and others across Southern Africa.

Placed in this context, it is possible to observe the core behavioural indicator of Ubuntu/Botho—the *compassion with which a leader deals with his subordinates.* But you will also notice how this connects with the spiritual leadership frame in the next section, where one's leadership is believed to be decreed/directed partly by spirit.

The other behavioural indicators of this Ubuntu/Botho philosophy are as follows:

- Respect—treating people the way they want to be treated.
- Community—doing things together and sharing tasks, as also demonstrated in the lekgotla process above. So, the idea of collective intelligence stands out strong with this behavioural indicator.
- Oneness with nature—connectedness not just with animals but with the elements of nature, plants, air, earth, water and fire. So, while others may speak of balance, there is no balance, just integration.

So, people and/or leaders who do not demonstrate these behaviours in their leadership are then regarded as 'izilwane'/'diphoofolo', which at a literal level can be interpreted as 'animal'—yet the more appropriate connotative meaning is that of a 'beast' or 'savage'.

It should also be emphasised here that the heart leadership or relational leadership is a great part of leadership but not in exclusion to cerebro-rational processes. Many of the traditional leaders are not praised just for their warmth but also for their wisdom, foresight and insight (cf: Du Preez (2010) for a number of character studies) as well as their strength—physical strength and courage.

So, it could be said that the conceptualisation of the African leadership style, at least in its idealised form, is holistic—encompassing not only the mind but also the doing (body), the feeling (heart) and the discerning (spirit).

Socio-Spiritual Leadership

Religion and spirituality are an essential part of many African communities, from traditional African spirituality which presents in different forms across the continent to modern religions, the most prevalent being Islam and Christianity in its various denominations.

Since religion and traditional leadership practices are part of the leader's identity, many leaders do bring these into the place of work or in organised systems, sometimes unconsciously as they form part of their culture. In many parts of West Africa, for example, the breaking of the kola nut is a ritual that symbolises welcome, which while embedded in a wider tradition permeates business meetings.

In Christian-led organisations, many meetings start and close with prayer—a practice that sometimes creates conflict if there are strongly opinionated individuals in teams that have different spiritual practices. In extreme situations, there have even been cases where some leaders revert to traditional healers to strengthen themselves and the workplaces (the core belief behind this practice being that there are not only physical aspects of the workplace but also spiritual/energetic elements that need to be attended to).

Islam is the major religion in many African countries, especially in the north of the continent. In Comoros, Libya and Western Sahara, at least 99% of the population was Muslim. These were the highest percentages of Islam on the continent. However, in many other African nations, while the majority of the population is Muslim, these countries have sizable populations from other faiths. In Egypt, for instance, Islam is the religion of 79% of the people. Given this, Islam influences leadership practices in many parts of the continent. In North Africa, Shariah law principles are embedded into core decisions about businesses and communities. These principles influence rules around products, holidays, design of workspaces and relationships. For example, in the Shariah law, a married woman is not allowed, for example, to shake hands with a man who is not her husband. In contrast, in Western culture, this may serve as a sign of confidence and welcome. This same principle also impacts the kind of spaces where a female leader spends time, including the level and type of interactions with men. She cannot be in a closed room with her male counterpart, and therefore, it becomes necessary to think about open-space meetings for one-on-ones.

The rules that drive diversity and inclusion in the West may be less important in organisations functioning in Muslim Africa, where gender roles are almost strictly defined and gender equality is seen in very different terms than that in the USA or EU. Beyond religion, the influence of Bedouin traditions in countries like Algeria and Morocco, for example, might emphasise this patriarchal orientation, which is likely to show up together with the hierarchical, family orientation of Bedouin traditions.

In Xhosa traditions, a nation of people in the southeast of South Africa, one's clan name confers respect and status within the community and by extension to the office. So, a meeting within the Xhosa tradition involves more than people introducing themselves by their names and positions, but by their clan name and lineage. So, to build rapport, a leader understands to call another by their clan name, as opposed to their name.

The concept of age and manhood seem to be important in the traditions of the Xhosa people, that then permeate the boardroom, in that the fact that one has undergone the standard Xhosa rite of passage into manhood matters to the teams and groups one leads. It matters to those one leads that this leader is a 'Man' by this definition. So, where a leader is perceived to not be a 'Man', his authority can be undermined. This has become interestingly problematic in modern offices where intergenerational conflict is no longer just about age but about the intersection of age and traditional rituals.

While this issue of rites of passage applies also to women, it is more nuanced, with marriage being a more salient issue for Xhosa women.

Proximity to traditional royalty is yet another factor that plays itself out in leadership practices and impinges on credibility of the leader. Perceptions of royal lineage, no matter how slight, are currency for building credibility and access and, by extension, influence.

In Nigeria and Zambia, the socio-spiritual factor to consider is tribe (this applies to many others but is very explicitly practiced in these nations). In many social structures in these countries, which 'tribe' one comes from plays a role in leadership credibility. While not empirically established, coming from Igbo tribes in certain parts of Nigeria may confer one with more credibility than coming from the Efik or Yoruba tribes—this seems to be a similar practice in Zambia, albeit less pronounced, with some tribes higher up the credibility hierarchy than others.

There are over 2500 language groups in Africa (World Atlas), and language is a critical determinant of leadership influence in both community and commercial settings. In many parts of Tanzania, in East Africa, a working understanding of Kiswahili is more useful than English, which is mostly limited to cities and certain community groups. So, speaking English is unlikely to win confidence for a leader in Tanzania; however, this will be different in South Africa and Kenya, which are seen as mostly Anglophone countries. This is more neutral in Zambia and Malawi, and then the game changes in Mozambique, Angola (Lusophone countries) and many Francophone African countries (Sierra Leone, Mali, Benin, etc.), where for the latter, the language of influence is French, while it is Portuguese for the Lusophone countries.

Language can be used to exclude, for example, people who cannot speak the Afrikaans language of the South African Dutch tribes and their descendants many times find themselves excluded from meeting conversations and social events, especially in businesses that are still led by predominantly Afrikaans leaders.

Insights for Leadership Development

With all that has been shared, it is important to go back to the caveat at the beginning of this chapter. For many Western scholars and those interested in understanding the African context to anything, but in this instance leadership, it is important to consider the following as ways that hopefully inform any type of analysis.

There's No Country Called Africa

Africa is a continent with 54 distinct countries that, while there are aspects many share in common, is mostly diverse in many levels, so studies of leadership might be more useful in exploring country lenses, as opposed to exploring uniformity across the continent. Much of what is referred to as 'North Africa' will have a lot more in common with Middle East and Southern Europe than Southern Africa, for example.

Models Versus Frameworks

In thinking about conceptualisations of knowledge and processes, it is important to understand that the cultural orientations of many countries and nations within the continent may have different ways of knowing and knowledge gathering, as opposed to the Westerners. I find the Cultural Orientation Framework that is proposed by Rosinski (2010) useful as a way of understanding the cultural orientations of different people, and I encourage many researchers, especially considering working on the African continent, to consider that there are different cultural orientations. It is important to understand that on the African continent a good majority of people maybe a lot less analytical and a lot more experiential, a lot less monochromic and a lot more polychronic in their time orientation—and therefore, as a way of understanding knowledge, existential—Phenomenological Frameworks would be more prevalent than logical positivist frameworks, especially in the social sciences.

So, a question about 'models' of leadership could be a non-starter or even a research bias in itself.

Region

Geography and culture, as well as nature and movement, across different parts of the continent may affect and vary the above. In West Africa, the lekgotla process, other than a different language, may follow slightly different processes. Power and authority in many West African countries is a lot more direct and a lot more assertive than in the eastern and southern parts of the continent. So, the same lekgotla experience may descend into boisterous chaos in many places in Nigeria but still progressive eventually because being loud and expressive may be valued in that area.

This would be different in the eastern and southern parts of the continent, where a more collective, hierarchical approach, even a ceremonial approach, is adopted.

Gendered-ness

The issue of gender and gendered-ness in Africa is complex, like many other aspects of a vast, diverse continent. In the eastern and southern parts of Central Africa, many cultures and ethnic groups are patriarchal in their nature; therefore, the valuing of the male voice in leadership is prevalent.

In West Africa, many communities are matriarchal and as such power dynamics for women are nuanced, where, while roles are formally clearly delineated, many females demonstrate agency and pro-activeness and perhaps a sense of perceived aggression in parts. Again, this is a gross generalisation of nuanced differences between different areas and individuals in the area.

The Southern African gender dynamics are mixed with some roles (e.g. people born in Royalty take on their agency, while many females are taught to defer to maleness and male authority, a dynamic that plays itself in taking up leadership roles).

Religion and Spiritual Practices

The continent of Africa has a diversity of religious and spiritual beliefs that critically influence beliefs, assumptions and behaviour of leadership as they do all of the social behaviour of many. To this day, many traditional spiritual practices of many groups across the continent coexist with modern religions of Christianity and Islam, which are by far the biggest of the world religions that exist on the African continent. A lot of this has been covered under Socio-Spiritual leadership Practices.

Colonialism and Modern Influences

A lot of the modern leadership practices are influenced by colonial education and tradition from the west and the north, which are by far still regarded as superior leadership practices. Many of these were adopted from the late 19th century to the early 21st century and were taken for granted as the definition of success. The implementation of scientific management principles and Tayloristic and behavioural psychological practices that arrived with missionaries, their schooling system as well as influences of multinationals became the taken-for-granted standard for 'excellence in leadership'—embedded within the management and reward practices. Many university curriculums emphasised these leadership practices as de facto standards in the boardrooms across the continent. Many of these have been ignored in this paper as there's a lot documented thereon, except perhaps where they intersect with indigenous perspectives as has already been applied elsewhere.

Conclusion

In conclusion, what are the perspectives on leadership in Africa? The final answer is: It's complicated. In this chapter and across this book, we show that 'Ubuntu leadership' is practiced in one form or another across many parts of the continent, especially in the eastern and southern regions of the continent, influenced by the Bantu tradition. The Lekgotla leadership approach, documented by scholars and practitioners like Ruel Khoza and Max Du Preez, is just one example of this.

Also practiced but sometimes not explicitly acknowledged is spirituality-based leadership or spiritual leadership, influenced by traditional leadership perspectives, e.g. the Dagara Tradition in West Africa, and otherwise practices influenced by Christian and Muslim spiritual beliefs.

As a result of the strong influence of colonialism and valuing of Western leadership practices and teaching, a good percentage of perspectives and approaches are imported from Insead, MIT, Oxford and other Western universities. The teaching of these in African universities often remains dominant, a feature which we hope this book will contribute towards changing.

Finally, many researchers and practitioners interested in leadership in Africa are likely to ask the wrong question if they do not consider that there could be other ways of knowing. In valuing the 'scientific method', for example, the research may already yield different results from what may be the truth in practice. So, there is a need to move away from a search for models and ways of doing towards learning more about ways of being.

> 'What the world can learn from Africa is the focus on humanness and spirituality, to complement [and possibly replace] industrial and western individualism [which goes with avarice and greed]'. (Magadlela & Rolle, 2014, p. 50)

References

Abebe, M. A., Tekleab, A. G., & Lado, A. A. (2020). Multilevel perspectives on leadership in the African context. *Africa Journal of Management*, *6*(3), 145–160.

Du Preez, M. (2010). *Of warriors, lovers and prophets: unusual stories from South Africa's past.* Penguin Random House South Africa.

Magadlela, D., & Rolle, K. (2014). Responsible leadership is an inside job: Reflections on the missing link in African leadership in the 21st century. *Journal of Coaching, Consulting and Coaching Psychology in Africa, 1*(1), 48–56.

Makhalima, M. C., & Magadlela, D. (2014). Prolog: Championing an Afro-centric approach to management. *Journal of Coaching, Consulting and Coaching Psychology in Africa, 1*(1), 33–47.

Mbigi, L. (2006). A vision of African management and African leadership: A southern African perspective. In H. Van den Heuvel, et al. (Eds.), *Prophecies and protests: Ubuntu in glocal management* (pp. 22–51). Rozenberg Publishers.

Rosinski, P. (2010). *Coaching across cultures: New tools for leveraging national, corporate and professional differences.* Hachette UK.

Saidi, C. (2010). The patriarchal myth: Deconstruction and reconstruction. In *Women's authority and society in Early East-Central Africa* (pp. 7–22). Boydell & Brewer.

Further Reading

Bennis, W. (2007). The challenges of leadership in the modern world: Introduction to the special issue. *American Psychologist, 62*(1), 2–5.

Kets de Vries, M. F. R. (1995). *Life and death in the executive fast lane: Essays on irrational organizations and their leaders.* San Francisco, CA, US: Jossey-Bass.

Makhalima, M. C., & Magadlela, D. (2014). Prolog: Championing an Afro-centric approach to management. *Journal of Coaching, Consulting and Coaching Psychology in Africa, 1*(1), 33–47.

Makhalima, M. C. (2013). What I learn from Nelson Mandela about Legendary Leadership: 5 ingredients of Legendary Leadership. https://bit.ly/2YURztl

Makhalima, M. C. (2020–2024). The leadership master class interviews: Humanising leadership series. [Radio broadcast]. Vuka Online Radio Podcast. https://podcasters.spotify.com/pod/show/vuka-online0

Mthembu, M. D. (2014). Exceptional leadership and Governance: The pillars for Africa's emerging future. *Journal of Coaching, Consulting and Coaching Psychology in Africa, 1*(1), 33–47.

Schcurinck, W., Vilakati, V., & Viljoen, R. (2016). Exploring the concept of African Spiritual Consciousness. *Journal of Coaching, Consulting and Coaching Psychology in Africa, 1*(2), 13–17.

Saidi, C. (2010). Rochester studies in African history and the diaspora. In *Women's authority and society in Early East-Central Africa* (pp. 188–190). Boydell & Brewer.

Somé, M. P. (1999). *The healing wisdom of Africa: finding life purpose through nature, ritual, and community*. New York: J.P. Tarcher/ Putnam.

Tichy, N. M.; Ulrich, D. O. SMR forum: The leadership challenge—A call for the transformational leader. *Sloan Management Review (pre-1986)*; Cambridge *26*(1), (Fall 1984): 59.

5

First Nation Approaches to Leadership

Terry L. Cross

National Indian Child Welfare Association, Portland, OR, USA

Introduction

This chapter provides an Indigenous perspective on leadership. It acknowledges the impossible challenge of describing diverse forms of leadership among Indigenous peoples, nations and organisations, and instead considers leadership from the perspective of worldview. It compares and contrasts the linear worldview of the West with the relational worldview of many Indigenous cultures. In doing so, it challenges leadership educators to examine how their own worldview constrains their understanding of leadership, both in their own and in other cultures. A discussion of the Great Law of the Haudenosaunee is used to illustrate a relational worldview concept of leadership. The chapter then discusses the value that is gained by including Indigenous concepts and contributions within the leadership development discourse.

How Indigenous Peoples See Leadership

There are likely almost as many views about leadership as there are specific peoples, cultural groups, nations or bands. As a result, it is impossible to coherently state how Indigenous peoples see

Mosaic Leadership: African, Asian, Middle Eastern and Indigenous Perspectives, First Edition. Edited by Jonathan Passmore, Badri Bajaj, and Mongezi C Makhalima.

Published 2026 by John Wiley & Sons Ltd.

leadership. However, I will discuss some commonalities among Indigenous peoples of North America, Australia and New Zealand, at the level of cultural worldview, and then examine how worldview influences concepts of leadership.

There are several risks in attempting to describe commonly held worldviews across diverse Indigenous populations. The greatest risk is the creation or reinforcement of stereotypes. I hope not to do that. The second risk is the oversimplification of complex phenomena. A third risk is that someone might assume that I am an expert on Indigenous leadership. I am not. What I am sharing is what I have learned and observed through a 50-year career that has included leadership—as a scribe leader (William Ron Allen, personal communication c. 2014), a servant leader, a thought leader, an executive director, a spokesperson, an advocate, and a chairperson of non-profit boards and one public commission.

I am writing from the perspective of a citizen of the Seneca Nation of Indians, one of the six nations of the Haudenosaunee Confederacy. I am also writing from my perspective as founder and long-time executive director of an Indigenous non-profit and as a senior fellow of the American Leadership Forum and from the perspective of an Indigenous leadership trainer, consultant and executive coach who has worked with Indigenous peoples across North America, Australia and New Zealand. Most importantly, I am writing from the perspective of a learner, a mentee of diverse Indigenous elders, spiritual advisors and senior leaders, and as a curious observer and student of our Indigenous ways.

Cindy Blackstock, an Indigenous scholar from the Gitxsan First Nation in the territory now known as British Columbia, Canada, is quoted as saying, 'As Indigenous peoples we tend to think our ancestors were mostly right as compared to Westerners who seem to believe their ancestors were mostly wrong' (Blackstock, 2014). I hope that I have honoured my ancestors and done it well enough. It has been my personal mission throughout my career to bring the Indigenous teachings of my ancestors into contemporary practice, and by practising them as best I can, decolonise myself and indigenise the organisation I founded.

What follows is one Indigenous leader's view of leadership and the cultural worldviews that have shaped Indigenous concepts of leadership past and present.

Worldview and Indigenous Peoples' Approaches to Leadership

Below, I describe Western and Indigenous worldviews as starkly different as I believe them to be. However, I recognise that in doing so, I will grossly oversimplify each. This contrast is necessary since, to understand what shapes concepts of leadership, it is important to examine how worldview shapes values and related action.

The Indigenous populations I've worked with tend to share a relational worldview. A relational worldview understands the human experience as a complex, ever-shifting balance among our thoughts and feelings, our physical existence, our relationships with the entirety of the context in which we live and the spiritual nature of our human experience. This worldview is often referred to as the circle of life. In North America, it is frequently depicted as a four-quadrant circle of mind, body, spirit and relationships. The relational worldview makes meaning through synthesis. It relies on holistic thinking to understand the patterns and cycles of our interconnectedness in all aspects of our human experience. The relational worldview stands in stark contrast to the predominant worldview of Western society, which is linear. The linear worldview is dependent upon reductionist thinking. The analysis is used to make meaning through breaking things down into their smallest parts.

Each of these two worldviews exhibits sets of associated values. Linear worldview cultures tend to value hierarchy, individuality, independence, progress, productivity, measuring things, acquiring wealth, facts, written knowledge and compartmentalisation. The linear worldview favours the scientific method and human existence as above and apart from nature. This linear orientation tends to conceive of leadership as determined by individual leaders, apart from culture. Thus, leadership is discussed in terms of the style of individual leaders and theories of leadership tend to discuss what leadership type is most effective (Bass & Bass, 2009, preface). Studies about leadership often examine whether transformational leaders are more effective than transactional (Bass, 1999) or whether servant leaders are more effective than authoritarian leaders (Jaworski, 1996, p. ix). The cultural value of hierarchy shows up in top-down leadership structures. Linear values on measurement, written knowledge and productivity show up in bureaucratic structures, policies and procedures and performance reviews.

In contrast, relational worldview cultures tend to value principles, patterns, wisdom, generosity, interdependence, collectivism, autonomy and holistic thinking (Cross, 1987, p. 13). The relational worldview favours wisdom versus knowledge, multi-generational observation and human existence as essentially an expression of nature. These values shape who leads and how various aspects of leadership are manifested. Within a relational worldview culture, leadership tends to serve essential functions within that culture. Valuing the group requires strong stewardship. Protecting the autonomy of individuals in a collective requires room for dissent and shared leadership, valuing wisdom and elderhood requires capacity for discernment. Valuing the spiritual nature of life inspires adherence to related virtues, character and integrity in service to the well-being of the group. Thus, leadership is less about individual style than about culturally determined roles, obligations and responsibilities. Across specific cultural groups, leadership structures may be diverse, but each will reflect the relational values within the worldview.

Relational leadership tends not to be aspirational but rather both an obligation and a gift (Young, 2006). Individuals are less likely to seek leadership positions and more likely to be thrust into or groomed for leadership because of their character or lineage. Relational culture leaders tend to be oriented towards stewardship and service rather than accomplishment and achievement. They also tend to be thought leaders, holders of cultural values and keepers of protocol.

Relational worldview values tend to emphasise humility and thus the Indigenous leader is discouraged from rising above the group (those who do are likely to be brought down). Instead, the Indigenous leader is usually the one to go first, the one to assume personal risk and the one who accepts criticism with grace for the sake of peace and harmony. Relational leaders are encouraged to cultivate the virtues of integrity, discernment, fairness, dedication and compassion and put the needs of the group before their own.

Finally, the relational worldview holds that the spiritual realm holds influence on the human experience equal to the physical. Thus, Indigenous leaders tend to rely heavily on spiritual experiences, protocols, prayers, rituals and ceremonies for inspiration, guidance, vision, resilience and revelation in fulfilling their leadership roles. Leaders are likely to be careful but courageous, slow to judgment yet decisive, strong and yet flexible. They are likely to be entertained by folly but informed by wisdom.

We can glean some perspectives on Indigenous leadership from the words of 18th, 19th and 20th century Indigenous leaders whose words were recorded. Following are a few quotes that help illustrate the concerns of Indigenous leaders and, by extension, the values they represented.

- Red Jacket, 1792: 'Our eyes are opened so that we can see clearly. Our ears are unstopped so that we have been able to distinctly hear the words which you have spoken.' (Vanderwerth, 1971)
- Joseph Brant, c. 1780: 'No person among us desires any other reward for performing a brave and worthy action, but the consciousness of having served his nation.' Joseph Brant. (n.d.). AZQuotes.com. Retrieved August 27, 2024, from AZQuotes.com Web site: https://www.azquotes.com/author/38514-Joseph_Brant
- Red Cloud, 1870: 'We do not want riches but we do want to train our children right.' (Vanderwerth, 1971)
- Chief Joseph, 1877: 'I want to have time to look for my children, and see how many of them I can find'; and 1879: 'I have been asked to show you my heart. What I have to say will come from my heart.' (Vanderwerth, 1971)
- Chief Seattle, 1853: 'Our religion is the traditions of our ancestors—the dreams of our old men, given them in the solemn hours of night by the Great Spirit.' (Vanderwerth, 1971)
- Sitting Bull, 1883: 'Now I will tell you my mind and I will tell everything straight,' (Vanderwerth, 1971)and 1877: 'Let us put our minds together and see what life we can make for our children.' (Vanderwerth, 1971)
- Black Elk, 1930: 'The power of the world always works in circles.' (Vanderwerth, 1971)

Historically, these leadership attributes and characteristics were intentionally nurtured, taught and shaped in youth by leaders of different types. Grooming of future leaders was recognised as essential to the survival of the group. Unfortunately, this careful attention to leadership development was interrupted and undermined by colonisation.

The history of the colonisation of Indigenous peoples is long and complex. It is a history of attempted genocide and pervasive deculturalisation (Spring, 2001). However, Indigenous peoples persist today despite the best efforts of European settler colonialism. Indigenous resistance has kept the cultures alive despite overwhelming odds. In no small part, the persistent survival of

Indigenous nations is due to the strength and structure of leadership. Indigenous nations are working to reclaim land, natural resources, sovereignty, culture and their children in a process that has been labelled 'decolonization' (Smith, 2002, pp.3-4; Cross et al., 2019, p. 101). Many are working to shed dysfunctional leadership approaches imposed by colonialism and to embrace the leadership structures and styles of their ancestors. Many have been able to retain their ancestral leadership structures. Two prominent examples are the Pueblos of the American Southwest, whose governments are hundreds of years old, and the Haudenosaunee (aka Iroquois) Confederacy, this author's identity.

The Great Law: An Enduring Example of Indigenous Leadership

The Great Law of the Haudenosaunee came into being almost nine centuries ago and has been maintained through rigorous oral tradition. Today nations of the Haudenosaunee Confederacy make it readily available through their cultural centres, museums and websites. The description that follows is based on this author's personal lifetime of learning and the Oneida Nation's website. In addition, there are numerous resources that may be consulted for reference (see Wallace, 1972; Wallace, 1946; Hertzberg, 1966).

The Great Law was brought to five Indigenous nations who spoke several dialects of a common language and culture but, at the time, were in constant conflict and strife. The Great Law was the dream of the peacemaker, Deganawida, to bring lasting and sustainable peace through establishing the Haudenosaunee Confederacy. This Confederacy, now of six nations, is the oldest continuously functioning democracy in the world. The Onondaga, Mohawk, Seneca, Oneida and Cayuga were joined by the Tuscarora in the early 1700s. The Great Law is an oral constitution. The Haudenosaunee record important documents in wampum belts. These belts of woven beads are memory triggers that are read at regular intervals so that each succeeding generation is able to recite the original oral agreements verbatim. In the Haudenosaunee belief system, you keep essential information in your head. Great care is taken to remember it exactly, and ritual and ceremony renew the sacred covenants that such belts represent. The Great Law is alive and as vital and clear today as it was in the 12th century.

The Great Law describes leadership in detail and divides that leadership into a balance of roles, functions and responsibilities that are like a woven wampum belt itself. The picture of leadership described by the Great Law gives leaders today direction and guidance about how to be effective leaders. It not only provides a blueprint for how to keep peace and harmony among nations but also informs us about how to ensure that the energy of any organisation can be directed towards the mission instead of internal conflict. Central to this blueprint is a foundation rooted in the White Roots of Peace, the essential values and spiritual teachings that are at the heart of the Confederacy.

At the founding of the Confederacy, the implements of war were buried beneath the Tree of Peace and forever abandoned in favour of being bound together in a lasting alliance of strength. Nine hundred years of unity is a strong testament to the wisdom of the Great Law's conceptions of leadership. Foremost, the value that supports the Confederacy is gratitude. Every official meeting or gathering begins with the Thanksgiving Address. A ritual opening that is far older than the Great Law. In reciting the Gan-on-yok (Thanksgiving Address), the first expression of gratitude is for the People. Specifically named are each type of leader as well as 'those with no particular title' because it is the workers, the cooks, the hunters and the farmers who make sure everyone is fed and the business, or ceremonials, can be conducted.

The Great Law names the Sachems or Chiefs to serve at the whim of the Clan Mothers, the matriarchal heads of extended families. The Sachems are statesmen who deliberate, speak, teach and provide spiritual guidance. They are the decision-makers and policymakers. They are mentors to the people and govern guided by stewardship, compelled to consider the needs of the seventh generation to come. Their authority to lead comes by way of appointment to their post by the clan mothers.

A type of leader called the Pine Tree Chiefs are servant leaders. They are recognised for their interest, hard work, dependability, wisdom and honesty. They sit with the formal leaders as advisors or key knowledge holders. Their authority as leaders comes only from their contributions and integrity.

The Great Law describes the role of the War Chief. They protect the people in times of conflict. They carry messages in service to the Clan Mothers and the Chiefs. They are managers, implementers and when needed commanders. In times of emergency, they may behave in autocratic ways, always aware that they will be held accountable by the clan mothers.

Clan Mothers select and can dismiss the Chiefs and War Chiefs. They are the holders of protocol and the holders of names and naming. They are responsible for the right conduct of rituals and ceremonies. They are the eyes and ears of the sachems and the voice of the people. They nurture and mentor potential chiefs and monitor the needs of the families. They are advocates for the children, the elderly and the infirm.

A group called the Faithkeepers are the operatives that implement the decisions of the leader. They manage the timing of the ceremonies according to ancient celestial knowledge. They ensure the ceremonies are being done correctly. Faithkeepers are responsible for convening people when necessary and for the communication of vital information to the community about ceremonial events. They find the helpers and conduct the protocols according to the policies set by the leaders. And finally, they are spiritual advisors to the people and also to the leaders. Faithkeepers are ultimately responsible for reminding everyone of the values behind the Great Law. They help ensure that everyone understands and appreciates why things are done according to the protocol. Their authority comes from their integrity as the holders of values that are foundational to the Great Law.

At every level of this leadership structure are checks and balances. No distinct group has power without the authority that comes from another segment of the leadership. It is a system of shared leadership and a recognition that different circumstances require particular types of leadership. It checks human nature and limits gender dominance. It gives authority and recognition to informal leaders to hold formal leadership accountable. It keeps leadership focused on the needs of the people and it encourages sustainability through advancing leaders of merit, stewardship and integrity.

Some authors have proposed that leadership styles represent a hierarchy of leadership and that leaders should strive to become the 'renewing' leader (Jaworski, 1996) or the 'visionary' leader. The Haudenosaunee approach is to embrace all types of leadership as equally important and to recognise that different circumstances or challenges are best served by specific leadership types. The Great Law outlined those leadership types almost a millennium ago but still provides us with valuable guidance for developing leaders today.

Insights into Leadership Development in Western Cultures

Each leadership role described in the Great Law has its own set of demands, energy, ethos and challenges. Each role requires talents, skills, discipline and effort commensurate with the responsibilities associated with the roles. The Great Law provides clarity regarding the functions of leadership. It is carefully structured to support a balance of power and ensure peace fulfilment of the duties of governance. It is so well crafted that the framers of the US Constitution used it as a model (Davis, 2023; S. Hrg. 100-610, 1987).

Developing leaders can benefit from understanding the types of leadership that each role exemplifies. The sachem role requires discernment, perspective, courage and skin 'seven thumbs thick' (Oneida Nation: The Great Law). The sachem must be grounded in mission, values and ethics, must be clear in communication and be future-oriented stewards of well-being. The pine tree chief must bring the value of specific knowledge or capacity to inform dialogue and decision-making. They must be dedicated to the mission. Both of these leadership functionaries gain respect by exhibiting humility, transcendence, revelation, vision and the shaping of a preferred future. They lead by recognising and encouraging potential in others. Their leadership type is the servant leader, empowering others and respecting the limits of leadership.

The war chief is trustworthy, able to respond to emergencies, keeps a cool head and is able to calm others in moments of crisis. They manage the day-to-day demands of deploying resources, implementing policy and monitoring procedures. When needed, they exercise power, control and authority within the constraints set by those who have bestowed authority upon them. They are the transactional leader and influence others by going first, assuming risk and exemplifying courage.

The clan mother is the steward. A servant leader who shapes the future through intentional development of the potential around her. This type of leadership pays attention to goals, cause, stability, fairness and protocol. This leader holds the organisation accountable to its own norms, values and rules and is able to be bureaucratic when procedures are needed for stability and accountability.

The faithkeeper leaders are detail-oriented holders of institutional memory and values. They ensure clear communication, productive meetings and attention to the tasks required to accomplish the day-to-day work of the organisation. The faithkeepers include technocrats whose expertise is valued for fulfilling the obligations and objectives of the organisation and ensuring that things are done at the right time.

Leaders today must embody elements of all of these leadership functions. They lead best when their leadership styles support surrounding themselves with co-leaders who embody the attributes most needed in various functions of the organisation. The effective leader knows which functions they excel at and which are more challenging. Knowing this allows them to engage co-leaders who mitigate their weaknesses and keep their worst tendencies in check.

The sachem leadership style is often focused outward, whereas the clan mother type is focused inward. The sachem type is focused on doing the right things, and the faithkeeper type is focused on doing things right.

Western cultures tend to centre concepts of leadership in the individual. Indigenous cultures tend to centre concepts of leadership in the systems of the culture. Western culture tends to assign a hierarchy of human value to specific leadership types. Indigenous cultures tend to place value on leadership as a process that serves and sustains the well-being of the group.

Western cultures might use Indigenous examples of leadership types to explore what types of leadership are required in different parts of an organisation. What consequences might result from bringing the wrong leadership energy to an organisational challenge? The Western leaders might explore what aptitudes, talents and characteristics leaders bring to their roles and how well their attributes align with the varied challenges of the diverse types of leadership needed in any organisation for success. The Western leader might also explore the consequences of misalignment of leadership aspirations with the demands of diverse circumstances in the organisation, and explore the stress that results when the leadership approaches that are needed are outside the comfort zone of the leader. How can that leader structure or staff the organisation so that each type of leader needed to bring a sustainable balance to the collective mission of the organisation is present? Finally, the Western leader might want to explore or embrace the value that shared leadership might bring to the organisation.

The most important thing Western leaders can do is reject the false colonial assumption that Indigenous ways of knowing have little to contribute to scholarly discourse, in this instance, insights about leadership. Branded as primitive, the valuable insights of Indigenous cultures have too often been overlooked. To date, Indigenous concepts have been given almost no consideration in the leadership development discourse in higher education. By recognising the legitimacy of Indigenous thought and engaging with Indigenous models, the Western leader can support the process of decolonisation. By welcoming Indigenous perspectives into leadership discourse, Western scholars can make space for Indigenous leaders to do the work of Indigenising leadership.

Conclusion

Concepts regarding leadership and the development of leaders are bound by the worldview of the observer. Historically, Indigenous populations had well-defined and functioning leadership structures which aligned with their worldview. The Great Law of the Haudenosaunee Confederacy and its leadership structure and guidance are a testament to relational Indigenous approaches. Its persistence over a millennium, despite the assault of colonisation, is evidence of its strength. The founding fathers of the USA found it so compelling that they appropriated much of its structure into the US Constitution (Barreiro, 1988; Davis, 2023). This chapter calls for expanding conceptualisations of leadership development in higher education and for supporting relational worldview leadership approaches in Indigenous nations and organisations.

References

Allen, W.R. Personal communication c. 2014. (note: Ron Allen, Chairperson of the Jamestown S'Klallam Tribe in Washington served several terms as president of the National Congress of American Indians. When asked how he became a leader, Ron remarked that he was asked by elder in a meeting to take notes. When it was time to report out the elders put him out front with his notes. He coined the label "scribe leader" to acknowledge being chosen for leadership due to service, capacity, and the faith of elders. This was also the author's experience.)

Barreiro, J. (1988). Indian roots of American democracy. Cultural encounter I. Special constitution bicentennial edition, 1988. *Northeast Indian Quarterly, 4*(4), 47–66.

Bass, B. M. (1999). Two decades of research and development in transformational leadership. *European Journal of Work and Organizational Psychology, 8*(1), 9–32. https://doi.org/10.1080/135943299398410

Bass, B. M., & Bass, R. (2009). *The Bass handbook of leadership: Theory, research, and managerial applications.* Simon and Schuster.

Black Elk (1930). The power of the world always works in circles. In J. G. Neihardt, P. Deloria, & R. DeMallie (Eds.), (2014)*The first cure. In Black Elk speaks: The complete edition* (pp. 121–126). University of Nebraska Press. https://doi.org/10.2307/j.ctt1d9njt6.26

Blackstock, C. (2014), Keynote speech. National American Indian Conference on Child Abuse and Neglect, Hollywood, FL.

Brant, J. (1780): *"No person among us desires any other reward for performing a brave and worthy action, but the consciousness of having served his nation."* Joseph Brant. (n.d.). AZQuotes.com. Retrieved August 27, 2024, from AZQuotes.com Web site: https://www.azquotes.com/author/38514-Joseph_Brant

Chief Joseph (1877). *"I want to have time to look for my children, and see how many of them I can find"*; and 1879: *"I have been asked to show you my heart. What I have to say will come from my heart."* (In. W. C. Vanderwerth, (ed). *Indian Oratory: Famous Speeches by Noted Indian Chieftains* (1971, p. 106-107). University of Oklahoma Press.

Chief Seattle (1853). *Our religion is the traditions of our ancestors—the dreams of our old men, given them in the solemn hours of night by the Great Spirit.* In W. C. Vanderwerth (Ed.), *Indian oratory: Famous speeches by noted Indian chieftains* (1971) (pp. 97–98). University of Oklahoma Press.

Cross, T. L. (1987). *Cross-Cultural skills in Indian child welfare: A guide for the non-indian* (2nd ed.). National Indian Child Welfare Association.

Cross, T. L., Pewewardy, C., & Smith, A. T. (2019). Restorative education, reconciliation, and healing: Indigenous perspectives on decolonizing leadership education. *New Directions for Student Leadership, 2019*(163), 101–115.

Davis, J. (2023). *The Haudenosaunee Confederacy and the Constitution. Library of congress blog.* Retrieved from https://blogs.loc.gov/law/2023/09/the-haudenosaunee-confederacy-and-the-constitution/

Hertzberg, H. W. (1966). *The great tree and the longhouse: The culture of the Iroquois*. Macmillan Co.

Jaworski, J. (1996). *Synchronicity: The inner path of leadership*. Berrett-Koehler Publishers.

Oneida Nation. (n.d.) *Clan systems*. Retrieved from https://oneida-nsn.gov/our-ways/our-story/clan-systems/

Oneida Nation. (n.d.) The great law. Retrieved from https://oneida-nsn.gov/our-ways/great-law-of-peace/viewed 8/10/2024.

S. Hrg. 100-610. (1987). Iroquois Confederacy of Nations, Hearing on S. Con. Res. 76 Before the S. Select Comm. on Indian Affairs, 100th Cong.

Seneca Cayuga Tribe. (n.d.) *The Senecas, their beliefs: Great Law of Peace*. Retrieved from https://sctribe.com/sites/default/files/2022-10/Great-Law-of-Peace.pdf.

Smith, L. T. (2002). *Decolonizing methodologies: Research and Indigenous peoples*. New York, NY: University of Otago Press.

Spring, J. (2001). *Deculturalization and the struggle for equality* (3rd ed.). New York, NY: McGraw-Hill.

Vanderwerth, W. C. (1971). *Indian oratory: Famous speeches by noted Indian chieftains*. United Kingdom: University of Oklahoma Press.

Wallace, P. A. W. (1946). *The white roots of peace*. University of Pennsylvania Press.

Wallace, A. (1972). *The death and rebirth of the Seneca*. New York: N.Y. Vintage Books.

Young, A. E. (2006). *Elders' teachings on indigenous leadership: Leadership is a gift* (Doctoral dissertation). University of British Columbia. https://dx.doi.org/10.14288/1.0064638

Section 2

Approaches to Leadership

Asia Perspectives

6

Kaizen

Ray Tak-yin Hui[1,2]

[1] *Faculty of Business and Law, University of Roehampton, London, UK*
[2] *NUCB Business School, Nagoya University of Commerce and Business, Nagoya, Japan*

The Big Idea

Kaizen (改善), a Japanese term meaning 'change for the better' or 'continuous improvement', is a philosophy focusing on small, incremental changes to improve efficiency and quality (Imai, 1986). It is composed of two Japanese words: 'KAI' and 'ZEN', where 'KAI' means reform, change, modify, examine and inspect and 'ZEN' means better, virtuous and goodness (Macpherson et al., 2015). Kaizen is deeply ingrained in Japanese corporate culture and reflects a commitment to constantly reflect and strive for improvement in all aspects of work as a daily routine activity (de Lange-Ros & Boer, 2001; Fukushige & Spicer, 2007; Kiran, 2019; Recht & Wilderom, 1998). The concept has been widely applied, for example, by Toyota Production System (TPS), where Kaizen involved all employees from the CEO to assembly line workers in suggesting and implementing improvements (Maarof & Mahmud, 2016). This inclusive approach ensures that improvement is a continuous, daily process rather than an occasional activity.

Mosaic Leadership: African, Asian, Middle Eastern and Indigenous Perspectives,
First Edition. Edited by Jonathan Passmore, Badri Bajaj, and Mongezi C Makhalima.

Published 2026 by John Wiley & Sons Ltd.

Principles of Kaizen

The core idea behind Kaizen is that small, consistent positive changes can lead to significant improvements over time, fostering a culture of efficiency, quality and productivity (McLoughlin & Miura, 2017). According to the Kaizen Institute (n.d.), Kaizen is built on five principles that collectively promote a culture of continuous improvement:

1. **Create Customer Value**: At the heart of Kaizen is the relentless pursuit of customer satisfaction. By understanding customer needs and preferences, organisations can continually refine their processes to deliver superior value.
2. **Create Flow Efficiency**: Kaizen advocates for optimising the flow of materials and information within an organisation. This involves minimising wastage and streamlining processes to enhance overall efficiency.
3. **Be Gemba-oriented**: Gemba, or the shop floor where value is created, holds pivotal importance in Kaizen. Leaders and employees are encouraged to observe processes firsthand, identify inefficiencies and implement improvements directly where the work is done. For example, implementing the 5S methodology (Sort, Set in order, Shine, Standardise and Sustain) to create an organised and efficient workspace.
4. **Empower and Engage People**: Central to Kaizen's success is empowering employees at all levels to contribute to continuous improvement. By soliciting ideas and insights from frontline workers, organisations can harness collective intelligence to drive innovation and efficiency. People's mindset could be transformed by engaging them in workshops and training organised by the organisation.
5. **Agility and Adaptability**: A culture rooted in Kaizen principles enables organisations to respond swiftly to market changes and challenges. By fostering a mindset of continuous and autonomous improvement, organisations remain agile and adaptable in dynamic business environments.
6. **Create Visual Standards**: Visual management tools are integral to Kaizen, facilitating transparency and accountability in process improvement efforts. By making standards, deviations and improvement progress visible, organisations can ensure consistency and sustained quality improvement. For example, SDCA

(Standardise, Do, Check and Act) and PDCA (Plan, Do, Check and Act) are valuable tools that should be used in cycles to improve standardisation.

Kaizen in Action: Frameworks and Methodologies

Kaizen employs several structured frameworks to guide continuous improvement initiatives, including 5S, PDCA and SDCA:

1. The 5S Framework
   The 5S methodology—Sort, Set in order, Shine, Standardise and Sustain—is a systematic approach to workplace organisation and cleanliness. By organising workspaces efficiently and maintaining cleanliness standards, organisations enhance productivity and reduce waste (Hirano, 1995). The five phases are:

   1. **Sort (Seiri)**: Remove unnecessary items from the workplace.
   2. **Set in Order (Seiton)**: Arrange necessary items in an orderly manner, so they are easy to find and use.
   3. **Shine (Seiso)**: Clean the workspace and keep it tidy.
   4. **Standardise (Seiketsu)**: Develop standards and procedures to maintain and monitor the first three Ss.
   5. **Sustain (Shitsuke)**: Ensure discipline and make 5S a habit in the workplace.

2. The PDCA Framework
   The PDCA (Plan-Do-Check-Act) cycle, also known as the Deming cycle, serves as a systematic method for problem-solving and process improvement. Through four-step iterative process, organisations can systematically achieve continuous improvement in their operations (Deming, 1986). The four steps are:

   1. **Plan**: Identify an opportunity for improvement and plan a change.
   2. **Do**: Implement the change on a small scale.
   3. **Check**: Review and analyse the results of the change.
   4. **Act**: If the change is successful, implement it on a larger scale. If not, refine the plan and repeat the cycle.

3. The SDCA Framework
   The SDCA (Standardise-Do-Check-Act) cycle complements the PDCA framework by emphasising the importance of standardising improvements. By establishing robust standards based on successful improvement initiatives, organisations ensure consistency and sustainability in their operational practices (Watson & DeYong, 2010). SDCA involves:

   1. **Standardise**: Establish standards and best practices based on previous improvements.
   2. **Do**: Implement the standardised processes.
   3. **Check**: Monitor and evaluate the results against the standards.
   4. **Act**: Take action to correct deviations from the standards and improve the processes further.

Benefits of Kaizen

Implementing Kaizen yields a multitude of benefits that contribute to organisational success:

- **Enhanced Productivity**: By eliminating inefficiencies and optimising workflows, Kaizen enables organisations to achieve higher levels of productivity and operational efficiency.
- **Improved Quality**: Continuous attention to detail and incremental improvements result in enhanced product and service quality, thereby boosting customer satisfaction and loyalty.
- **Employee Empowerment**: Involving employees in the Kaizen process fosters a sense of ownership, engagement and commitment to organisational goals. This empowerment cultivates a positive workplace culture built on collaboration and continuous learning.
- **Cost Reduction**: Identifying and eliminating waste not only improves operational efficiency but also leads to significant cost savings for organisations.
- **Agility and Adaptability**: A culture rooted in Kaizen principles enables organisations to respond swiftly to market changes and challenges. By fostering a mindset of continuous improvement, organisations remain agile and adaptable in dynamic business environments.

Expanding Kaizen's Influence

Beyond its foundational principles and methodologies, Kaizen continues to evolve and expand its influence in contemporary management practices (Suárez-Barraza, 2023). Organisations increasingly integrate Kaizen principles into broader strategic initiatives, such as lean management and total quality management (TQM), to drive sustainable growth and competitive advantage.

How to Apply It

Kaizen, emphasising continuous improvement through small, incremental changes, offers a distinctive and effective approach to leadership and coaching in organisations. This philosophy, rooted in Japanese management practices, enhances leadership and coaching effectiveness in fostering continuous improvement among employees throughout their work processes (Miller et al., 2014).

Implementing Kaizen in Leadership

1. Cultivate a Continuous Improvement Mindset:
   Kaizen promotes input from employees at all levels. Leaders should create an environment where employees feel comfortable suggesting and implementing improvements autonomously without fear of criticism. This can be achieved through regular team meetings, suggestion boxes and formal feedback channels. Recognising and rewarding employees for their contributions to improvements further encourages participation and ownership.

2. Engage Employees at All Levels:
   Kaizen promotes the involvement of employees at all levels. Leaders should create an environment where employees feel comfortable suggesting improvements without fear of criticism. This can be achieved through regular team meetings, suggestion boxes and creating formal channels for feedback. Recognising and rewarding employees for their contributions to improvements can further encourage participation and ownership.

3. Gemba Walks:
   Leaders should spend time on the shop floor (Gemba) where the actual work is done. This allows them to observe processes first-hand, understand the challenges employees face and identify opportunities for improvement. Gemba walks should be conducted with a spirit of inquiry and collaboration, rather than inspection and judgement. This hands-on approach helps leaders make informed decisions and build stronger relationships with their teams.

4. Standardise and Document Processes:
   Standardisation is crucial for sustaining improvements. Leaders should work with their teams to document best practices and create standard operating procedures (SOPs). These standards should be clearly communicated and regularly reviewed for relevance. Visual management tools like process maps and flowcharts can make these standards easily accessible and understandable.

Conclusion

In this chapter on Kaizen, I explore its principles as a method of continuous improvement through small, incremental changes. Kaizen emphasises employee involvement, leadership engagement on the shop floor (Gemba) and the importance of standardising processes for sustained efficiency, quality and productivity. I reviewed Kaizen's frameworks like 5S, PDCA and SDCA and suggest the model is a useful one for leaders in their own self-development journeys.

References

de Lange-Ros, E., & Boer, H. (2001). Theory and practice of continuous improvement in shop-floor teams. *International Journal of Technology Management, 22*(4), 244–358.

Deming, W. E. (1986). *Out of the crisis*. USA: MIT Press.

Fukushige, A., & Spicer, D. P. (2007). Leadership preferences in Japan: an exploratory study. *Leadership and Organization Development Journal, 28*(6), 508–530.

Hirano, H. (1995). *5 pillars of the visual workplace: The sourcebook for 5S implementation*. Japan: Productivity Press.

Imai, M. (1986). *Kaizen: The key to Japan's competitive success.* USA: McGraw-Hill Education.

Kaizen institute (n.d.). KAIZEN Foundations are one of the pillars of creating a KAIZEN Culture. Kaizen Institute. Retreved from https://kaizen.com/insights/article-master-kaizen-foundations.

Kiran, D. R. (2019). Terminology used in Japanese management practices. In D. R. Kiran (Ed.), *Production planning and control* (pp. 87–102). UK: Butterworth-Heinemann.

Maarof, M. G., & Mahmud, F. (2016). A review of contributing factors and challenges in implementing Kaizen in small and medium enterprises. *Procedia Economics and Finance, 35*, 522–531.

Macpherson, W., Lockhart, J., Kavan, H., & Iaquinto, A. (2015). Kaizen: A Japanese philosophy and system for business excellence. *Journal of Business Strategy, 36*(5), 3–9.

McLoughlin, C., & Miura, T. (2017). *True kaizen: Management's role in improving work climate and culture.* UK: Taylor & Francis.

Miller, J., Wroblewski, M., & Villafuerte, J. (2014). *Creating a kaizen culture: Align the organization, achieve breakthrough results, and sustain the gains.* USA: McGraw-Hill Education.

Recht, R., & Wilderom, C. (1998). Kaizen and culture: on the transferability of Japanese suggestion systems. *International Business Review, 7*(1), 7–22.

Suárez-Barraza, M. F. (2023). *KAIZEN-21: The philosophy of continuous improvement and operational innovation in the new global environment.* UK: Emerald Publishing Limited.

Watson, G. H., & DeYong, C. F. (2010). Design for six sigma: Caveat emptor. *International Journal of Lean Six Sigma, 1*(1), 66–84.

7

Mengzi's Five Virtues—Ren, Yi, Li, Zhi and Xin

Dan Qin[1] *& Ray Tak-yin Hui*[1,2]

[1] *NUCB Business School, Nagoya University of Commerce and Business, Nagoya, Japan*
[2] *Faculty of Business and Law, University of Roehampton, London, UK*

The Big Idea

Mencius or Mengzi ('Master Meng'; c. 371 – c. 289 BCE) is a renowned Chinese Confucian philosopher, who is often referred to as the 'Second Sage' after Confucius. One of his key contributions was his belief in the innate goodness of human nature. He argued that all humans are born with a sense of morality and righteousness, which can be nurtured through education and self-discipline. He also emphasised the responsibility of rulers to provide for the well-being of their people, advocating for just and humane governance.

Mencius identified four innate moral qualities in human beings, which he called Siduan (四端; four beginnings/ Sprouts). Siduan includes **Ren** (仁; benevolence), **Yi** (義; righteousness), **Li** (禮; rites) and **Zhi** (智: wisdom; Mencius). Later, Dong Zhongshu added the fifth virtue, **Xin** (信; trustworthiness) and made it the well-known five virtues (Thacker, 2003). These virtues, initially intended for personal and political morality, have found relevance in contemporary discussions on ethical business leadership. Mencius's philosophy is grounded in the intrinsic goodness of human nature and the cultivation of moral virtues.

1. **Ren (仁; benevolence)** is the essence of humaneness and compassion. It is the virtue that drives individuals to care for others and act with kindness. Mencius believed that Ren is the

Mosaic Leadership: African, Asian, Middle Eastern and Indigenous Perspectives, First Edition. Edited by Jonathan Passmore, Badri Bajaj, and Mongezi C Makhalima.

Published 2026 by John Wiley & Sons Ltd.

foundation of all moral actions and is inherent in every person (Van Norden, 1997, 2019). This virtue encourages empathy and altruism, promoting a society where people look out for one another. In contemporary terms, Ren can be seen in acts of charity, volunteerism and community service.

2. **Yi (義; righteousness)** represents moral rectitude and the commitment to do what is right, regardless of personal cost. It is the internal compass that guides individuals to act with integrity and honour. Mencius emphasised that Yi involves a sense of duty and justice, often requiring one to make sacrifices for the greater good (Wǔcháng, 2009). In modern contexts, Yi can be observed in whistleblowers who expose corruption or individuals who stand up against injustice.
3. **Li (禮; rites)** pertains to the observance of rituals, customs and social norms that maintain societal harmony (Wǔcháng, 2009). It encompasses manners, etiquette and respect for tradition. Mencius saw Li as essential for creating a structured and orderly society where everyone knows their role and behaves accordingly. Today, Li can be reflected in professional conduct, cultural ceremonies and the observance of laws and regulations.
4. **Zhi (智: wisdom)** involves the ability to make sound judgements and decisions based on moral principles (Van Norden, 2019). It is not just about knowledge but also about applying that knowledge ethically. Mencius regarded wisdom as crucial for discerning right from wrong and for guiding one's actions in a virtuous manner (Crossan et al., 2015; Tiwald, 2020). In the present day, Zhi can be seen in ethical leadership, critical thinking and informed decision-making.
5. **Xin (信; trustworthiness)** was later added by Dong Zhongshu and is considered the foundation for the other virtues (Wǔcháng, 2009). It is the virtue of being reliable, sincere and honest, building the foundation of trust in relationships and society. Trustworthiness ensures that individuals can depend on each other, fostering a sense of security and cooperation. In contemporary settings, Xin is vital in business ethics, personal relationships and public trust in institutions.

Mencius's virtues provide a robust framework for ethical leadership in business, emphasising the importance of compassion, integrity, wisdom, propriety and trustworthiness. By integrating these virtues into their leadership approach, business leaders can create more ethical, harmonious and successful organisations.

How to Apply It

The integration of Mencius's five virtues, benevolence, righteousness, propriety, wisdom and trustworthiness, into business leadership can have profound implications for organisational culture and effectiveness.

Promoting Benevolent Leadership (Ren)

Ren (benevolence) in leadership involves fostering a culture of kindness, mutual respect and well-meaning intentions within the organisation. Leaders who cultivate benevolence create a trusting workplace environment where team members do not expend mental and emotional energy worrying about each other's intentions. The benevolent atmosphere allows teams to focus on forward-looking goals and elevate company performance. Moreover, benevolence can be cultivated through both formal and informal practices. Formal benevolence might involve structured tools like feedback systems, rewards and developmental programs, while informal benevolence hinges on authentic, spontaneous acts of kindness and respect among colleagues. Both forms of benevolence are crucial for long-term success and talent retention in profit-oriented organisations. To embody Ren, leaders should prioritise empathy and compassion in their interactions. This includes:

- **Active Listening**: Paying close attention to employees' concerns and needs, showing genuine interest and care.
- **Supportive Environment**: Creating policies and practices that support work–life balance, mental health and overall well-being.
- **Inclusive Culture**: Encouraging diversity and inclusion, ensuring that everyone feels valued and respected.

Upholding Ethical Standards (Yi)

Yi (righteousness) implies a commitment to fairness and ethical practices, ensuring that decisions benefit not just the organisation but also society at large. It means leading by example and making tough decisions that reflect moral integrity (Van Norden, 2008). Righteousness pertains to upholding ethical standards and moral integrity in business practices. This virtue is essential for establishing a transparent and honest corporate culture, where leaders are deeply connected to the operational realities of their organisations and address ethical failings proactively (Crossan et al., 2015). Leaders must embody ethical conduct and serve as role models, demonstrating a commitment to doing what is right even when faced with challenging situations. Leaders can practise Yi by maintaining high ethical standards and promoting a culture of integrity. This involves:

- **Transparent Decision-Making**: Ensuring that decisions are made transparently and fairly, with input from relevant stakeholders.
- **Ethics Training**: Providing regular training on ethical behaviour and decision-making, reinforcing the importance of integrity.
- **Accountability Mechanisms**: Implementing systems to hold individuals accountable for unethical behaviour, ensuring justice and fairness.

Demonstrating Respect and Cultural Sensitivity (Li)

Li (rites) in leadership involves adhering to societal and organisational norms and showing respect and courtesy in all interactions. Leaders who practise propriety may be seen as maintaining a professional demeanour that fosters a respectful and dignified workplace. This virtue underpins the creation of a stable platform of core competencies that drive organisational value and helps in developing meaningful partnerships within the industry ecosystem. Leaders must be conscious of their behaviour and the cultural norms of their organisation, ensuring that their actions align with both internal and external expectations. To practise Li, leaders should demonstrate respect and cultural sensitivity in their interactions. This includes:

- **Cultural Awareness**: Educating themselves and their teams about different cultural practices and norms, promoting mutual respect.

- **Respectful Communication**: Encouraging courteous and respectful communication, addressing any disrespectful behaviour promptly.
- **Adherence to Norms**: Upholding organisational norms and traditions, fostering a sense of belonging and stability.

Cultivating Wisdom and Sound Judgement (Zhi)

Zhi (Wisdom) in business leadership encompasses strategic thinking, sound judgement and the ability to navigate complex challenges. Transformational leaders utilise wisdom to move beyond tactical optimisation and engage in deep strategic exploration, harnessing available opportunities and resources to innovate and grow. Developing wisdom involves continuous learning and an unwavering commitment to understanding the broader implications of business decisions, ultimately supporting the organisation and contributing positively to society (Crossan et al., 2015). Leaders can develop Zhi by seeking continuous learning and applying wisdom in decision-making. This involves:

- **Lifelong Learning**: Encouraging a culture of continuous learning and development, staying informed about industry trends and best practices.
- **Critical Thinking**: Promoting critical thinking and problem-solving skills, enabling teams to tackle complex challenges effectively.
- **Balanced Decisions**: Making decisions that consider both short-term and long-term impacts, ensuring sustainable growth.

Building Trust and Reliability (Xin)

Xin (Trustworthiness) involves demonstrating reliability, loyalty and a steadfast commitment to the organisation and its stakeholders. Leaders who exhibit faithfulness inspire trust and confidence among their team members and external partners. This virtue is critical for leaders as it underscores the importance of being dependable and maintaining a consistent focus on long-term organisational goals. Faithfulness reinforces the leader's commitment to their role and the organisation, driving sustained success and organisational cohesion (Crossan et al., 2015). To embody Xin, leaders should focus on building trust and reliability. This includes:

- **Consistency**: Ensuring that actions and words are consistent, following through on commitments and promises.
- **Transparency**: Being open and honest in communications, sharing information and updates regularly.
- **Reliability**: Demonstrating dependability in all interactions, being someone that employees and stakeholders can count on.

Challenges

Applying Mencius's virtues in business leadership involves several challenges that can complicate their effective implementation. Obstacles to applying social norms in general also hamper the application of Mencius's ideas. For example, the subjective nature in the interpretation of these virtues can significantly hinder consistent applications. Additionally, systematic cognitive barriers can blind individuals to their own unethical behaviours, thereby hampering the ability to maximise value creation in the business context (Bazerman, 2020).

Applying Mencius's virtues also faces a unique challenge. Mencius emphasised that virtues like benevolence and propriety are inherent in individuals and need proper nurture to flourish (Van Norden, 2019). However, the complexities of modern business environments may challenge the nurturing of these virtues, making it difficult to align personal aspirations with organisational goals.

Conclusion

In this chapter, we have explored the concept of Mengzi's four innate moral qualities in human being and thus in leaders, which includes **Ren** (仁; benevolence), **Yi** (義; righteousness), **Li** (禮; rites), **Zhi** (智: wisdom; Mencius) and fifth virtue **Xin** (信; trustworthiness) added by Dong Zhongshu. Together these can provide a useful framework for leaders to hold in mind.

References

Van Norden, B. W. (2019). Mencius. In E. N. Zalta (Ed.), *The stanford encyclopedia of philosophy* (Fall 2019 ed.).

Wǔcháng, S. (2009). Three fundamental bonds and five constant virtues. *Berkshire Encyclopaedia of China, 5*, 2252–2255.

Van Norden, B. W. (trans.), (2008). Mengzi: With Selections from traditional commentaries, Indianapolis: Hackett Publishing.

Van Norden, B. W. (1997). Mencius on courage. In P. A. French, T. E. Uehling, & H. K. Wettstein (Eds.), *The philosophy of religion* (pp. 237–256). Notre Dame, IN: University of Notre Dame Press.

Crossan, M., Seijts, G., & Gandz, J. (2015). *Developing leadership character*. US: Routledge.

Bazerman, M. H. (2020). A new model for ethical leadership. *Harvard Business Review, 98*(5), 90–97.

Thacker, T. C. (2003). Wu chang (Five constant virtues). In X. Yao (Ed.), *Encyclopaedia of confucianism* (pp. 660). Abingdon, UK: Routledge.

Tiwald, J. (2020). Song-Ming confucianism. In E. N. Zalta (Ed.), *Stanford encyclopaedia of philosophy summer* (2020th ed.). USA: Stanford.

8

Vasudhev Kutumbhkam

Badri Bajaj

Department of Humanities & Social Sciences, Jaypee Institute of Information Technology, Noida, India

The Big Idea

'Vasudhaiva Kutumbakam' is a Sanskrit phrase that conveys the idea that 'the world is one family'. This concept originated from the ancient Indian texts, the Maha Upanishad. The Maha Upanishad is a collection of philosophical writings. This phrase captures the essence of universalism—the idea that all people are related and there is oneness of humanity regardless of their race, religion, ethnicity or nationality. It supports the notion that all people are members of a single family and promotes empathy, understanding and respect for one another among people and groups. This age-old Indian concept fosters inclusivity and harmony by highlighting how interconnected everyone is.

In leadership development, the idea of 'Vasudhaiva Kutumbakam' can be used to promote a sense of empathy, inclusivity and belongingness. Leaders can draw motivation to expand their perspectives, embrace diversity and acknowledge the inherent value and dignity of every person. Moreover, it can inspire them to nurture healthy relationships, get together efficiently and contribute to the welfare of other people, both within their immediate circles and the wider community. By fostering an inclusive and empathetic leadership style, leaders may create a more cohesive and collaborative environment. Leaders having 'Vasudhaiva Kutumbakam' as their core philosophy can better handle conflicts with empathy and openness,

Mosaic Leadership: African, Asian, Middle Eastern and Indigenous Perspectives, First Edition. Edited by Jonathan Passmore, Badri Bajaj, and Mongezi C Makhalima.

Published 2026 by John Wiley & Sons Ltd.

leading to more effective and lasting resolutions. Leaders following the 'Vasudhaiva Kutumbakam' ideology can inspire their teams and organisations to contribute positively to society.

This tool can assist leaders in handling cross-cultural interactions, building compatible and harmonious relationships with people and fostering inclusive environments where people feel valued and respected. Leadership development initiatives can make use of the concept of 'Vasudhaiva Kutumbakam' when there are cases where they encounter conflicts or misunderstandings. It can facilitate resolution. As the principle highlights shared humanity and common goals, leaders can learn to tackle conflicts with empathy, openness and an eagerness to collaborate towards mutually beneficial solutions. Leaders can apply the concept of 'Vasudhaiva Kutumbakam' in their leadership styles. This coaching tool can assist leaders in fostering inclusive leadership practices and promoting team cohesion. It can help cultivate a sense of belonging among team members from different backgrounds. This encourages leaders to reflect on their beliefs, biases and attitudes towards others on a personal level. By learning the idea of 'Vasudhaiva Kutumbakam', leaders can develop self-awareness and empathy in themselves. They can promote a sense of interconnectedness with humanity. This would lead to enhanced personal growth and well-being. The idea of 'Vasudhaiva Kutumbakam' can be used in coaching to encourage global citizenship and a feeling of social responsibility, particularly for leaders who want to improve society or effect social change. All things considered, 'Vasudhaiva Kutumbakam' can be an influential principle in coaching leaders. It can assist leaders to operate interpersonal dynamics, foster inclusive environments and embrace a wider perspective of interconnectedness and unity.

How to Apply it

Applying the concept of 'Vasudhaiva Kutumbakam' to leadership coaching involves guiding leaders to understand the concept and cultivate a mindset of empathy, inclusivity and belongingness. Coaching leaders for cultivating the 'Vasudhaiva Kutumbakam' concept may start with explaining to the leader what 'Vasudhaiva Kutumbakam' means—that is, 'the world is one family'. It is important to emphasise that this age-old Indian concept fosters inclusivity and harmony by highlighting how interconnected everyone is. Emphasise that the concept of 'Vasudhaiva Kutumbakam' can transform their leadership style to be more inclusive and empathetic. Support the leaders to take into account their views, values and perspectives for inclusion and diversity. Help the leader to identify any assumptions and stereotypes that they might be holding about people on the grounds of religion, race or nationality or other factors. Help leaders recognise and address unconscious biases that may be affecting their decision-making process and interactions with their team members.

Using the key message of 'Vasudhaiva Kutumbakam', assist the leaders to develop compassion and understanding for people from diverse backgrounds. Guide them to explore ways to practice empathy in daily interactions. Discuss with them empathy-building techniques, such as active listening and perspective-taking, to enhance their interpersonal relationships with other people. Talk about the actions the leader may take to encourage inclusion and a feeling of association in both their personal and professional settings. Invite leaders to explore how to implement inclusive practices, such as diverse hiring, equitable opportunities and creating safe spaces for dialogue. Encourage them to explore ways to build bridges and strengthen connections with individuals from diverse backgrounds.

Invite leaders to examine strategies for fostering understanding and fortifying ties with individuals from diverse backgrounds. Encourage them to look at how far they have come in implementing the idea of 'Vasudhaiva Kutumbakam'. Motivate them to reflect on their progress. Help the leaders establish objectives so they can apply 'Vasudhaiva Kutumbakam' concepts to their everyday lives. Make a plan for follow-up sessions to review progress, deal with the challenges that arise, plan actions and celebrate successes.

Conclusion

'Vasudhaiva Kutumbakam' leadership development tool can help leaders to understand this important concept and inculcate the mindset of empathy, inclusivity and belongingness with people from diverse backgrounds. Leaders can make a positive impact on society or contribute to social change by leveraging the concept of 'Vasudhaiva Kutumbakam'. By promoting the idea of oneness and inclusivity, leaders can build a positive organisational culture that values diversity and fosters mutual respect.

9

The Art of War

Ho C. Law[1,2]

[1] *Research & Psychology, Colombo Institute, Colombo, Sri Lanka*
[2] *Cambridge Coaching Psychology Group, Empsy Limited, Cambridge, UK*

The Big Idea

Sun Tzu's The Art of War 孫子兵法, a classic Chinese military treatise written around the 4th century BC, provides a timeless framework for understanding leadership, offering valuable insights for modern leaders and coaches. By embracing its principles, leaders can enhance their strategic thinking, operational effectiveness and ethical conduct in practice, navigating the complexities of today's business world with wisdom and agility. Although focused on warfare, its principles offer profound insights into leadership strategy. While readers can read the original chapter by the author (Sun Tzu, 2010) or the earlier translation of *Sun Tzu's The Art of War* (Griffith, 1963), this chapter focuses on leadership development while incorporating the latest critical thinking (Jackson, 2024; Law, 2010).

Historical and Cultural Context

The Art of War emerged during the Warring States period in ancient China, a time of intense conflict and strategic manoeuvring. Sun Tzu 孫子, a military strategist, presented his work to King Ho Lu of Wu 吳, demonstrating its effectiveness through a famous anecdote involving the training of female soldiers. The Chinese idiom 殺一儆百 kill one to warn a hundred means to

Mosaic Leadership: African, Asian, Middle Eastern and Indigenous Perspectives, First Edition. Edited by Jonathan Passmore, Badri Bajaj, and Mongezi C Makhalima.

Published 2026 by John Wiley & Sons Ltd.

punish an individual as an example to others. The story highlights the importance of leadership, discipline and accountability.

The Art of War Model of Leadership

The book comprises 13 interconnected essays covering various aspects of warfare, from strategic planning and operational leadership to tactical dispositions and the use of spies:

1. Planning 計
2. Operation/implementation (Waging War) 作戰
3. Offensive Strategy 謀攻
4. Tactical (Military) Disposition 形
5. Power 勢
6. Weaknesses and Strengths 虛實
7. Operational Leadership (Military Operation) 軍爭
8. Nine Changes 九變
9. Manoeuvring the Army 行軍
10. Topology (Terrain) 地形
11. Nine Terrains 九地
12. Incendiary Attacks 火攻
13. Employing Spies 用間

Applying these essays to a leadership model applicable for coaching, the approach emphasises a systems thinking that predates Western operational research (Forrester, 1968). Using a systems approach to capitalise on the interconnectivity of the 13 essays, the principles can be translated to a useful leadership model for coaching, as shown in Figure 9.1.

Key Principles

1. **Strategic Planning**: Sun Tzu stresses meticulous planning as the foundation for success. Leaders must consider five fundamental factors:

   - Tao 道(Ethical/Moral Principle): A shared vision grounded in ethics is crucial for inspiring and motivating teams.
   - Heaven 天(Meteorology): Understanding and leveraging environmental factors, including weather.
   - Earth 地(Geography): Strategic positioning and utilising geographical advantages (Essays 10 & 11).

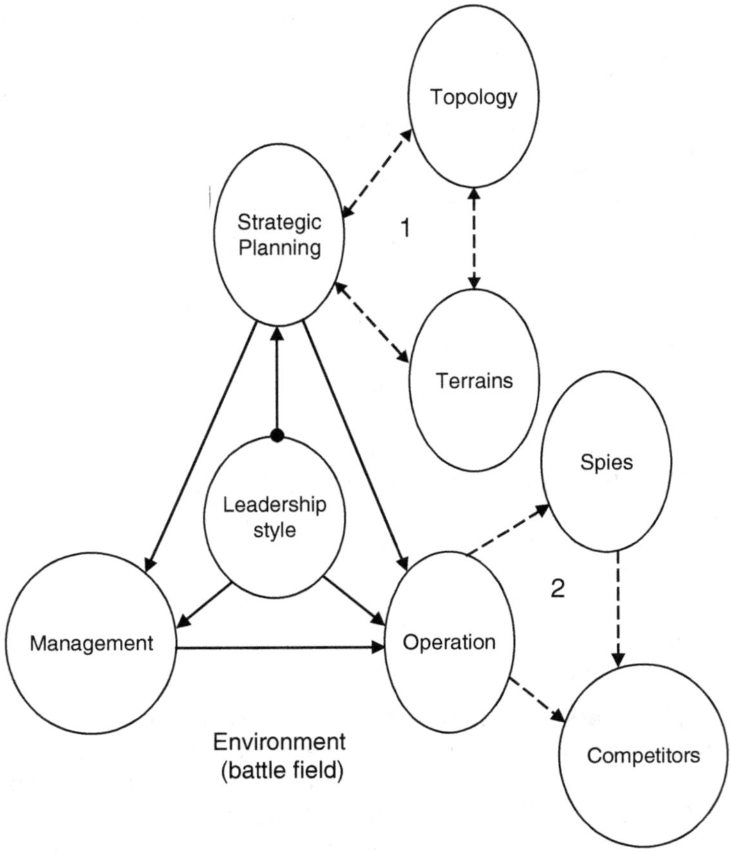

Figure 9.1 Sun Tzu's Leadership Model.

- The Commander 將(Leader): Possessing virtues like wisdom, trustworthiness, humanity, courage and strict authority.
- Method 法: Effective governance, organisation and utilisation of resources.

2. **Operational Leadership**: This involves gathering intelligence, utilising informants and implementing the strategic plan. Sun Tzu categorises five types of spies, highlighting the importance of 'foreknowledge' in gaining a competitive edge.
3. **Peak Performance**: Achieving peak performance involves continuous preparation, learning and seizing opportunities. True excellence lies in making no mistakes and achieving victory effortlessly.

4. **Nine Modes of Operation**: Sun Tzu outlines nine operational modes based on different situational contexts, providing guidance for leaders to adapt their approach based on the challenges they face.
5. **Weaknesses and Strengths**: Understanding and leveraging the interplay of weaknesses and strengths, both within oneself and the competitor, is crucial for success.

How to Apply It

While written as a military text, Sun Tzu's approach can be used in leadership development. For instance, the leadership triangle in Figure 9.1 can be extracted and further expanded (see Figure 9.2). This effectively describes three types of leadership styles:

i) **Power Leadership**: Managing large organisations with direct and indirect approaches, adapting to circumstances and making timely decisions (Essay 5).
ii) **Operational Leadership**: Implementing strategic plans (Key principle 1) through meticulous measurement, estimation, calculation, comparison and seizing opportunities (Essays 1–4,7 & 9).

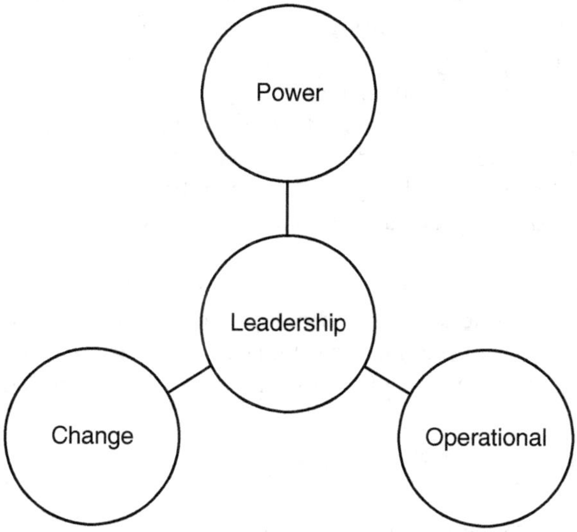

Figure 9.2 Sun Tzu's Types of Leadership Styles.

iii) **Change Leadership**: Embracing change, adapting tactics and exploiting weaknesses while avoiding strengths (Essays 6 & 8).

Sun Tzu's principles provide modern leaders with timeless guidance for navigating the complexities of leadership. At the foundation is an emphasis on ethics; leaders must anchor their vision in strong ethical principles to foster trust and commitment within their teams. Trust, as Sun Tzu implied, is the bedrock of effective leadership, and without it, even the most ambitious goals may falter.

Strategic thinking is another vital aspect, pushing leaders to develop comprehensive, well-informed strategies that consider all variables and anticipate potential challenges. This kind of foresight is essential in today's fast-paced, unpredictable environment. But strategy alone is not enough. Leaders must also focus on operational effectiveness, executing their plans with precision by efficiently using resources and making informed, timely decisions.

Adaptability is equally critical in an ever-changing world. Sun Tzu's insights emphasise the importance of embracing change, adjusting tactics as necessary and handling complex situations with agility. Leaders who remain flexible can better navigate uncertainty and turn challenges into opportunities.

Finally, self-awareness and commitment to personal growth are key to sustainable leadership. Recognising both strengths and areas for improvement allows leaders to foster a culture of continuous learning and development, benefiting not only themselves but also their teams. By embodying these principles, modern leaders can lead with strength, wisdom and resilience.

In Sun Tzu's leadership, the focus is towards outcomes—what is the desired goal? Furthermore, Sun Tzu's principle implies that the first step of action towards that goal is 'preparation'. The leader needs to make the appropriate preparations to ensure their success.

Like warriors, modern leaders have a commitment to secure peace through ethical actions (the primacy of ethics, 道Tao). To ensure this is honoured, a Chinese system coaching practice must be evaluated in terms of the benefits to all stakeholders, as Sun Tzu said:

百戰百勝，非善之善也;不戰而屈人之兵，善之善者也。

> 'The best leadership is not to conquer by force, but to enable people to follow without any resistance'. (Essay 3)

Implications

Sun Tzu's philosophy offers a rich, holistic approach to leadership that encompasses strategic thinking, operational effectiveness, ethical conduct and adaptability. His teachings remind us that effective leadership isn't just about making good decisions in isolation but requires a comprehensive understanding of various aspects that together drive success. By integrating these elements, leaders can create cohesive, adaptable strategies that remain resilient in the face of challenges.

Proactive planning stands as a core principle in Sun Tzu's philosophy. Leaders must emphasise meticulous preparation, giving careful thought to both opportunities and potential obstacles. With foresight and a readiness to tackle challenges before they arise, leaders can position their teams to seize opportunities with confidence and resilience. This approach aligns with the idea that success favours those who anticipate rather than react.

The importance of intelligence in decision-making is also a key lesson from Sun Tzu. Leaders who gather and analyse information thoroughly are better equipped to make informed choices and gain a competitive edge. By valuing data and insight, they can move beyond assumptions and make grounded, impactful decisions that propel their teams forward.

Adaptability and agility are crucial in today's fast-paced, constantly evolving environment. Sun Tzu's emphasis on these qualities reflects the need for leaders to remain flexible and responsive to changes. Leaders who can modify their tactics and strategies as circumstances shift are better positioned to overcome obstacles and capitalise on emerging opportunities.

Ethical leadership is perhaps one of the most timeless aspects of Sun Tzu's philosophy. Acting with integrity and maintaining a strong moral compass is essential for building trust and inspiring teams. Leaders who consistently demonstrate ethical conduct create a positive culture, one where team members feel valued, committed and motivated to give their best.

Conclusion

In conclusion, *The Art of War* offers a profound, enduring framework for modern leadership. Through self-awareness, strategic planning, decisiveness and adaptability, leaders can forge a pathway to success that honours Sun Tzu's timeless wisdom. By internalising and applying these principles, leaders can create a resilient, competitive organisation poised for long-term achievement in an unpredictable world.

References

Forrester, J. W. (1968). *Principles of systems* (2nd ed.). Pegasus Communications.

Griffith, S. B. (1963 translated) *Sun Tzu The art of war*. Oxford University Press.

Jackson, M. (2024). *Critical systems thinking – A practitioner's guide.* Wiley.

Law, H. C. (2010). An Asian perspective on leadership coaching: Sun Tzu and the art of war. In J. Passmore (ed.) *Leadership coaching.* (pp. 93–114). Kogan Page.

Tzu, S. (2010). *The art of war*. London: CreateSpace Independent Publishing Platform.

10

The Wu-Wei (Non-Doing) Model of Leadership Development

Qing Wang

School of Psychology and Cognitive Science, East China Normal University, Shanghai, China

The Big Idea

The concept of wu-wei (non-doing) represents a fundamental aspect of Chinese cultural and philosophical Taoist tradition. The term 'Tao' can be translated into 'the Way' or 'the Path', encapsulating the central concept within Taoist thoughts. Emerging alongside Confucianism, Taoism offers a distinct philosophical and epistemological perspective, emphasising harmony with the natural order, spontaneity, simplicity, humility and the pursuit of balance in existence.

Central to Taoist philosophy is the concept of *Yin* and *Yang* (you may read this idea again in this book), symbolising the complementary forces inherent in a variety of phenomena. Yin represents receptivity, pliancy and passivity, while Yang embodies activity, strengths and rational control. The opposition between Yin and Yang is naturally regarded as the balanced interplay between the receptivity and rational control dualities, which underscores the dynamic equilibrium that Taoists seek to cultivate in individuals' lives and society.

Most Western philosophers have been willing to grant that a condition of rational decision, choice and action is essential for human development. For example, if someone does not strive to manage a team at the workplace, we would view this as practically irrational from a common-sense perspective. However, the concept of

Mosaic Leadership: African, Asian, Middle Eastern and Indigenous Perspectives, First Edition. Edited by Jonathan Passmore, Badri Bajaj, and Mongezi C Makhalima.

Published 2026 by John Wiley & Sons Ltd.

wu-wei (無為) in Taoism, often translated as 'non-doing' or 'effortless action', offers a distinct proposition that connotes a mode of action characterised by spontaneity, naturalness and effortlessness. Derived from the '*Tao Te Ching*', attributed to the ancient Chinese sage Laozi, the concept of *wu-wei* embodies a paradoxical notion, suggesting that effective action arises not from deliberate striving or forceful intervention but rather from a state of receptivity and alignment with the natural flow of the universe, nature and organic systems, acting in accordance with their rhythms rather than against them. Meanwhile, *wu-wei* does not denote passivity or inaction but rather a harmonious engagement with one's surroundings, wherein one acts in accordance with the inherent rhythms and patterns of the Tao, the underlying principle of existence. Laozi employs imagery of water, which effortlessly conforms to the contours of its environment, as a metaphor to illustrate the epistemic naturalness and receptivity. By relinquishing the impulse to exert control or impose one's will upon the world, individuals can attain a state of inner tranquillity and allow circumstances to unfold organically. *Wu-wei* also advises individuals to refrain from actions that run counter to the Tao, which entails respecting the intrinsic importance of what lies outside the self, recognising the limits of one's power and refraining from futile struggles against the inevitable currents of change. Although *wu-wei* may appear paradoxical or elusive to the rational mind, it offers a profound insight into the nature of effective action and the cultivation of harmony within oneself and the world. Through the practice of *wu-wei*, individuals aspire to attain a state of effortless grace and authentic spontaneity, thereby realising the inherent wisdom and power of the Tao.

Difference Between Non-doing and Deliberate Action

The differences between non-doing and deliberate doing in Taoism reflect distinct philosophical orientations towards action, agency and engagement with the world. As we know, non-doing emphasises a mode of action characterised by spontaneity, naturalness and effortlessness according to the underlying principle of existence. Rather than striving for predetermined outcomes or imposing rigid plans, individuals practicing non-doing seek to act in accordance with the unfolding of events, responding intuitively to the needs unfold moment-to-moment. While *wu-wei* emphasises non-interference of and surrendering to the natural flow of events, this concept does not imply passivity or inaction but rather a state of dynamic receptivity and responsiveness to the ever-changing circumstances of life, similar to the idea of acceptance and openness in mindfulness. In contrast, deliberate doing entails a more proactive and intentional approach to action, prioritising the exercise of agency and the imposition of human will upon the external world and social systems. This mode of conduct often involves the formulation of specific objectives and goals, conscious development of action plans, strategic execution and implementation of deliberate steps and evaluative monitoring in pursuit of predetermined goals (basically everything that we do in Western models).

While *wu-wei* advocates for a harmonious engagement with the natural order and a surrendering of the ego-driven desire for control, deliberate doing emphasises the exercise of conscious intentionality and the pursuit of instrumental goals. I believe both approaches have their place within contemporary management and coaching, with practitioners navigating a dynamic balance between spontaneous responsiveness and purposeful action in their immediate environments. I will introduce a coaching model informed by *wu-wei* in the next section.

How to Apply It

The practice of *wu-wei* extends beyond individual conduct to permeate various aspects of life, including interpersonal relationships, artistic creation, ethical behaviours and a variety of areas in human life. In the context of management and leadership coaching, *wu-wei* finds expression in the Taoist concept of 'ruling without ruling' or 'governing by non-interference'. By cultivating a state of inner stillness and attunement to the Tao, the enlightened practitioners of *wu-wei* exercise restraint and allow the natural order to govern affairs, transcend ego-driven desires and align themselves with the spontaneous unfolding of reality instead of micromanaging or imposing rigid structures, thereby fostering harmony and minimising disruption in their organisations.

Applying the concept of *wu-wei* to leadership development involves guiding leaders to cultivate a non-doing mindset that emphasises receptivity, adaptability and mindfulness. Interestingly, leaders need to do something in order to achieve non-doing. Here, I present a blossom-shape model informed by *wu-wei* and suggest specific ways that the principles of *wu-wei* can be integrated into leadership development conversations (see Figure 10.1).

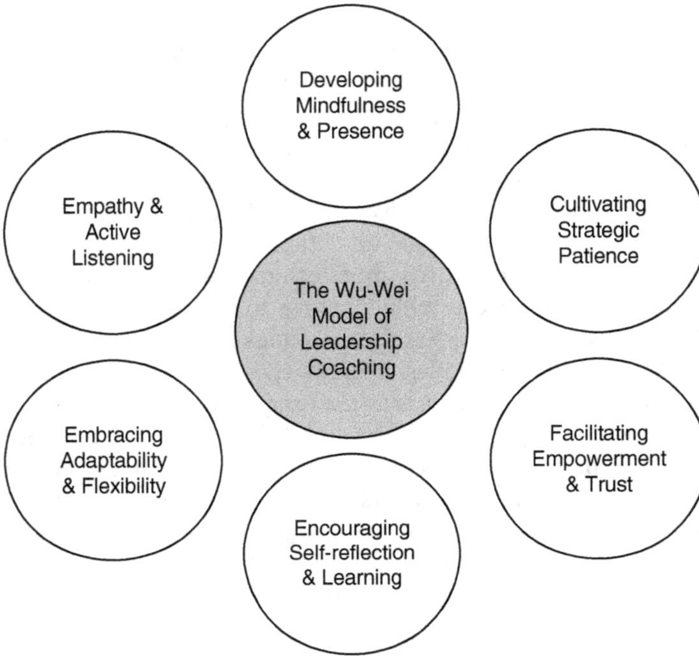

Figure 10.1 The Wu-Wei (Non-Doing) Model of Leadership Development.

Developing Mindfulness and Presence. The *wu-wei* informed approach encourages leaders to cultivate a mindful attitude and a strong awareness of the present moment. By developing a deeper connection with their inner selves, their surroundings and people and perhaps the larger environment, leaders can enhance their ability to discern the most appropriate course of action in any given situation, rather than reacting impulsively or being driven by ego-driven desires and purposes.

Embracing Adaptability and Flexibility. Leaders can be encouraged to adopt a mindset of flexibility and adaptability, learning to embrace uncertainties and view system change as opportunities. By recognising that change is inevitable, leaders would realise that rigid adherence to predetermined plans in a top-down approach may hinder organisational effectiveness and healthy dynamic. By remaining open to new possibilities and responsive (not habitual reaction) to emerging challenges, leaders can navigate complex and uncertain environments with greater ease and grace.

Facilitating Empowerment and Trust. Leadership development can emphasise the importance of empowering others and fostering a culture of trust within the organisation. What leaders do not do may influence people to a greater extent than what they do to their employees. Aligning with the principles of *wu-wei*, leaders need to learn to relinquish the need for micromanagement and create a safe and non-judgemental space for people's thoughts, feelings, concerns and vulnerabilities to flow without criticism or repercussion. In addition, leaders would promote active participation and collaboration by leveraging and maximising team members' existing strengths and capabilities, allowing team members the autonomy to make decisions and taking ownership of their work as well as cultivating a sense of collective responsibility and initiative.

Practicing Active Listening and Empathy. The *wu-wei* principle denotes listening and healthy silence rather than telling or instructing. In this aspect, leadership development is about integrating empathy with active listening, genuinely listening to the perspectives and concerns of others without imposing their own agenda, not hearing the words but also discerning the underlying emotions, intentions and implicit messages that the narrator wishes to convey. Through the cultivation of this aspect, leaders can foster a climate of mutual respect and create a supportive environment wherein employees are empowered to navigate challenges, capitalise on opportunities and actualise their potential.

Cultivating Strategic Patience. Patience embodies a non-reactive and accepting approach towards the unfolding of experiences and events. Over time, leaders can learn to cultivate strategic patience, recognising that meaningful change often emerges gradually and requires a long-term perspective. Strategic patience does not mean simply waiting there for nothing; instead, it involves cultivating a non-judgemental and compassionate stance towards internal and external events, refraining from impulsive actions and allowing solutions to emerge organically and observing the pathway of events with curiosity and equanimity. In this way, leaders can avoid unnecessary disruptions or engagement of cognitive rumination of mental decisions.

Encouraging Self-Reflection and Learning. Paradoxically, *wu-wei* can be learned and itself is a learning journey. Leadership development approaches can promote self-reflection and continuous learning in order to gain deeper insights into their own values, aspirations, limitations and strengths as essential components of effective leadership development. By regularly examining their beliefs, assumptions and behaviours, leaders can learn how to release attachment to outcomes and striving for perfection, to trust intuitions and inner wisdom, to seek out the most effortless and harmonious action and to follow a path for growth and refinement with less resistance and greater simplicity.

Conclusion

Incorporating the principles of *wu-wei* into leadership development requires a shift away from conventional notions of leadership as directive and control-oriented towards a more nuanced understanding of leadership as facilitative and adaptive. By embracing the concept of non-doing, leaders can be more attuned to the complexities of human interaction and organisational dynamics and cultivate a leadership style that is characterised by authenticity, wisdom and effectiveness in guiding their organisations towards sustainable success.

Further Reading

Lao Tzu. (2009). *Tao Te Ching: An illustrated journey*. Translated by Stephen Mitchell. Frances Lincoln.

Slote, M. (2018). *The philosophy of Yin and Yang: A contemporary approach*. The Commercial Press.

Watts, A. (1975). *Tao: The watercourse way*. Pantheon.

11

Seven Core Precepts of Bushido

Shigetsune Yamoto[1] *& Ray Tak-yin Hui*[1,2]

[1] *NUCB Business School, Nagoya University of Commerce and Business, Nagoya, Japan*
[2] *Faculty of Business and Law, University of Roehampton, London, UK*

The Big Idea

Bushido (武士道), the way of the warrior, is a code of conduct and a way of life for the samurai, the military nobility of feudal Japan (Bennett, 2020). Bushido is described as 'the chivalric, moral, and ethical system of ideas and correct behavior developed by the samurai class' (Cummins, 2022, p. 3). The term is composed of two parts: **bushi** (武士; military gentleman) and **do** (道; the pattern behind the universe). This ancient code, which has influenced Japanese culture for centuries, emphasises virtues that are universally applicable and timeless (Horvat, 2018). According to Nitobe (2019), the seven core precepts of Bushido—Gi (Rectitude), Yu (Courage), Jin (Benevolence), Rei (Respect), Makoto (Honesty), Meiyo (Honour) and Chugi (Loyalty)—provide a comprehensive framework for leadership and management (Nitobe, 2019; see Table 11.1).

Gi (Rectitude)

Rectitude is the most important virtue of Bushido (Nitobe, 2019). It refers to the ability to make fair and righteous decisions. For the samurai, rectitude was not just about following the law but about

Mosaic Leadership: African, Asian, Middle Eastern and Indigenous Perspectives, First Edition. Edited by Jonathan Passmore, Badri Bajaj, and Mongezi C Makhalima.

Published 2026 by John Wiley & Sons Ltd.

Table 11.1 The Seven Core Precepts of Bushido and Meanings.

Japanese	English	Meaning
義	Gi	Rectitude, Righteousness
勇	Yu	Courage, the Spirit of Daring and Bearing
仁	Jin	Benevolence, Compassion
礼	Rei	Respect, Etiquette
誠	Makoto	Honesty, Sincerity, Truthfulness
名誉	Meiyo	Honour
忠義	Chugi	Loyalty, Devotion

adhering to a moral code that transcended or sacrificed personal gain for the right reason (Nitobe, 2019). In modern leadership, this translates to righteousness in decision–making, ensuring that actions are guided by ethical principles rather than convenience or personal benefit (Helmold & Helmold, 2021).

Yu (Courage)

Courage, both physical and moral, is essential for overcoming fear and taking decisive action. The samurai demonstrated physical bravery on the battlefield, but moral courage was equally valued—standing up for what is right, even in the face of opposition (Nitobe, 2019). Contemporary leaders can draw on this principle to inspire confidence, take calculated risks and address challenges head-on, fostering a culture of resilience and determination (Helmold & Helmold, 2021).

Jin (Benevolence)

Benevolence or compassion is the quality of being kind and humane (Nitobe, 2019). The samurai were expected to show mercy and kindness, particularly to the weak and the vulnerable. This precept emphasises the importance of empathy and consideration for others. In leadership, Jin encourages leaders to act with kindness, support their teams and prioritise the well–being of their employees and stakeholders, creating an environment of trust and cooperation (Helmold & Helmold, 2021).

Rei (Respect)

Respect, or courtesy, is fundamental to harmonious relationships. Rei is not merely an external form of courtesy but an internal expression of respect and sincerity. It is a tangible means of expressing respect and appreciation for others (Nitobe, 2019). The samurai adhered to strict codes of conduct and showed respect to superiors, peers and subordinates alike. This principle underscores the importance of treating others with dignity and consideration. Modern leaders who practice rei foster a culture of mutual respect, enhance collaboration and promote a positive and inclusive organisational culture (Helmold & Helmold, 2021).

Makoto (Honesty)

Honesty or sincerity is about being truthful and genuine in all dealings. For the samurai, makoto meant more than just telling the truth—it involved acting with integrity and ensuring that one's words and actions were aligned (Nitobe, 2019). In contemporary leadership, this translates to transparency, accountability and authenticity. Leaders who embody makoto build trust, inspire loyalty and maintain credibility (Helmold & Helmold, 2021).

Meiyo (Honour)

Honour is the reputation and moral character that a person builds through their actions, but its foundation lies in the inner worth and virtue of the individual (Nitobe, 2019). For the samurai, maintaining one's honour was paramount, often considered more valuable than life itself. This precept highlights the importance of upholding one's principles and behaving in a manner that garners respect. Leaders who prioritise honour strive for excellence, uphold ethical standards and cultivate a legacy of trustworthiness and respect (Helmold & Helmold, 2021).

Chugi (Loyalty)

Loyalty is the unwavering commitment to one's duties and allegiances. The samurai were expected to be loyal to their lords, their comrades, and their code of conduct (Nitobe, 2019). This principle emphasises dedication, faithfulness and responsibility. Loyalty is not mere blind obedience but is based on high ethical standards and a sense of justice. Therefore, a warrior is also expected to have the courage to make an ethical decision when his lord's command is unjust. In a modern context, Chugi encourages leaders to demonstrate loyalty to their organisation, their team and their mission, fostering a sense of unity and shared purpose (Helmold & Helmold, 2021).

How to Apply It

Integrating the precepts of Bushido into modern leadership and management involves both philosophical alignment and practical application. Here are some ways to incorporate these principles into various aspects of leadership and management:

Decision-Making and Integrity

Leaders can apply the principle of Gi (Rectitude) by establishing clear ethical guidelines and ensuring that all decisions align with these standards. Regular ethics training and open discussions about moral dilemmas can reinforce the importance of integrity. By prioritising justice and fairness, leaders build a foundation of trust and respect within their organisation.

Building a Courageous Culture

To foster Yu (Courage), leaders should encourage risk-taking and innovation. This can be achieved by creating a safe environment where team members feel supported in exploring new ideas and taking bold steps. Recognising and rewarding courageous actions, whether they lead to success or failure, helps to build a resilient and dynamic organisational culture.

Promoting Compassion and Empathy

Jin (Benevolence) can be integrated into leadership practices by prioritising employee well–being and demonstrating empathy. Leaders should practice active listening, provide support during difficult times and advocate for policies that promote work–life balance. Acts of kindness and understanding from leaders set a tone of compassion and care throughout the organisation.

Cultivating Respectful Relationships

Rei (Respect) can be fostered by promoting a culture of inclusivity and respect. Leaders should model respectful behaviour, acknowledge and value diverse perspectives and address any instances of disrespect or discrimination promptly. Training programmes on cultural competence and respectful communication can further support this effort.

Ensuring Transparency and Authenticity

Makoto (Honesty) requires leaders to be transparent in their communications and actions. Open-door policies, regular updates and honest feedback sessions help to build a culture of sincerity. Leaders should also reflect on their own authenticity, ensuring that their actions align with their words and values.

Upholding Honour and Ethical Standards

To embody Meiyo (Honour), leaders should commit to high ethical standards and lead by example. Recognising and celebrating ethical behaviour within the organisation reinforces the value of honour. Leaders can also establish mechanisms for accountability, ensuring that everyone in the organisation is held to the same ethical standards.

Demonstrating Loyalty and Commitment

Chugi (Loyalty) can be demonstrated through consistent support for team members and dedication to the organisation's mission. Leaders should actively engage with their teams, understand their needs and provide the necessary resources for success. Showing appreciation for employees' loyalty and contributions helps to foster a strong sense of unity and shared purpose.

By integrating the seven core precepts of Bushido into leadership practices, modern leaders can draw on the timeless wisdom of the samurai to create ethical, resilient and compassionate organisations. These principles offer a robust framework for guiding behaviour, making decisions and fostering a culture of excellence and integrity.

Conclusion

Bushido, the samurai code of conduct, emphasises seven core precepts: Rectitude, Courage, Benevolence, Respect, Honesty, Honour and Loyalty. These virtues guide ethical leadership, promoting integrity, empathy and resilience. By integrating Bushido's timeless principles, modern leaders can foster ethical decision-making, compassionate team dynamics and sustained commitment to organisational values, enhancing trust and collaboration.

References

Bennett, A. (2020). *Bushido explained: The Japanese samurai code: a new interpretation for beginners*. USA: Tuttle Publishing.

Cummins, A. (2022). *The book of bushido: The complete guide to real samurai chivalry*. London, UK: Watkins Media Limited.

Helmold, M., & Helmold, M. (2021). Lean management and new work concepts. In M. Helmold (Ed.), *New work, transformational and virtual leadership: Lessons from COVID-19 and other crises* (pp. 121–135). Switzerland: Springer.

Horvat, A. (2018). Bushidō and the legacy of "Samurai Values" in contemporary Japan. *Asian Studies*, *6*(2), 189–208.

Nitobe, I. (2019). *Bushido: The Samurai code of Japan: With an extensive introduction and notes by Alexander Bennett*. Tuttle Publishing.

12

Shokunin Katagi

Kazuhiko Kato[1], *Ray Tak-yin Hui*[1,2], *& Shigetsune Yamoto*[1]

[1] *NUCB Business School, Nagoya University of Commerce and Business, Nagoya, Japan*
[2] *Faculty of Business and Law, University of Roehampton, London, UK*

The Big Idea

Shokunin katagi (職人気質), or the 'spirit of the craftsman', embodies the Japanese concept of dedication, pride, meticulous attention to detail and devotion to the highest quality that craftsmen bring to their work (Mihic, 2020). In Japanese, 'shokunin' (職人) refers to a craftsman or artisan who has mastered their craft through years of training and dedication, encompassing not only technical skill and knowledge but also a deep pride and respect for tradition and craftsmanship responsibilities (Daijirin, 2006). 'Katagi' (気質) translates to temperament or disposition, highlighting the intrinsic qualities that define a person's approach to their profession (Daijirin, 2006). Together, 'Shokunin katagi' encapsulates the spirit, mindset, values and 'Waza' (技; skill-set) that define a true 'Takumi' (匠; artisan or craftsman)—qualities such as dedication, attention to detail, pride in workmanship and a continuous pursuit of excellence (Funabiki, 2003; Tanoue, 1999).

Although modern Japanese management, which emphasises efficiency and standardisation, has shifted its focus from craftsmanship to intensive division of labour, shokunin katagi is deeply rooted in Japan's cultural heritage and influences modern people management (Gamble, 2001), especially in talent management and leadership succession. It goes beyond technical proficiency, emphasising

Mosaic Leadership: African, Asian, Middle Eastern and Indigenous Perspectives, First Edition. Edited by Jonathan Passmore, Badri Bajaj, and Mongezi C Makhalima.

Published 2026 by John Wiley & Sons Ltd.

a commitment to mastery, continuous improvement and the creation of high-quality work. This philosophy integrates technical expertise, creativity and a dedication to craftsmanship excellence.

Core Principles

The essence of shokunin katagi can be distilled into several core principles (Mihic, 2020):

1. **Pride and Responsibility:** Shokunin take immense pride in their work, viewing craftsmanship as a means of personal fulfilment and societal contribution (Funabiki, 2003). This pride is rooted in a sense of responsibility to uphold the standards of their craft, deliver excellence to customers and contribute positively to their communities. It reflects a deep-seated commitment to creating products of enduring value and beauty.
2. **Respect for Tradition and Innovation:** Shokunin honour traditional techniques and cultural heritage while remaining open to innovation (Funabiki, 2003). They strike a balance between preserving time-honoured methods passed down through generations and integrating new ideas, materials or technologies that enhance their craft. This dynamic approach ensures the evolution and relevance of their work in contemporary contexts.
3. **Attention to Detail:** Every aspect of a shokunin's work is infused with meticulous attention to detail. From selecting the finest materials to executing intricate techniques, every decision is deliberate and aimed at achieving perfection. This dedication ensures that each piece bears the hallmark of the artisan's skill and care, distinguishing it from mass-produced alternatives.
4. **Mastery and Skill Development:** Shokunin dedicate themselves to mastering their craft through rigorous training and years of practice (Mihic, 2020). This pursuit of excellence not only hones technical skills but also fosters a deep understanding of the materials, techniques and cultural context surrounding their craft.
5. **Continuous Improvement (Kaizen; 改善):** Central to shokunin katagi is the concept of kaizen, or continuous improvement (Mihic, 2020). Shokunin constantly seek ways to refine their techniques, innovate within traditional boundaries and elevate the quality of their workmanship. This principle extends beyond personal skill development to encompass refining processes and

embracing new technologies where they enhance quality without compromising tradition (Imai, 1986).

6. **Ethics and Integrity:** Ethics and integrity are fundamental to Shokunin katagi (Mihic, 2020). Artisans adhere to high ethical standards in sourcing materials, transparency in their processes and honesty in their interactions with customers. This ethical foundation reinforces trust and respect, which are crucial elements in sustaining their craft over generations.

The Inheritance of Shokunin Katagi

The inheritance of Shokunin katagi is deeply rooted in the master–apprentice relationship, a bond that transcends mere technical instruction and encompasses a profound transmission of values, philosophies and dedication to the craft (Nagata, 2007; Sasaki, 2008). The master, or shisho (師匠), is an experienced and highly skilled craftsman, who embodies the spirit, values and techniques of the craft and is responsible for passing these on to the next generation. The apprentice, or deshi (弟子), is a learner and a student who commits to learning the craft under the guidance of a master (Nagata, 2007).

Traditionally in Japan, an apprentice lived with the master for years until the master decided they were ready to become independent (Nagata, 2007). In the workshop, the master usually did not teach or train the apprentice directly. Instead, the apprentice would silently observe from a discreet distance, hoping to 'steal' the knowledge and skills (技を盗め, Gijutsu wo nusumu) necessary to transcend to higher levels over a period of up to 10 years (Buntrock, 1998). The master typically held a very high position, while the apprentice occupied a lower status in everyday life. This hierarchical relationship may be rooted in Confucianism. To acquire more advanced skills from the master, apprentices competed with each other by showcasing their growth and advancement, thereby gaining more attention and teachings from the master. Ultimately, only a few apprentices would be qualified and recognised to inherit the Shokunin katagi from their master, eventually becoming the next generation of masters.

In Shokunin katagi, Shu Ha Ri (守破離) represents the journey or stages of learning to master craftmanship (Zeami, 2006). It highlights the craftsman's commitment to continuous improvement (kaizen), respect for tradition and the pursuit of excellence in their work. The concept can be broken down into three stages:

1. **Shu (守):** To protect or adhere to. This initial stage involves faithfully following the teachings and techniques of the master or tradition. It is the stage of learning and imitating the fundamentals. A beginner strictly follows the instructions of the master, repetitively practising the basic forms and techniques to build a solid foundation.
2. **Ha (破):** To break or detach. In this stage, the practitioner begins to innovate upon the learned fundamentals, integrating their own insights and variations. Once the basics are mastered, the practitioner starts to introduce their own style and modifications, adapting the forms to suit their understanding.
3. **Ri (離):** To separate or depart. This is the final stage where the practitioner transcends the traditional forms, creating their unique style and becoming independent. The practitioner has now developed their own techniques and approaches, moving beyond the original teachings to explore new creative possibilities.

How to Apply It

Integrating the principles of Shokunin Katagi into leadership can significantly enhance the development of managers and leaders, fostering a culture of excellence, continuous improvement and ethical responsibility.

1. **Fostering Pride and Responsibility:** Leaders can cultivate a sense of pride and responsibility in their teams by emphasising the importance of their contributions to the organisation and society. This can be achieved by recognising and celebrating individual and team achievements, creating a shared vision of excellence and highlighting the impact of their work on customers and the community. This also involves setting challenging yet achievable goals, providing constructive feedback and guiding subordinates to see their role as integral to the organisation's success. Leaders should model this pride by demonstrating their own commitment to high standards and ethical behaviour.

2. **Balancing Tradition and Innovation:** Leaders should strive to balance respect for established processes and traditions with the need for innovation. This involves creating an environment where team members feel valued for their knowledge and encouraged to

suggest improvements. Leaders can facilitate this by holding regular brainstorming sessions, rewarding innovative ideas and ensuring that any changes respect the organisation's core values and heritage. In addition, managers should also encourage subordinates to document and share successful innovations, fostering a culture of continuous learning and improvement.

3. **Emphasising Attention to Detail:** Leaders can instil meticulous attention to detail in their teams by setting clear expectations for quality and precision. This involves providing the necessary resources and training for team members to perform their tasks to the highest standard. Leaders should also lead by example, demonstrating meticulousness in their own work and decision-making processes.
4. **Skill Development and Continuous Improvement (Kaizen):** Leaders should prioritise ongoing skill development and mastery within their teams by providing continuous learning opportunities. This can include workshops, mentorship programmes and access to resources that support skill enhancement. Leaders should also encourage a growth mindset, where challenges are viewed as opportunities for development and continuous improvement.

Conclusion

The chapter discusses *Shokunin katagi*, the 'spirit of the craftsman,' which emphasises pride, responsibility, attention to detail and continuous improvement. Rooted in Japan's cultural heritage, it integrates tradition and innovation through a master–apprentice system. These principles can enhance leadership by fostering excellence, ethical responsibility and skill development within organisations.

References

Buntrock, D. (1998). The political economies of Japan's crafts, yesterday and today. Paper presented at the 86th ACSA Annual Meeting and Technology. Association of Collegiate Schools of Architecture. USA.

Daijirin (2006). *Daijirin* (3rd ed.). Tokyo: Sanseidoo Shoten.

Funabiki, T. (2003). *Nihonjinron' saikō [A rethinking of 'Nihonjinron].* Tokyo, Japan: Nihon Hōsō Shuppan Kyōkai.

Gamble, J. (2001). Modelling the invisible: The pedagogy of craft apprenticeship. *Studies in Continuing Education, 23*(2), 185–200.

Imai, M. (1986). *Kaizen: The key to Japan's competitive success.* USA: McGraw-Hill Education.

Mihic, T. (2020). *Re-imagining Japan after Fukushima.* Australia: Australian National University Press.

Nagata, M. L. (2007). Apprentices, Servants and other workers: apprenticeship in Japan. In S. L. Kaplan, B. De Munck, & H. Soly (Eds.), *Learning on the shop floor historical perspectives on apprenticeship* (pp. 35–45). New York: Berghahn Books.

Sasaki, S. (2008). Overview of research concerning vocational education and vocational training in modern Japan. In F. Rauner & R. McClean (Eds.), *Handbook of technical and vocational education and training research* (pp. 62–68). Bonn: Springer.

Tanoue, S. (1999). *Master's skill: Takumi no waza.* Japan: Society of Automotive Engineers of Japan.

Zeami (2006). *The flowering spirit: Classic teachings on the art of Nō.* Japan: Kodansha International.

13

Han Fei's Philosophy: Fa, Shu and Shi

Changrong Lu[1] & Ray Tak-yin Hui[1,2]

[1] *Nagoya University of Commerce and Business, Nagoya, Japan*
[2] *Faculty of Business and Law, University of Roehampton, London, UK*

The Big Idea

Han Fei (281–233 BCE), a prominent Chinese philosopher of the Warring States period, is one of the most influential figures in the school of Legalism (法家). Like other Legalists, he assumed that human beings are overwhelmingly selfish, so we should not expect them to behave morally (Graen, 2008; Schneider, 2018). His ideas, often viewed as pragmatic and sometimes ruthless, provide a distinct perspective on governance and leadership (Goldin, 2012). Han Fei's philosophy revolves around three central concepts: **Fa** (法; law and methods), **Shu** (術; techniques) and **Shi** (勢; power or positional advantage) (Witzel, 2016; Yang, 2012). These principles, when integrated into modern leadership, offer a structured and result-oriented approach to management and organisational effectiveness (Graen, 2008).

1) **Fa**: (Law and methods) refers to the establishment and enforcement of clear laws and rules of regulations (Yang, 2012). According to Han Fei, laws are the foundation of a well-governed state. The leaders should ensure that everyone is aware of their duties and the consequences of their actions. This principle

Mosaic Leadership: African, Asian, Middle Eastern and Indigenous Perspectives, First Edition. Edited by Jonathan Passmore, Badri Bajaj, and Mongezi C Makhalima.

Published 2026 by John Wiley & Sons Ltd.

emphasises the importance of transparency, consistency and accountability (Chen, 2000).

2) **Shu**: (Techniques) represents the techniques and strategies employed by leaders to manage and control their subordinates (Graen, 2008; Yang, 2012). Han Fei believed that effective governance required more than just laws; it also necessitated the use of strategic management techniques. This includes techniques like understanding human nature, utilising incentives and disincentives and employing tactics to ensure compliance and productivity (Ke, 2019).
3) **Shi**: (Power or positional advantage) is conveyed by the resources controlled by a leader that can be used to influence subordinates, denoting the power or positional advantage inherent in a leader's legitimate position (Graen, 2008). Han Fei argued that the effective use of power was crucial for maintaining order, achieving goals and commanding respect and obedience. This principle is the authority and influence that empower leaders to enforce Fa (laws) and implement Shu (techniques). Therefore, it represents the legitimate power and command that a leader holds, enabling them to make decisions, resolve conflicts and inspire their teams (Graen, 2008).

Relationship Between Fa, Shu and Shi

The three principles of Fa, Shu and Shi, while distinct, are deeply interconnected and function cohesively to create an effective leadership framework.

- **Fa (Laws and methods) as the Foundation**: Fa provides the structural backbone of an organisation. It establishes the rules and guidelines that ensure a predictable and stable environment (Witzel, 2016). Without Fa, there would be chaos and inconsistency, undermining the leader's ability to govern effectively. Fa ensures that everyone knows what is expected of them and the consequences of failing to meet those expectations (Graen, 2008). This clarity and consistency are crucial for maintaining order and fairness. Therefore, Han Fei advocated that law should be used as teaching or training materials and the leaders should serve as teachers.

- **Shu (Techniques) as the Operational Mechanism**: While Fa sets the ground rules, Shu represents the practical application of those rules. Shu involves the techniques and strategies that leaders use to motivate and manage their teams within the framework established by Fa. Han Fei proposed three main *Shu*, including (1) assigning competent talents to the right positions, (2) checking results of performance with expectations or standards and (3) controlling the power of sparing and termination to evaluate competencies of subordinates (Graen, 2008). From the perspective of modern human resource management, Shu includes employee selection, performance management and disciplinary actions. Shu is about the day-to-day operations and the methods leaders use to get the best out of their teams. It ensures that the organisation runs smoothly and that employees are productive and engaged (Wiebke, 2010).
- **Shi (Power or Positional Advantage) as the Enabling Force**: Shi is the authority and influence that empower leaders to enforce Fa and implement Shu (Graen, 2008). It is the power that gives leaders the ability to make decisions, resolve conflicts and inspire their teams. Without Shi, leaders would lack the authority to enforce laws and the influence to effectively use techniques (Graen, 2008). Shi ensures that leaders have the respect and obedience of their team members, which is necessary for maintaining order and achieving organisational goals. In simpler terms, Shi is what gives leaders the actual power to lead. It's not just about having rules (Fa) or knowing how to manage people (Shu); it's about having the recognised authority to make sure those rules and techniques are followed (Graziani, 2015). Shi is the glue that holds everything together, ensuring that leadership is effective and respected.

How to Apply It

Applying Han Fei's principles of Fa, Shu and Shi to modern leadership and coaching can significantly enhance managerial effectiveness and organisational performance. Here is how these concepts can be practically implemented:

1) Establishing Clear Policies and Accountability (Fa)
   To apply the principle of Fa, leaders should focus on setting clear expectations, ensuring that rules are applied uniformly

and maintaining a fair and just environment. This helps minimise ambiguity, reduce biases and promote a culture of accountability. Leaders who embrace Fa are seen as reliable and just, fostering trust and respect among their team members. This includes the following:

- **Creating Clear Guidelines**: Draft detailed policies covering various aspects of organisational behaviour and decision-making. These guidelines should be easily accessible and communicated effectively to all employees. Regular training sessions and accessible documentation ensure that all employees understand their roles, responsibilities and the consequences of their actions. This reduces ambiguity and fosters a sense of fairness and predictability within the organisation.
- **Performance Metrics**: Develop and implement measurable performance standards. Using key performance indicators (KPIs) and regular performance reviews, leaders can objectively assess employee contributions and identify areas for improvement. This approach aligns individual goals with organisational objectives, fostering a performance-driven culture.
- **Consistency in Enforcement**: It is crucial to apply rules uniformly to all employees. Inconsistencies can lead to perceptions of favouritism and unfairness, which can undermine morale and trust. Leaders must ensure that disciplinary actions and rewards are applied consistently to maintain a culture of accountability.

2) Utilising Effective Management Techniques (Shu)
Leaders adept in Shu are those who can adapt their strategies to the specific needs of their organisation and workforce, leveraging both rewards and discipline to achieve desired outcomes. Leaders can integrate Shu into their management practices by employing a variety of techniques to optimise team performance and achieve strategic goals. This includes:

- **Talent Management:** Assigning the right people to the right roles is fundamental. Leaders should invest in robust recruitment and selection processes to ensure a good fit between job requirements and employee capabilities. This also includes succession planning and career development programmes to nurture and retain talent.
- **Training and Development:** Invest in ongoing training and development programmes to equip employees with the skills and knowledge necessary for their roles. Furthermore, it is

important to identify and nurture high-potential employees through mentoring, training programmes and leadership development initiatives. This not only improves individual performance but also enhances overall organisational capability.

- **Performance Management:** Implement regular performance appraisals to monitor progress against established standards. This involves setting clear, achievable goals, providing constructive feedback and recognising and rewarding achievements. Effective performance management systems motivate employees and drive continuous improvement.
- **Incentives and Disincentives:** Use a balanced approach to motivate employees. Financial incentives like bonuses, promotions and salary increments can drive performance, while non-financial incentives, such as recognition, professional development opportunities and a positive work environment, also play a significant role. Conversely, clear consequences for underperformance or misconduct ensure adherence to organisational standards.

3) Exercising Authority and Inspiring Confidence (Shi)
Understanding and effectively using Shi involves balancing authority with empathy and ensuring that power is exercised in a manner that supports organisational objectives. This includes:

- **Legitimate Authority:** Cultivate respect and trust among team members by leading with integrity and empathy. This involves being transparent, honest and approachable while also maintaining the necessary authority to lead effectively. Legitimate authority fosters respect and obedience from employees.
- **Enforcing Policies**: Use one's position and authority to inspire commitment to the organisation's mission, values and policies. A leader should ensure that policies are not just in place but actively enforced. This includes holding individuals accountable for their actions and maintaining order within the organisation.
- **Decision-Making:** Demonstrate decisiveness and confidence in making tough decisions. Leaders should be prepared to take responsibility for their choices and stand by their principles. Additionally, use authority judiciously to make decisions that are in the best interest of the organisation. This includes resolving conflicts, allocating resources effectively and setting strategic directions. Involving employees in the

decision-making process where appropriate can also enhance buy-in and commitment.

- **Inspirational Leadership:** Beyond authority, leaders should inspire and motivate their teams. This involves setting a compelling vision, leading by example and demonstrating a genuine commitment to the well-being and development of employees. Inspirational leadership can drive engagement, innovation and loyalty.

Conclusions

The chapter explores Han Fei's Legalist philosophy, emphasising the importance of Fa (laws), Shu (management techniques) and Shi (power or authority) in leadership. It underscores how these principles function together to create effective governance by establishing clear rules, applying strategic management techniques and exercising legitimate power. By integrating these concepts into modern leadership, leaders can enhance accountability, team performance and organisational success through structured, result-oriented management that balances authority with empathy and ethical leadership.

References

Chen, Q. (2000). *Han Feizi, with new collations and commentary.* Shanghai: Guji.

Goldin, P. R. (2012). Introduction: HAN Fei and the Han Feizi. In P. R. Goldin (Ed.), *Dao companion to the philosophy of Han Fei* (pp. 1–21). Dordrecht: Springer Netherlands.

Graen, G. B. (2008). Linking Chinese leadership theory and practice to the world: leadership secrets of the Middle Kingdom. In C. C. Chen & Y. T. Lee (Eds.), *Leadership and management in China* (pp. 272–297). UK: Cambridge University Press.

Graziani, R. (2015). Monarch and minister: Reflections on an impossible partnership in the building of absolute monarchy in the Han Feizi. In Y. Pines, P. R. Goldin, & M. Kern (Eds.), *Ideology of power and power of ideology in early China*. Brill: Leiden.

Ke, Y. (2019). The morality of Chinese legalism: Han Fei's advanced philosophy. Masters Theses 838.

Schneider, H. (2018). *An introduction to Hanfei's political philosophy: The way of the ruler*. UK: Cambridge Scholars Publishing.

Wiebke, D. (2010). *The dynamics of maters literature: Early Chinese thought from confucius to Han Feizi*. USA: Harvard University Press.

Witzel, M. (2016). The leadership philosophy of Han Fei. In C. Rowley & D. Ulrich (Eds.), *Leadership in the Asia Pacific* (pp. 47–61). London: Routledge.

Yang, S. J. (2012). Shen Dao's theory of fa and His influence on Han Fei. In P. R. Goldin (Ed.), *Dao companion to the philosophy of Han Fei* (pp. 47–63). Dordrecht: Springer Netherlands.

14

IKIGAI: A Japanese Approach to Leadership

Sok-Ho Trinh

School of Business - Occupational & Business Psychology, University of Roehampton, London, UK

The Big Idea

Ikigai is a deeply rooted Japanese concept often translated as one's 'reason for being'. It is a profound motivation that drives purpose in everyday life. Ikigai reflects a harmony between personal fulfilment and social responsibility. Rooted in Shintoism and Buddhism, it emphasises balance, humility and respect, guiding individuals to find meaning through their roles within family, community and nature.

The M-IKIGAI™ framework (Figure 14.1) has adapted this original concept specifically for leadership, adding meaning and contribution to the original dimensions of passion, mission, profession and vocation (Garcia & Miralles, 2017). This model offers a path for leaders to align their values and actions with the traditional Japanese principles of service, integrity and long-term vision, encouraging them to lead in ways that promote community well-being (Kumano, 2018) and sustainability (Buettner, 2009).

Ikigai in Japanese Society and Its Cultural Roots

The word Ikigai combines 'iki' (生き), meaning life, and 'gai' (甲斐), meaning worth or value. Japanese culture views Ikigai not as a career or ambition but as a holistic approach to life, where personal joy is intertwined with communal welfare (Ishida, 2014). In Okinawa,

Mosaic Leadership: African, Asian, Middle Eastern and Indigenous Perspectives, First Edition. Edited by Jonathan Passmore, Badri Bajaj, and Mongezi C Makhalima.

Published 2026 by John Wiley & Sons Ltd.

Figure 14.1 The M-IKIGAI™ concept. Adapted from Garcia & Miralles's Ikigai.

known for its high number of centenarians (Buettner, 2009; Sone et al., 2008), Ikigai is evident in practices like Yuimaru (mutual support), where daily life emphasises shared responsibilities and cooperation. Here, residents find fulfilment in simple, communal activities that strengthen social bonds, showing how purpose is naturally woven into daily life.

Japanese Leadership and the Principles of Ikigai

In Japan, Ikigai extends beyond personal purpose (Mogi, 2018) to leadership. Leaders of family-owned businesses or Shinise view themselves as caretakers of legacies. Such leaders prioritise long-term sustainability and community service, valuing integrity, humility and patience over profit. This leadership philosophy sees work as a social duty rather than a path to personal gain.

Historically, samurai culture embodied aspects of Ikigai through the Bushido code, the 'way of the warrior', emphasising loyalty, self-discipline and service. Samurai leaders saw their lives as commitments to their community, reinforcing that a meaningful life is one of duty and humility.

Modern Japanese leaders often use Nemawashi, a consensus-building practice in which decisions are carefully discussed with all involved parties. This approach reflects Ikigai's values by promoting respect and harmony and ensuring that leadership actions support collective well-being. Nemawashi enables leaders to consider the broader impact of their actions, fostering a culture of trust, respect and long-term thinking.

M-IKIGAI™ Framework: Five Core Dimensions for Purpose-Driven Leadership

The M-IKIGAI™ framework translates the Ikigai concept into dimensions that support purpose-driven leadership. Each dimension encourages leaders to pursue values that resonate with Japanese principles:

1. What you love (Passion): Leaders are encouraged to find purpose in service-oriented activities, reflecting humility and a focus on communal welfare over individual ambition.
2. What the world needs (Mission): Japanese leadership is grounded in social duty and centres on addressing community needs, from environmental stewardship to corporate responsibility.
3. What you are good at (Profession): In Japan, lifelong skill refinement is valued. Leaders seek mastery and precision in their roles, aligning with the principle of continuous improvement.
4. What you can be paid for (Vocation): Leaders view their work as valuable not only for financial rewards but also for serving societal needs and creating a lasting impact.
5. What you find meaningful (Contribution): This additional dimension deepens leaders' connection to their purpose, grounding their decisions in integrity, social responsibility and self-reflection.

How to Apply It

Ikigai and the M-IKIGAI™ framework provide a culturally aligned method for leaders to integrate purpose and community focus into their roles:

1. **Concept Demystification**: Leaders understand M-IKIGAI™'s dimensions and explore how each aligns with traditional Japanese values. Reflecting on these dimensions, leaders can

identify ways to incorporate humility, resilience and integrity into their roles. For example, a leader may assess how their skills can benefit others or how they might prioritise community needs in decision-making.

2. **Reflection on M-IKIGAI™ dimensions**: Leaders explore each dimension of M-IKIGAI™ through introspective questions:
   - **Passion**: 'What parts of my role bring fulfilment through service?'
   - **Mission**: 'What societal or organisational needs can I uniquely address?'
   - **Profession**: 'What skills can I refine to contribute more effectively?'
   - **Vocation**: 'How can my work support others sustainably?'
   - **Contribution**: 'What values guide my leadership and connect me to a broader purpose?'

   This reflection helps leaders align their motivations with values deeply embedded in Japanese culture.
3. **Insights from traditional Japanese practices**: Leaders can draw on Naikan (reflection on relationships and gratitude) and Kintsugi (appreciating resilience in adversity). Naikan encourages leaders to reflect on how their actions impact others, fostering humility and a sense of duty, while Kintsugi emphasises seeing setbacks as growth opportunities, reinforcing resilience.
4. **M-IKIGAI™ reflection and application**: Leaders identify their core themes from the M-IKIGAI™ reflection and apply them in their roles. For example, they might incorporate Nemawashi in decision-making to build consensus and encourage inclusiveness. This practice aligns leadership actions with harmony and respect, enhancing team trust.
5. **Goal setting aligned with Japanese values**: Leaders set goals that align with M-IKIGAI™ principles, focusing on sustainability, community impact and harmony:
   - **Long-term impact goals**: Leaders may establish goals to mentor others, ensuring skill-sharing for future generations.
   - **Community engagement goals**: Goals extend beyond organisational success, like supporting local causes, to reinforce the importance of societal engagement.
   - **Balance and harmony goals**: Leaders set personal and organisational practices to maintain balance and perspective and foster resilience and humility.

By setting goals grounded in these values, leaders can integrate M-IKIGAI™ principles into actionable strategies, creating a legacy of purpose, integrity and service.

Conclusion

Ikigai and the M-IKIGAI™ framework offer a culturally enriched model that aligns with Japanese leadership values. It encourages leaders to approach their roles with humility, community responsibility and resilience. By connecting deeply with the Ikigai's essence, leaders can foster harmony, promote collective good and ensure that their actions contribute to long-term societal well-being.

The M-IKIGAI™ model invites modern leaders to view leadership as a balance of personal fulfilment and social alignment. Practices like Naikan, Kintsugi and Nemawashi reinforce the Ikigai's emphasis on harmony, trust and respect, providing a path for leaders to create a meaningful impact.

References

Buettner, D. (2009). *The blue zones: Lessons for living longer from the people who've lived the longest.* Washington, D.C.: National Geographic Society.

Garcia, H., & Miralles, F. (2017). *Ikigai: The Japanese secret to a long and happy life.* London: Hutchinson.

Ishida, M. (2014). Does traditional Japanese culture help people cope with stress using the concept of Ikigai (Reason for Being)? *Journal of Education, Society and Behavioural Science, 4*(11), 1592–1600. https://doi.org/10.9734/BJESBS/2014/4189

Kumano, M. (2018). On the concept of well-being in Japan: Feeling Shiawase as Hedonic well-being and feeling Ikigai as Eudaimonic well-being. *Applied Research in Quality of Life, 13*, 419–433. https://doi.org/10.1007/s11482-017-9532-9

Mogi, K. (2018). *The little book of Ikigai: The essential Japanese way to finding your purpose in life.* London: Quercus.

Sone, T., Nakaya, N., Ohmori, K., Shimazu, T., Higashigawa, M., & Tsuji, I. (2008). Sense of life worth living (Ikigai) and mortality in Japan: Ohsaki study. *Psychosomatic Medicine, 70*(6), 709–715. https://doi.org/10.1097/PSY.0b013e31817e7e64

15

Advaita Vedanta

Rupinder Kaur

Institute of Coaching and Mentoring (IOCM), Pune, India

The Big Idea

In this chapter, we draw on Advaita Vedanta (Indich, 1995), an ancient Indian philosophy, as a foundational way of developing leadership wisdom. Vedanta is rooted in the metaphysical view of reality as a single, interconnected whole known as 'Brahman'.

The word Vedanta literally means the end of Vedas—the Vedas being the scriptures of Hindus. Vedanta is one of the world's most ancient spiritual philosophies and one of its broadest, based on the Vedas, the sacred scriptures of India.

'Advaita' is a Sanskrit word, with *a-* meaning 'no' and *dvaita* meaning 'two'. 'A*dvaita*' translates to 'not two'. It is a school of Hindu thought and philosophy, which suggests that all is one, and all is the Brahman. It is the philosophical foundation of Hinduism; but while Hinduism includes aspects of Indian culture, Advaita Vedanta is universal in its application and is equally relevant to all countries, all cultures and all religious backgrounds. Paul Deussen beautifully said, 'On the tree of Indian wisdom, there is no fairer flower than the Upanishads (ancient Indian Scriptures) and no finer fruit than the Vedantic philosophy'. According to Vedanta, however, the real 'answers' to the foundational questions of existence, life and leadership are not straightforward. This insight is called *jnana*. It is revolutionary wisdom, turning one's consciousness towards 'Brahman'.

Mosaic Leadership: African, Asian, Middle Eastern and Indigenous Perspectives, First Edition. Edited by Jonathan Passmore, Badri Bajaj, and Mongezi C Makhalima.

Published 2026 by John Wiley & Sons Ltd.

The word Brahman, in Vedic text, refers to someone who, having analysed his own experiences, has discovered the true knowledge of self. The knowledge of self is the ultimate wisdom, which cannot be sought from outside, and therefore, the longest journey is one of 'Self-Awareness' focusing on the inner core.

This non-dualistic perspective of 'Brahman', emphasising the oneness of all existence and integration of the whole, offers practical insights into the mechanics of how we lead, development of a leader and the cultivation of wisdom.

By connecting Vedanta's philosophy to the concept of lucid wisdom, we present it as a practical approach to becoming a wise and effective leader. Wisdom is difficult to acquire on one's own. It is the teacher, the *guru*, who guides one along the spiritual path. From ancient times to the present, the *guru* has played an important role in transmitting the Hindu traditions of wisdom and practice. The Vedantic perspective is dependent on the presence of a 'guru' or 'teacher', which places emphasis on the importance of a teacher who is spiritually enlightened or wiser than the leader.

Going Deeper—Connecting Wisdom With Vedantic Principles

One of the primary distinctions that Vedanta makes is the difference between intelligence and intellect. Intelligence is acquired from schools and universities, while the intellect is developed through one's personal effort in thinking, reasoning and questioning before accepting anything. Intellect is developed by following the practices of Vedanta.

It is made up of four core principles and practices: Atma Bodha (Self-Discovery), Viveka (Discernment), Vairagya (Detachment) and Karma Yoga (Selfless Service) as mechanisms to educate the individual about the interconnectedness and the interdependent nature of leadership. (Refer to Table 15.1 for operational definitions of each of these pillars.)

The Vedantic approach to leadership challenges egotistical development and fosters positive agentic humility that is usually hard to witness in the modern world (Tahora et al., 2019).

A key concept explored is the Vedantic philosophy of **maya**, which refers to the illusion that material reality is separate and distinct, while in truth, everything is interconnected. In the context of knowledge management, maya represents the flawed thinking that perceives events, problems, and individuals as isolated from their

Table 15.1 Vedantic Pillars.

Atma Bodha (Self-Discovery): Develop self-awareness and authentic leadership rooted in deeper values and purpose.
Viveka (Discernment): Strengthen critical thinking and long-term decision-making, discerning between essential and non-essential.
Vairagya (Detachment): Cultivate detachment from results, leading with calm, resilience and focus on the quality of effort.
Karma Yoga (Selfless Service): Promote leadership as service, acting selflessly for the greater good of the organisation and society.

broader environment. This illusion prevents leaders from seeing the whole picture, leading to fragmented thinking and ineffective decision-making.

Common barriers to knowledge flow within teams include the belief that one's understanding of reality is singular and complete, a tendency to engage in debates aimed at 'winning' rather than fostering collaborative learning, and an overemphasis on individual knowledge rather than recognising the value of collective insights (Bhattacharjee, 2011). These barriers often arise from the ego-driven assumption that one's perspective is the most accurate and that others must be convinced of it.

Leaders too often attribute disproportionate value to intelligence over intellect (Gaur, 2018).

Human beings are skilled at gathering peripheral data and making inferential conclusions based on the collected information. We also are endowed with a keen sense of logic leading to proficiency in knowledge in the chosen subject matter, thus giving us an illusion that we know a lot if not all.

This deep sense of outside knowledge though does not necessarily translate into knowledge about self, which is the underlying principle of Vedantic philosophy. The unending desire to acquire more and more knowledge leads to an unbalanced and impoverished self, sometimes incapable of taking decisions that are rooted in empathy, humility and compassion over achievement, drive and competition.

The concept of **Vedanta** as a philosophical framework is designed to help leaders overcome these challenges. In Vedantic thought, everything in the universe is interconnected, and no problem or event can be fully understood in isolation. Maya, the illusion of separateness, fosters human attachment to material objects and personal achievements, leading to competition and division rather than collaboration and growth. By understanding the concept of maya, leaders can begin to address the cognitive biases and assumptions that hinder knowledge flow.

Vedanta explores the practical transformative power of interconnectedness and acceptance of self and the world as a fundamental aspect of practical wisdom. The moment the self becomes a part of the larger integrated whole, this awareness allows leaders to engage with the world with compassion, humility and wisdom (Callahan and Chakrabarti, 2020).

The discovery of interconnectedness can happen only if there is a commitment to the discovery of self or, in Vedantic terms, 'atma-vicara' meaning self-inquiry. Leaders are encouraged to develop practices such as **meditation** for self-awareness, reflection and learning about the self. This opens the doors to the interconnectedness of all things and creates the conditions for dialogue and collaboration (Tahora et al., 2019).

The two pillars, Viveka and Vairagya help in achieving a state of balance.

Viveka is the ability to discern the real from the unreal, the permanent from the impermanent and the essential from the non-essential. It is a faculty of discrimination that allows one to see the true nature of reality.

Viragah means freedom from both attachment and aversion, and Vairagya is the corresponding state of dispassion. It is important to understand that Vairagya or dispassion not only means freedom from attachment but also means freedom from aversion. Dispassion arises when one understands what one is really seeking and recognises the nature of happiness gained from worldly objects. As understanding grows, the mind slowly becomes free from binding likes and dislikes which makes leaders focus on the short term to long term and greater good.

How to Apply It?

Vedanta is a way of life, and therefore, it is universal in application and aims at developing wise leaders in a holistic way. The application of Vedantic principles takes the form of interconnected aspects of leadership canvas as below (Figure 15.1)

Figure 15.1 The Wise Leader Framework.

Self-Discovery—Spiritual Awakening

The Vedantic philosophy of leadership starts with self-discovery, which is the foundational exercise for all leaders. Leaders should strive to continuously understand their actions, their beliefs and the alignment between their actions and beliefs. The way to do that is to engage with the self in a curious non-judgemental way and accept it.

Vision—Dharma

Vedanta embodies the interconnectedness of nature and thus human beings. This principle suggests that all leaders need to take into account the effects of their decisions with the larger impact on lives, societies and ecosystems. Their vision of business cannot be separated from its beneficial or detrimental effect on humanity. Therefore, the pursuit of short-term goals should not be taken up at the cost of long-term impact.

Leadership Position—Brahman

The Vedantic principles urge us to see leadership not only as a position and posture but also as a responsibility and privilege to serve others. A brahman is the one wise leader who embodies the traits of balance. Humility, focus and endurance while being true to self and others. This journey of inner coherence is what leaders should strive to reach.

Action—Karma

All leaders have to take action which is aligned with the larger purpose of the organisation. What is imperative, Vedantic principles say, is to align personal purpose with a larger purpose to establish congruence of action, congruence of thought and impact in outcomes. A wise leader is open to different perspectives, thoughts, and beliefs and accepts external conditions while being courageous enough to hold on to his convictions rooted in principles.

The four pillars of Vedantic leadership wisdom are embedded in a leader's way of feeling, thinking, acting and being in the world. A congruent way of thinking, feeling, acting and being helps the wise leader reach a state of Stith Prajna (absolute stability), which is the essence of a wise leader.

The Vedic principles of Vasudha-eva-Katumbakam, which emphasises that the whole world is one big family that prepares leaders to lead through compassion, humility and support (Sathiyaseelan et al., 2022).

Conclusion

This chapter draws upon India's ancient wisdom gathered through scriptures. The purpose of this chapter is to connect ancient Indian metaphysical perspectives for developing wise leaders who thrive on practical wisdom to run ethical, compassionate and bold organisations.

We draw on the principle of Vedantic philosophy to synthesise the principles for developing wise leaders. The core principle of Vedanta is the belief in unified consciousness, which binds us all in a shared destiny. This shared destiny also believes the world to be an interconnected and complex web of interdependencies.

References

Bhattacharjee, A. (2011). Modern management through ancient Indian wisdom: Towards a more sustainable paradigm. *PURUSHARTHA-A journal of Management, Ethics and Spirituality*, *4*(1), 14–37.

Callahan, G., & Chakrabarti, S. (2020). Vedantic Leadership. In *The Routledge companion to inclusive leadership* (pp. 154–167). Routledge.

Gaur, V. (2018). Wisdom of Vedanta for management educators of 21st century. *Journal of Business and Retail Management Research, 13*(2).

Indich, W. M. (1995). *Consciousness in advaita vedanta.* Motilal Banarsidass Publ.

Sathiyaseelan, A., Balasundaram, S., & Zirkler, M. (2022). Indian perspectives of mindful leadership. In International Research Conference on Mindfulness.

Tahora, S., Shah, S., & Rooney, D. (2019). Vedanta philosophy's contribution to wisdom development for leadership: Grounding Indian practical wisdom in higher knowledge and purpose. In *Applying wisdom to contemporary world problems* (pp. 309–336).

16

Yin–Yang Therapy to Leadership

Wen Tingting[1] *& Yang Wensheng*[2]

[1] *Shanghai Communications Polytechnic, Shanghai, China*
[2] *Shanghai Jiao Tong University, Shanghai, China*

The Big Idea

There are numerous Western psychological approaches, but sometimes they may not be suitable for Chinese clients. In response, we have created the Yin–Yang Therapy, which is designed to help individuals achieve the behavioural change they are seeking.

The Yin–Yang Therapy integrates traditional Chinese culture with modern psychological theories. Based on the Yin–Yang concept from the *Book of Changes*, it develops a six-dimensional strategy and technique, which aims to assist clients in resolving psychological distress and fostering personal growth. This approach emphasises the Yin–Yang mindset, viewing psychological issues as stemming from excessive stubbornness over initiative. It strives to restore the dominance of initiative by adjusting inner forces, enabling clients to escape troubles and regain inner peace. This perspective reflects Chinese cultural wisdom, while aligning with modern psychology's understanding of individual internal motivation and mental states. Additionally, the Yin–Yang Therapy focuses on observation, listening, and locking techniques, emphasising the consultants' careful observation of clients' behaviours and words, active listening to their needs and concerns, and effective guidance through targeted conversations. These techniques facilitate effective client–consultant relationships and smooth coaching processes.

Mosaic Leadership: African, Asian, Middle Eastern and Indigenous Perspectives,
First Edition. Edited by Jonathan Passmore, Badri Bajaj, and Mongezi C Makhalima.

Published 2026 by John Wiley & Sons Ltd.

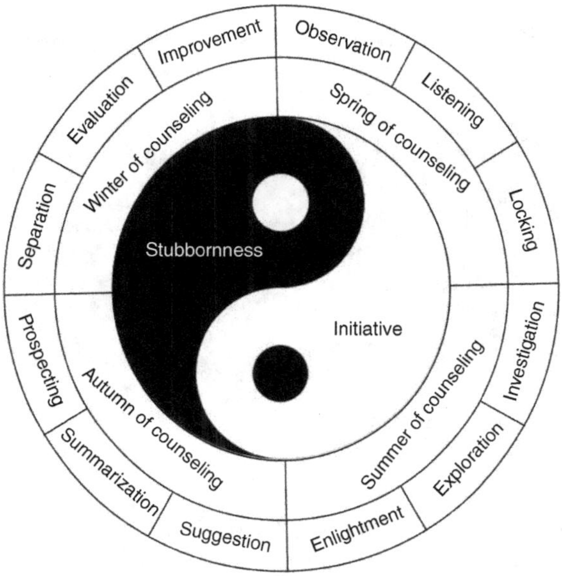

Figure 16.1 Yin & Yang—Four Seasons.

Yin–Yang shares similarities with Western psychological theories and techniques, such as behavioural and cognitive therapies, but applies them flexibly to each individual clients' needs, bridging the Eastern and Western gap to create a new approach to behavioural change (Figure 16.1).

This therapy has developed six psychological strategies: time (future and past), action (cognition and behaviours), comparisons (the basic point and the absolute point), body (stability and mobility), compassion (inward and outward) and benefits (abandoning and striving). It is based on a four-stage process model inspired by nature's four seasons: spring, summer, autumn, and winter, which include techniques such as 'Heart Metaphor', encouraging individuals to exercise subjective initiative and express their inner emotions. The following medical box (each box has different drawers) (Figure 16.2) shows the essence of the Yin–Yang Therapy:

The first major principle is to advance by retreating and overcoming hardness with softness. The second principle is to capitalize on the situation and allow the negative to dissipate while the positive grows. The wisdom of the four seasons refers to spring,

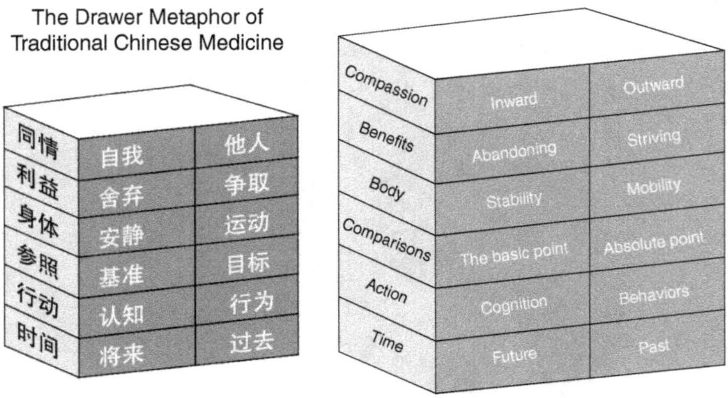

Figure 16.2 Six Psychological Strategies.

summer, autumn, and winter. Spring marks the beginning, summer the midpoint, autumn the harvesting, and winter the conclusion. Each of the four seasons has a distinct working principle:

1. **Spring**: Concealing one's abilities and nurturing strength (the beginning of the conversation);
2. **Summer**: Riding the waves and pursuing dreams (intervening and taking action);
3. **Autumn**: Practicing thrift to avoid danger and guarding hopes (resolving issues);
4. **Winter**: Withdrawing after success and soaring high (resting and recuperating).

How It Works

The fundamental concept of Yin–Yang holds that the essence of psychological distress lies in a person's stubbornness, outweighing their initiative. Stubbornness mainly manifests in aspects such as greed, suspicion, arrogance, ignorance, and resentment, but these should not be categorically rejected as they also correspond to progressiveness, caution, self-confidence, purity, and power, respectively.

It is necessary to observe (observe oneself and others), listen (actively ask questions, listen attentively, and cautiously express oneself), and lock in (the topic of conversation, determine the priority order, and transform the topic into a goal). The goal setting follows the STAR principle, which stands for:

- Specific
- Time for completion
- Agreed
- Realistic.

Conclusion

In practice, the Yin–Yang Therapy describes it as the four seasons and every season has its priorities. While exhibiting uniqueness and effectiveness in some aspects, it may not suit all clients or issues. Therefore, its application requires a comprehensive consideration of clients' specific circumstances and needs. Overall, Yin–Yang psychology offers a novel and practical approach, combining Chinese wisdom with modern psychology, providing a new avenue for addressing psychological challenges. Its effectiveness awaits further research and practice for validation.

17

The Hwarang—The Flower Youths

Haesun Moon

Ontario Institute of Studies in Education (OISE), University of Toronto, Toronto, Canada

The Big Idea

As early as the 6th century, an elite group of young warriors known as the Hwarang (or 'Flower Youths') emerged in ancient Korea's Silla Kingdom (57–676 A.D.). More than just skilled fighters, these young men were cultural and spiritual leaders devoted to a set of guiding principles that are holistic in nature and relational in practice.

The Hwarang were trained in more than martial skills; their development included rigorous cultivation of the mind, body and spirit. The guiding principles illustrate ethical and relational leadership—one rooted in courage, compassion and collective well-being. While they were a warrior force behind uniting three kingdoms into one unified Silla, they were also cultural influencers with profound character.

How to Apply It

In a world where leadership is often equated with technical expertise and individual achievement, we risk losing sight of something far more profound. The Hwarang warriors, much like other non-Western leadership models, remind us that at the heart of

Mosaic Leadership: African, Asian, Middle Eastern and Indigenous Perspectives, First Edition. Edited by Jonathan Passmore, Badri Bajaj, and Mongezi C Makhalima.

Published 2026 by John Wiley & Sons Ltd.

leadership lies character. While the Hwarang stories we know may be romanticized, there is still valuable wisdom to glean. For the Hwarang, leadership wasn't just about martial prowess; it was about cultivating loyalty, compassion, justice and relational harmony. Their approach to leadership was about who you are, not just what you can do. This stands in stark contrast to many contemporary models that prioritize skills over values and individual success over collective well-being.

Modern leadership loves binaries—skills versus character and technical expertise versus empathy. Too often, we measure leadership success by market performance, stakeholder satisfaction or productivity metrics. This focus sidelines character traits—often dismissively labelled as 'soft skills'—despite their crucial role in shaping a leader. The Hwarang, like many East Asian traditions, challenges this by showing that leadership starts from within.

East Asian leadership places the leader within a web of relationships. It's about stewardship—nurturing bonds among people, nature and community and measuring success by the harmony and well-being that emerge. In traditional East Asian teachings, the leader is a servant first, creating space for everyone to contribute. The Hwarang understood this—their strength lay in collective harmony rather than personal dominance. The Hwarang dismantle the myth of the heroic, lone leader. Where contemporary narratives celebrate the charismatic visionary, the Hwarang model emphasizes the collective. Each member was trained not only to excel personally but also to uplift the group. Their success was not individual feats but the cohesion and harmony they nurtured.

A significant challenge in modern leadership training is its hyper-individualistic focus—leaders are often trained in classrooms, far removed from those they serve. This disconnect perpetuates a gap between skills and character. In contrast, the Hwarang and East Asian approaches emphasize community-based learning, engaging directly with people, and integrating skills with shared responsibility.

For today's leaders, I invite a shift in focus. As a communication scientist, I encourage leaders to prioritize character development and explore how coaching can support this journey. Instead of asking, 'What skills do I need?' ask, 'How can I cultivate a character that uplifts others?' Skills are necessary, but they are not the foundation. Leaders who focus on loyalty, empathy, courage, and justice create environments where people thrive and resilience is shared. Here are a few coaching prompts to consider:

- **Reflective Journaling**: 'Think of a recent interaction where your character was tested. How did you respond? How could you align your actions more closely with your core values?'
- **Values Alignment Check**: 'How do your daily decisions reflect your core values? Where might you feel a disconnect, and what might bridge that gap?'
- **Community Engagement Challenge**: Spend time in direct service to your community and then reflect on how it influenced your understanding of leadership.

Adopting a relational, character-centred approach means stepping away from hyper-individualism. True strength comes from being embedded in the community—from knowing when to step forward and when to listen. By nurturing relationships and embodying core values, leaders can transform their organizations into spaces where everyone's potential is recognized, and success is measured by collective well-being.

Reimagining leadership through the wisdom of the Hwarang and East Asian traditions reveals a path rooted in connection, character and collective growth. This is the kind of leadership that doesn't just achieve goals—it cultivates belonging, purpose and resilience. And isn't that precisely what our world needs now more than ever?

Conclusion

The Hwarang teach us that leadership is not about exerting power but about living by values that foster community, courage and care. By adopting their principles of character, holistic development and relational intelligence, modern leaders can create organizations that uplift and inspire—rooted in values that are timeless and profoundly human.

18

Ba

Mamoru Itoh

COACH A Co. Ltd, The Taos Institute, Tokyo, Japan

The Big Idea

About the Concept of 'Self and Others'

Scientifically, we can separately observe the human mind and body, but we cannot separate the mind and body of a living person. There is a tendency to think that when the brain makes decisions without regard to responses from the body, we are being objective and accurate, but the body's responses show reactions to information that are different from those of the brain. The brain and the body are considered as one and make decisions as such. By interpreting and deciding while at the same time connecting with other people's thoughts and interpretations, we can deal with the various problems and challenges we are currently facing due to the limitations caused by a self–other dichotomy. To deal with complex problems, the self cannot be separated or exist in isolation. The self is also recognised in the context of connections and linkages, and if the self merely tries to refer to itself as an object, it is inevitable that self-contradiction will occur at some point. When the living self tries to analyse the static self in isolation from the self, self-contradiction arises.

High-Context Versus Low-Context Cultures

English-speaking cultures are generally low-context. In contrast, Japan is a high-context culture, where indirect communication, unspoken understanding, and attentiveness to the surrounding

Mosaic Leadership: African, Asian, Middle Eastern and Indigenous Perspectives, First Edition. Edited by Jonathan Passmore, Badri Bajaj, and Mongezi C Makhalima.

Published 2026 by John Wiley & Sons Ltd.

atmosphere play a central role. Japan's high-context nature can be attributed to the fact that it is an island nation and has developed with little cultural and racial diversity. Additionally, Japan is a sedentary rice farming society, where people spend many years in a single community, making it easy to create shared assumptions. Many problems encountered by Japanese global companies in English-speaking countries lie not in the communication itself but in the difference in communication styles. Westerners use direct and clear expressions, while Japanese prefer indirect and ambiguous expressions. This can be seen in the difference between prioritising the individual or the organisation.

Japanese Culture

Japanese people communicate without subjects. For example, when confessing feelings to someone, Japanese people did not say 'I love you.' Nowadays, under the influence of Western culture, we say 'I LOVE YOU,' but before, we would walk down the street at night, stop for a moment, and usually the man would say, 'The moon is beautiful, isn't it?.' The women would respond, 'Yes, it is indeed beautiful.' A heart-to-heart communication where people saw the same thing and experienced the same feeling; that was 'I love you' and 'I love you too.' In such communication, there is no subject. People did not say, 'I love you.' In fact, when the word 'love' was first introduced to Japan, there was no direct translation for it. Some dictionaries translated 'love' as 'to cherish,' which may have been the closest equivalent.

As well, there was no sport of swimming or mountain climbing in Japan, with a few exceptions. The concept of 'conquering nature' did not exist either. The Japanese did not think of themselves as separate from nature. Since they viewed themselves as part of nature, they did not have the concept of nature as an object. There is a term '霊験あらたか' (r*eigen arataka*), which refers to the manifestation of blessings from the gods, Buddha, or spiritual beings. It means that by going to a shrine or temple to pay your respects, you are inspired by the gods or Buddha, and as a result, your wish is fulfilled or some mysterious event occurs. This did not happen only in special places or times but extended to mountains themselves—especially Mount Fuji in Japan—as well as trees, waterfalls, and the changing of the seasons, and people have naturally put their hands together to worship God in nature. So, there must have been no thought of conquering it. The word 'nature' itself did not exist, and with the arrival of the Western term 'nature,' the original Japanese term '自然' (*jinen:* the absence of human intervention) was adapted to represent the concept.

Systemic Thinking

Systemic thinking is rooted in *dialogue, social constructionism*, and the concept of 'Ba' (場)—a philosophical notion introduced by Kitaro Nishida, which refers to a *shared space for emerging relationships* (Nonaka & Konno, 1998). Later, Nonaka and Konno (1998) and Shimizu (2000) refined the concept of Ba to include environments and situations in which people create and share knowledge with each other.

The Concept of Ba

'Context is what is co-created in the space of communication. And since context is co-created, people can share the same context in the communication space. In a new civilization, there is an inevitability that there will be a revolution in communication that includes this kind of embodiment. Generally, the *stage for co-creation* in which people engage their bodies in co-creative communication is called "Ba"'. (Shimizu et al., 2000, p. 17)

More specifically, it refers to the physical and metaphorical space in which people engage in relationships and dialogue to co-create knowledge. In 'Ba', people share each other's knowledge and resources and influence each other to create new knowledge. Here, knowledge creation means the mutual development or mutual transformation of things such as understanding, meaning and expertise. It does not mean teaching, gathering, discovering, or creating information or facts. It also does not assume that one person can transmit what is called knowledge to another person. In other words, while things can be shared, it is impossible for the receiver to interpret the shared content in the same meaning as the sender intended. Maturana calls this 'the illusion of instructive interaction'. He says, 'It is impossible. What matters is not the information or facts that are shared and discovered. Rather, what is important is the newness in the understanding that can arise from the interaction in the process of sharing, discovering, and analyzing'.

In 'Ba', it is not the knowledge itself that is important, but rather the knowledge creation of the people present within the relationships and the process. The focus is on the relational aspect of people doing something together. Creating knowledge is essential for innovation and newness, and therefore, in the context of an organisation, it is a company's capacity to successfully and sustainably continue developing. Hence, dialogue is not directed towards finding a single answer or solving a problem, but rather, it has meaning in its ability to persist within the organisation over time.

Previous theories believed that if each individual advances his or her relationship individually so that the relationship between them works well, overall order will emerge. This is often referred to as bottom-up thinking, meaning building up the individual to create the whole from the individual. However, if we think about it carefully, contradictions arise among various relationships while building up only such individual relationships.

Those familiar with simulations using game theory to create self-organising order among multiple units will understand this concept well. It becomes clear that relationships between individuals alone are insufficient, and the creation of 'Ba' is also necessary. One conclusion from this is that the nature of the harmony between individual creation and the creation of the whole emerges from the dual existence of life.

The *dual existence of life* means that life appears simultaneously with two different modes of existence: localised existence and omnipresent existence. For example, in quantum mechanics, there are simultaneously a localised form of existence called a particle and an omnipresent form of existence called a wave. To concretely think about co-creation, it is necessary to understand how this dual existence of life operates within humans. This is referred to as the *duality of the self*. The self reflects both localised and omnipresent forms of life and, therefore, exists with two distinct domains: the self-centred domain and the spatial domain. The self-centred domain creates individuality (absolute diversity), while the spatial domain, in cooperation with others, creates wholeness. The self-centred self forms individual relationships with the self-centred selves of others. This operates in a bottom-up manner. On the other hand, in the spatial domain, there is no individuality like absolute diversity, and like waves, it self-organises a common 'Ba' by synchronising with each other.

How to Apply It

Ba and Improvisation

The *stage for co-creation* can be seen as improvisation. There is no pre-prepared scenario, and roles are not assigned in advance. There is no director. The actors (who do not necessarily have to be actors) stand on the stage, paying attention to their own and others' gazes, facial expressions, body movements and breathing. When someone speaks, they predict the other's role and, based on that, predict their own role. When they speak, they do so from that role. Simultaneously, the relationships within the roles create the *co-creation relationship* that builds the stage. The consciousness of co-creating becomes the life of improvisation, and eventually, the roles, the progress of the play and the purpose of the play are shared. The flow of the play itself is created. This does not occur only on the stage; the audience's reactions also influence the play's progression. The entire play, including the audience, takes on a life of its own. The connections and interactions of those participating, while engaging their whole beings, carry out co-creative communication. This stage for co-creation is called 'Ba'.

Engaging in Dialogue Inside the Ba

Leaders view dialogue as a co-creative process, not just an exchange of information. The following seven concepts can be practiced on a daily basis:

1. **Constructing Reality:** understanding that reality is created through dialogue and creating positive reality in dialogue.
2. **Relational Scenarios:** understanding the habitual patterns in a conversation and having the ability to flexibly change them.
3. **Choices:** being aware of the choices presented in dialogue and jointly creating new choices with the other person.
4. **Positioning:** Being aware of one's own and the other person's position and taking a position that is empathetic to both parties.
5. **Dual Involvement:** Pay attention to the content of the dialogue as well as the relationship. It is important to be aware of word choice, tone and nonverbal elements.
6. **Pluralistic Presence**: Recognising the diversity of oneself and others and finding ways to leverage it.
7. **Embodiment:** Embodying the value of dialogue not only through words but also through actions and attitudes. Communicate while incorporating your whole being.

Here, the phrase 'communicating while incorporating your whole being' suggests that when the brain is disconnected from the body, it becomes enlarged, ultimately leading to the denial of humanity. Additionally, incidents where young people fail to empathise with others' pain and easily cross limits, even taking lives, are phenomena born from a culture that undervalues the whole being. The background of this is an excessive focus on self-and-other-separating information. Self-and-other-separating information is an attitude and way of thinking that divides the world into two: the self and the world other than the self, where the self sees things other than itself from a self-centred way and interprets their meanings. The logic that has been used in this subject–object dichotomous thinking is objectification logic. However, it has become clear that this logic has significant limitations. That limitation is that it cannot be used for things that cannot be presented in a way that is separate from the self. Examples include meaning, value, beauty, ethics, a sense of responsibility and markets. Additionally, while we consider biology and life to be different concepts, life cannot be separated from self and thus cannot be explained through self-and-other-separating scientific methods.

Conclusion

In systemic thinking, even when facing the individual, the individual is never separated from others or the environment. Based on the premise that humans exist within relationships, existence is viewed as being within relationships, and thus co-creation is encouraged. Systemic thinking can be described as a process that liberates human existence and purpose from the individual framework and develops relationships and dialogue.

References

Nonaka, I., & Konno, N. (1998). The concept of Ba: Building a foundation for knowledge creation. *California Management Review*, *40*(3), 40–54.

Shimizu, H., Kume, T., Miwa, Y., & Miyake, Y. (2000). 場と共創 (Ba and Co-creation). Tankobon Press.

Islamic Perspectives

19

Islam and Self-reflective Leadership

Suzan Bou Naseredine

Qatar Foundation Schools, Counseling Department, Doha, Qatar

The Big Idea

People in Asia and the Middle East contend with significant issues that can profoundly impact their well-being. However, they avoid coaching in the belief that it will not acknowledge their religious beliefs. Furthermore, experience and research evidence have highlighted the value of self-awareness and reflection in leadership roles.

Self-reflection and accountability are considered crucial in Islam, and most leaders from the Gulf are encouraged through their faith to take personal responsibility, be accountable for one's actions and evaluate one's thoughts and actions.

Know yourself so that you come to know Allah (Subhanahu wa ta'ala (SWT)—Glory be to Him) as said in Arabic. This view is echoed in Islamic culture: 'Whosoever knows himself knows his Lord.' This hadith implies that gaining knowledge about oneself leads to knowledge about Allah.

Islam encourages the practice of introspection and inner reflection as a way to connect with God. Studying ourselves and our abilities redirects our attention back to the existence of God. I found that using quotes from the Quran can work as an aid in supporting the exploration of the self. For example, referring to Surah Ash-Sharh (94:5–6), Allah (SWT) reassures: "Indeed, with hardship [will be] ease. Indeed, with hardship [will be] ease.' If a client is

Mosaic Leadership: African, Asian, Middle Eastern and Indigenous Perspectives, First Edition. Edited by Jonathan Passmore, Badri Bajaj, and Mongezi C Makhalima.

Published 2026 by John Wiley & Sons Ltd.

facing hardships, this verse offers solace and provides hope and comfort through their struggles.

Through self-reflection, a person can evaluate his actions as opposed to the actions of others. This method is important in strengthening one's character development and spiritual being as well. This self-reflection in Eastern culture is called 'Muhasabah'—the more the person reflects on oneself the more recognition that it is our self-perceptions that create negative thoughts, emotions and thus behaviours. Reminding the client that there is a reason for everything and that Allah (SWT) has put them into such experiences as a test. By this being said, Allah will ask the person what was their reaction and behaviour, what was chosen to be done and not what were the expectations of what others should do. Leadership coaching is a powerful way to enhance one's skills, performance and impact as a leader. It requires a person to reflect on their own strengths, challenges and goals. Self-reflection is indeed a critical skill for leaders who want to grow, develop and adapt in this changing world while preserving the culture and traditions. Reflective practice is essential for fostering a culture of accountability, growth and resilience in leadership coaching. Through self-reflection, we gain insights into our own behaviours, values and attitudes, enabling us to adjust our actions and decision-making processes accordingly. Something I've realised is that self-reflection is a cornerstone of leadership development. It is a key leadership skill, a powerful technique that helps leaders think back to past experiences while also helping to plan for their future development.

The self-reflection process can be done through journaling using several prompts provided by the coach or from the Koran. Throughout a leader's leadership journey, self-reflection must be the major pillar across all aspects of the leadership role, focusing on different areas of self-knowledge such as personal ambitions and goals, individual and organisational values, personality types, thinking styles, emotional intelligence, and reflective learning. For a leader to maintain consistency, this kind of reflection must be done regularly, preferably daily. It is greatly important to find the time to practise this process to hold ourselves accountable and ask God for repentance when recognising faults and shortcomings. This will automatically lead to decreased anxiety and improved well-being.

From the Islamic perspective, self-reflection is a profound exploration into the inner journey of the soul. It involves contemplating one's intentions, actions and relationship with the Creator. This process gives the client the chance to assess their adherence to Islamic principles and values, preparing for personal development and spiritual growth. In Islam, self-reflection is a fundamental process to strengthen the connection with Allah (SWT). In addition, through self-reflection guided by the Quran, a person can get a better understanding of their inner thoughts and behaviours. There are a few Prophetic guidance keys on self-reflection that a leader must reflect on, for example:

1. **Intentions:** reflecting on one's intentions helps in aligning the actions with the faith.
2. **Accountability:** holding oneself accountable for their actions and behaviours and taking responsibility for one's deeds.
3. **Gratitude:** reflecting on the blessings and showing gratitude and appreciation is a way of strengthening faith.
4. **Self-improvement:** seeking to be a better person each day is an inner journey in Islam and is a main pillar of leadership coaching.

How to Apply It

To develop leadership skills, self-reflection through the journaling technique can be a valuable tool for almost every client. The key is to start and maintain the practice. There are no rules for journaling except to keep the practice once started. The process can be undertaken in the morning or evening, but a regular place and time helps. There are several ways that a leader can do self-reflection; here are a few steps:

1. Through journaling, the leader can perform self-reflection utilising mindfulness as a first step, which is also called 'Muraqabah,' an Arabic word for meditation. Praying five times a day makes this step easier. It filters the unwanted thoughts. The entire focus and devotion will be on Allah. The nearest a servant comes to his Lord is when he is prostrating himself, so make supplication (in this state). [Sahih Muslim, no. 482]
2. Expressing yourself through writing is the second step. This step can take the form of writing or speaking. Usually, I recommend writing so that the client can go back and reflect on the healing process and journey. A combination of drawing and writing can work well. The use of language or sentence structure does

not matter, as there is no one to judge one's thoughts except Allah (SWT).

3. Manifesting positivity is the third step. So, whoever does an atom's weight of good will see it. And whoever does an atom's weight of evil will see it. [Surah Az-Zalzalah 99:7–8]
4. Through this verse, the client understands that challenging their perspectives and thought process is crucial and critical.
5. Self-reflection circle for leadership development is a group practice. The sessions involve small groups of leaders coming together regularly to reflect, share experiences and support each other in their leadership journey. Following each meeting, attendees record their insights, reflections and thoughts in their personal journal.

With each practice, individuals should choose those that work best for them and seek to sustain this for the benefits to emerge over time.

Conclusion

In this short chapter, we have highlighted the importance of self-reflection in leadership from an Islamic perspective, emphasising the alignment of actions with faith. Through journaling, meditation and accountability, leaders can strengthen their personal development and connection with Allah (SWT).

20

Five Solar Moments Model

Dina Khalid AlAlami

AOEC, Academy of Executive Coaching, Abu Dhabi, UAE

The Big Idea

The five daily prayers are moments of reflection that are designed to 'ground' Muslims during their day. In those moments of connection with God, the Muslim also connects with their core purpose: to raise their consciousness and practise elevated morality through service to improve life. In the Noble Koran, it is called to become the 'Khalifa'.[1]

While a religious practice, this practice informs all aspects of life including leadership, and we have conceptualised this as the Five Solar Moments Model reflecting the five moments during a day of 'grounding'.

How to Apply It?

The basis of the model is the five daily prayers that Muslims practise in their connection with God. The model can be used by a trainer, coach, or leader themselves. It can be used as described, guided by faith, or by a secular leader, guided by their values.

When using this model, the leader can use the moments to reflect during the day. The model anchors its actions and accountability while performing the daily prayers, but equally this could be a mindfulness moment.

An individual's actions are stacked in those moments like 'coats hanging on the branches of a strong-rooted tree'. The tree analogy

Mosaic Leadership: African, Asian, Middle Eastern and Indigenous Perspectives, First Edition. Edited by Jonathan Passmore, Badri Bajaj, and Mongezi C Makhalima.

Published 2026 by John Wiley & Sons Ltd.

is used to depict the individual as the tree, rooted in their soil (their culture, values and 'specific being'). The soil and associated programming feed the tree. At different times of the day, the tree performs its actions in light of the sun.

The model uses the well-established prayer habit during these 'solar moments'. The repetitive routine builds structure and consistency, just like the prayers have a structure, rhythm and tempo to quieten the mind. Like breathing in meditation, the leader can sit with themselves, unwinding from the stressful, fast-paced office work, and focus on a given decision or issue.

The model invites the leader to follow the specific timings of the five daily prayers (Kaltner, 2016) (approximate times):

1. Dawn moment (before sunrise)
2. Noon moment (12:30–4 p.m.)
3. Mid-afternoon moment (4–6 p.m.)
4. Sunset moment (6–7:30 p.m.)
5. Night moment (7:30–9 p.m.)

The leader would follow the self-inspection model sequence during these moments. They take a moment (this might be 2–5 minutes) where they connect with their inner self/voice and go over a set of questions, which follow the structure of the 'Fatihat al-Kitab',[2] the first surah or chapter in the Noble Koran.

1. **Gratitude**: 'What am I grateful for now?'

   The first question starts with gratitude for what is and what is possible.

2. **Compassion**: 'How can I practise self-compassion? How can I practise compassion for others?'

   The second question uses compassion as a base for dealing with oneself/others, including plants and inanimate objects.

3. **Justice and accountability**: 'Am I ready for the Day of Judgment?' 'Am I ready to live with the consequences of my actions?' 'What if the whole world can see my actions and consequences?'

   This question brings forward the sense of justice that comes with accountability for one's actions. Justice happens on the Muslim Day of Judgement, and what goes around comes around. What you send out into the world will find you and come back, so you better do good!

4. **Vulnerability**: 'What is within my control?' 'What is not?'
   As a human, I only have control over how I respond (not react) to events in my life. I cannot control others or life. I am aware of my limitations and seek God's help in my life and when making decisions.

5. **Guidance**: 'O Allah, if what I am doing is good for me, grant me strength and success. If not, guide me to what is better and remove from my path what is not beneficial for me.'

The last question asks for guidance from God and within one's inherent inner leader. It is a combination of following God's path, self-leadership and discipline to carry it out.

To illustrate this, imagine a leader is about to make a decision in their office, 'What is?' What is happening now that I need to be aware of? What are my limiting beliefs? Where am I coming from? From a place of love or fear? Who am I now acting in this way?

A Muslim's base is 'Taqwa,'[3] which is being mindful of God when acting. It is the reference point when making decisions to act or not. So, the internal dialogue would be like this: 'Will this action bring me closer to God and righteousness or push me away?'

In this reflective moment, options of what is possible would also undergo a similar scrutiny,

'What is aligned with my values and identity?' Culture and belief systems vary widely and the individual needs to reflect on their own values, which may or may not be faith-based (Hofstede, 2001).

Values like acting with integrity, 'Amana' (Qurṭubī, 2003a) are paramount for Muslims. They encompass the concept that life is a mission with responsibilities and purpose. Going through life with 'Amana'[4] as a guiding principle is the way of Muslims.

In the reflective moment, the leader must answer questions like 'What resources can I tap into now'? Again, the resources must be lawful and reflect their values.

When answering the resources question, abundance is available as one of God's qualities and names. The reference to names of God like 'The Abundant- Ar Rahman,' 'The Bestower-Al Wahab,' and 'The Generous-Al Kareem' allows the leader to feel hopeful and aspirational when pursuing goals.

As the moment approaches its end, the leader can conclude by asking for guidance. Muslims can find external wisdom within themselves. Imam Al ibn Abi Talib once said in his poetry, 'You think yourself but a speck, while the great universe dwells within you.' (Al Ibn Abi Talib, (n.d.b)).

Conclusion

This chapter explores the 'Five Solar Moments Model,' which integrates the structure of daily Muslim prayers into leadership reflection. The model, based on gratitude, compassion, accountability, vulnerability and guidance, encourages leaders to practice mindfulness and self-inspection throughout the day. By reflecting on their values and decisions, leaders can align their actions with ethical principles and achieve personal growth. This model supports both faith-based and secular approaches to leadership, fostering integrity, responsibility and self-awareness in decision-making processes.

Notes

1 Qurṭubī, A. (2003). *Al-Jāmiᶜ li-Aḥkām al-Qurʾān* (Vol. 1). This work provides commentary on the Qur'anic verse about humans being appointed as vicegerents (khalifa) on Earth, highlighting the responsibilities that come with this role.
2 Al-Ghazālī, A. H. (2004). *The Beginning of Guidance (Bidāyat al-Hidāyah).* Al-Ghazālī discusses the spiritual significance of Surah Al-Fatiha and why it is recited in every unit of the prayer. He emphasizes the need for mindful recitation of "Fātiḥat al-Kitāb" to truly connect with its meanings.
3 Al-Ghazālī, A. H. (2010). The Beginning of Guidance (Bidāyat al-Hidāyah) (A. Mangera, Trans.). White Thread Press.In this concise manual, Al-Ghazālī outlines the fundamentals of acquiring guidance through God-consciousness (taqwa).
4 *Reference to Amāna: Commentary on Quranic verses related to Amāna, such as Surah Al-Ahzab (33:72), which discusses the trust given to humanity.* Qurṭubī, A. (2003). *Al-Jāmiᶜ li-Aḥkām al-Qurʾān (Vol. 11). Dar al-Kutub al-Ilmiyya.*

References

Ali ibn Abi Talib, I. (n.d.) *You think of yourself as a speck while the great universe dwells within you.* [Poem]. In *Collected Poems of Imam Ali* (Diwan Ali Ibn Abi Talib). Retrieved from (https://adabworld.com on Aug. 24, 2024)

Al ibn Abi Talib, I (n.d.). *Diwan al-Imam 'Ali* (pp. 86). Beirut, Lebanon: Dar al-Kutub al-'Ilmiyya.

Hofstede, G. (2001). *Culture's consequences: Comparing values, behaviors, institutions, and organizations across nations* (2nd ed.). Sage Publications.
Kaltner, J. (2016). *Islam: What nonmuslims should know* ((Revised & expanded edition.). ed., pp. 34). Fortress Press.
Qurṭubī, A. (2003a). *Al-Jāmiᶜ li-Aḥkām al-Qur'ān* (Vol. 1).
Qurṭubī, A. (2003b). *Al-Jāmiᶜ li-Aḥkām al-Qur'ān* (Vol. *11*). *Dar al-Kutub al-Ilmiyya.*

21

Qadr of Allah (Divine Destiny)

F. K. Tia Moin

University of Reading, Reading, U.K.
The Inclusion Coach Ltd, London, U.K.

The Big Idea

Qadr (pron. kud-urr) of Allah is a concept that originates from the religion of Islam. It is estimated that there are over 2 billion Muslims (followers of Islam), and it is the second largest religion in the world. Islam is also the dominant religion in the Middle East, North Africa and some countries in sub-Saharan Africa (Lugo et al., 2011). Islamic culture significantly influences leadership values in these regions.

The word 'Qadr' is Arabic and can be translated as 'divine decree'. It refers to the concept of predestination, a belief in God (Allah)'s plan. According to the Koran, the holy book of Islam, everything that happens (down to the precise falling of a leaf from a tree) has already been written and only happens by the will of Allah:

> He has the keys to the unseen: no one knows them but Him. He knows all that is in the land and sea. No leaf falls without His knowledge, nor is there a single grain in the darkness of the earth, or anything, fresh or withered, that is not written in a clear Record. (Al-Qu'ran 6:59 – translated by M.A.S. Abdel Haleem, 2008).

The belief in Qadr can be both an obstacle and a resource. For example, the occurrence of devastating floods in Bangladesh is often explained away as an 'act of God', impeding the efforts of local

Mosaic Leadership: African, Asian, Middle Eastern and Indigenous Perspectives, First Edition. Edited by Jonathan Passmore, Badri Bajaj, and Mongezi C Makhalima.

Published 2026 by John Wiley & Sons Ltd.

and aid organisations to survive such crises. Yet, it is the very belief in Qadr that offers people solace, comfort and acceptance of what has happened, such that they do not waste time questioning events and why they happened so that they can focus on moving on (Schmuck, 2000). Thus, a belief in Qadr can have benefits as well as limitations.

A Common Misconception

Limitations arise from a common misconception in understanding Qadr, believing that your fate is entirely out of your hands. A person may believe that they have no control or sway in changing the direction of future events because everything has already been preordained and determined—described by psychologists as an external locus of control (Rotter, 1966). When considered alongside motivational theories such as self-determination theory (Deci & Ryan, 2008), which places emphasis on the importance of feeling like we have a choice in our actions (known as 'ikhtiyar' in Arabic), and goal theory (Locke & Latham, 2019), which highlights the importance of plausible goals, it is clear to see why this misconception could interfere with the coaching process which relies heavily on these principles.

Under this limited interpretation of Qadr, the leader who experiences a setback may have a tendency to attribute any failure to destiny, the will of Allah. This can lead to a feeling of powerlessness, lack of accountability and giving up hope. Any efforts may be hampered by an underlying belief that actions will be fruitless because the outcome is already 'written' by Allah and cannot be changed. The lack of assertion or effort could also result in missed opportunities or even detrimental outcomes, compromising their stance as a leader.

A Constructive Interpretation

The concept of fate and free will has been debated heavily by Islamic scholars. It is argued by some that Qadr does not refer to an unchangeable fate, rather it refers to Allah's precise *foreknowledge* of events, including the choices one is going to make. This interpretation accepts that there is no interference by Allah in a person's free will and capacity to make choices (ikhtiyar), with all people being accountable for their own actions—a concept that is repeatedly reinforced in the Koran (Saleem & Rizvi, 2019—suggested reading). A synonymous term often used interchangeably with Qadr is 'taqdir'—the literal translation is similar to the term 'of measure'. While Qadr implies Allah's precise knowledge and power of how future events will unfold, taqdir implies latent possibilities, presumably through the exercise of free will (Al-Quran 2: 256; 54: 49; 15: 21, as cited in Wan Zakaria, 2015).

There is a common expression in modern Islamic culture of 'tying your camel', which is useful when someone responds to Qadr with 'what's the point?' Tying your camel refers to an authentic 'hadith' (At Tirmidhī, n.d.; Sunan al-Tirmidhī 2517), an authenticated account by a companion of the prophet Muhammed's (peace be upon him) teachings in Islam. In this hadith, a traveller asked the prophet whether he should bother tying his camel to prevent it from wandering off or place his trust in Allah since the fate of the camel was already determined. The prophet replied that he should tie the camel *and* place his trust in Allah (referred to as 'tawwakkul'). The concept of responsibility is emphasised, and it is encouraged that a person can influence their own fate through making thoughtful choices and striving, often paired with prayer ('dua') to Allah.

Under this interpretation, the leader who experiences a setback will be motivated to explore solutions, alternative plans or approaches and ways to overcome challenges to achieve their desired goals and outcomes. They may also pray for guidance (known as the 'ishtikhara' prayer), after which they trust their intuition to make decisions under God's guidance and accept whatever good or bad happens as Qadr, allowing them to move on quickly to other presenting opportunities.

When Fate Can't Be Changed

Finally, a belief in Qadr supports a leader's resilience when faced with disappointing outcomes in spite of their efforts or in situations outside of their control (e.g. such as those presented during the COVID-19 pandemic or a devastating flood). Since these events are seen to be an act of God, engaging in feelings of regret suggests questioning Allah's plan, which is seen as a lack of faith. Certainly, Muslims are encouraged to believe that even bad things happen for good reasons and that potentially an even worse crisis had been averted or the benefit might not be apparent yet—either in this world (the 'dunya') or in the next world (the afterlife: 'akhira').

The rapid acceptance can sometimes even contribute towards feelings of gratitude as well as resilience, which we know has positive outcomes for well-being (Hu et al., 2015; Portocarrero et al., 2020).

How to Apply It?

The leader or their coach could first explore whether *free will* or *fate* is the key determinant of the situation. In other words, is influencing the outcomes feasible in the situation (see Figure 21.1)? The individual should consider alternative courses of action that are permissible by way of Islam (an internal locus of control); or whether outcomes cannot be changed regardless if one exercises free will or because of an act of God (external locus of control).

Asking questions which support the client to recognise their ability to exercise choices (i.e. tying the camel) is recommended before deciding that something is not destined to be. Self-reflective questions might include:

- How do you know this outcome is Qadr of Allah? What other outcomes are possible?

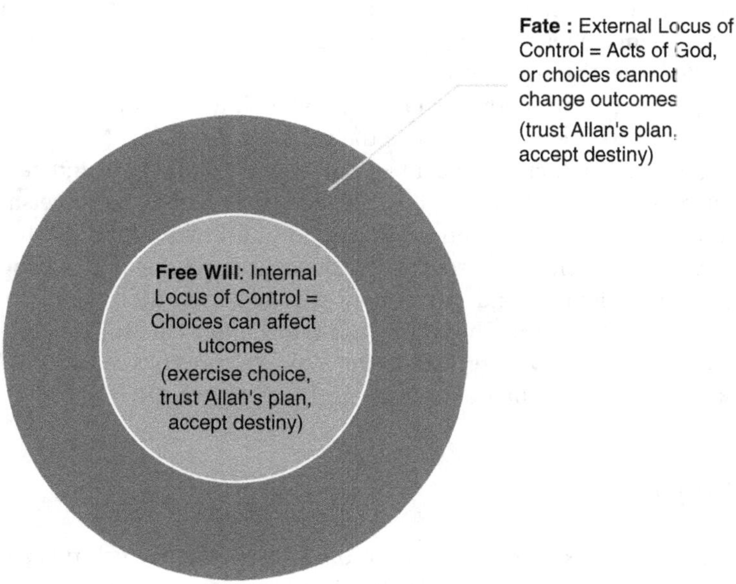

Figure 21.1 *Internal versus External Locus of Control: Free Will versus Fate.*

- What do you think Allah would want you to do/choose in this situation?
- If you have prayed for guidance, what does your gut tell you to do now?
- Which opportunities are opening up for you now? And which are closing?

When it comes to dealing with negative outcomes of situations that can't be changed, leverage the concept of fate (Qadr) to develop acceptance of what has happened and build resilience. Questions might include:

- Do you accept this as Qadr of Allah?
- How does that shape how you feel about the situation?
- Do you believe Allah has a better plan for you/the situation?
- Are you ready to explore what that plan might be?

Considerations: It is conceivable that alongside religious beliefs, a person's natural levels of optimism, hope or self-efficacy will affect their agency. However, beyond this, structural or environmental contexts may also influence someone's perceived locus of control (suggested reading: Anderson et al., 2016). Consider whether your worldview and cultural or historical perceptions might differ from your clients in terms of appreciating and recognising whether there are feasible 'options' that your client could explore.

Qadr (predestination) or fate is strongly linked to how much a person feels they can influence their environment. We know that higher levels of perceived control can increase motivation and performance at work as well as reduce stress and absenteeism (Spector, 1986). Thus, understanding how best to interpret a belief in Qadr can help the executive coach support clients in achieving self-determination and motivation to achieve the outcomes they desire. Furthermore, a belief in Qadr can support clients in accepting and facing adversity, facilitating feelings of resilience and possibly even feelings of gratitude when things go wrong.

Conclusion

This chapter explores the concept of *Qadr* (divine decree) in Islam and its impact on leadership, highlighting both constructive and limiting interpretations. Understanding *Qadr* can shape leaders' resilience and accountability. By embracing a balanced perspective—acknowledging both free will and divine destiny—leaders can make thoughtful decisions and persevere through adversity, fostering resilience, acceptance and gratitude in challenging circumstances. This nuanced understanding can support the development of effective leadership traits, integrating religious beliefs with our understanding of motivation for improved leadership outcomes.

References

Abdel Haleem, M. A. S. (2008). *The Qur'an (2010 reprint with corrections).* Oxford University Press.

Anderson, C., Turner, A. C., Heath, R. D., & Payne, C. M. (2016). On the Meaning of Grit. . .and Hope. . .and Fate Control. . .and Alienation. . .and Locus of Control. . .and. . .Self-Efficacy. . . and. . .Effort Optimism. . .and. . .. *The Urban Review, 48*(2), 198–219. https://doi.org/10.1007/s11256-016-0351-3

At Tirmidhī. (n.d.). Sunan al-Tirmidhī 2517. In *Sunan At-Tirmidhi (Jami` at-Tirmidhi)* (Vol. 4). Sunnah.com. https://sunnah.com/tirmidhi

Deci, E. L., & Ryan, R. M. (2008). Self-determination theory: A macrotheory of human motivation, development, and health. *Canadian Psychology, 49*(3), 182–185. https://doi.org/10.1037/a0012801

Hu, T., Zhang, D., & Wang, J. (2015). A meta-analysis of the trait resilience and mental health. *Personality and Individual Differences, 76*, 18–27. https://doi.org/10.1016/j.paid.2014.11.039

Locke, E. A., & Latham, G. P. (2019). The development of goal setting theory: A half century retrospective. *Motivation Science, 5*, 93–105. https://doi.org/10.1037/mot0000127

Lugo, L., Cooperman, A., O'Connell, E., & Stencel, S. (2011). *The future global muslim population projections for 2010-2030.* Pew Research Center: Forum on Religion & Public Life.

Portocarrero, F. F., Gonzalez, K., & Ekema-Agbaw, M. (2020). A meta-analytic review of the relationship between dispositional gratitude and well-being. *Personality and Individual Differences, 164*, 110101. https://doi.org/10.1016/j.paid.2020.110101

Rotter, J. B. (1966). Generalized expectancies for internal versus external control of reinforcement. *Psychological Monographs: General and Applied, 80*(1), 1–28. https://doi.org/10.1037/h0092976

Saleem, H. M., & Rizvi, K. H. (2019). Khalifa Abdul Hakim on the doctrine of free will and predestination, good and evil in Islam. *Bazyaft, 34*(1). https://doi.org/10.57156/bazyaft3414929

Schmuck, H. (2000). "An Act of Allah": Religious explanations for floods in Bangladesh as survival strategy. *International Journal of Mass Emergencies & Disasters, 18*(1), 85–95. https://doi.org/10.1177/028072700001800105

Spector, P. E. (1986). Perceived control by employees: A meta-analysis of studies concerning autonomy and participation at work. *Human Relations, 39*(11), 1005–1016. https://doi.org/10.1177/001872678603901104

Wan Zakaria, W. F. A. (2015). Qadar in classical and modern Islamic discourses: Commending a futuristic perspective. *International Journal of Islamic Thought, 7*(1), 39–48. 10.24035/ijit.07.2015.004

22

Ershad Leadership

Raja'a Yousef Allaho

ICF, EMCC, Kuwait

The Big Idea

Leadership involves the responsibility of guiding a group in making decisions that align with the organisation's agreed goals. Effective leadership requires personal and professional skills to inspire and influence others to take action, make decisions and follow instructions aimed at achieving these goals. This ability to lead is grounded in the capacity to build personal and professional relationships with followers, fostering an environment where everyone contributes their energy and works together to ensure that the organisation's objectives are met.

What Is Islamic Leadership?

Jūratė Kuklytė (2017) has defined Islamic leadership as 'managerial knowledge acquired from revealed and other Islamic sources of knowledge that results in applications compatible with Islamic beliefs and practices.'

Islamic leadership is about serving organisations and their members to reduce uncertainty, foster collaboration and address managerial and social challenges through the application of high moral standards and religious principles.

Mosaic Leadership: African, Asian, Middle Eastern and Indigenous Perspectives, First Edition. Edited by Jonathan Passmore, Badri Bajaj, and Mongezi C Makhalima.

Published 2026 by John Wiley & Sons Ltd.

Abdullah bin Balqasim Albakri (2020) classifies leadership traits into three categories: leadership, behavioural, and ethical. Each category is supported by verses from the Quran. These are summarised in Table 22.1.

How to Apply It?

The ERSHAD leadership emphasises these traits and skills and can be developed through a parallel coaching process.

When we search for the meaning of ERSHAD in Arabic, we find the following Breakdown in the Arabic Dictionary: al-Maany al-Jami.'

1. Guided (Rashada, *verb*, past root)
   He guides (rashada), he who is guided (marshud)
   It also means 'to be inflicted,' 'to be enlightened' and 'to be set on the right path.'
2. Phrases with guidance or guided or he who is guided (ar-rushd, *noun*)
   1. '[he] has reached the age of puberty or maturity.'
   2. '[he] has returned to his senses, come to,' or has returned to normal, to their normal selves. It is also used in opposite, to have *lost* one's senses.
   3. It also refers to the legal age of responsibility for one's actions.

Other meetings of Guidance 'AlRushed':

- Practicing truth (honesty)
- Achieving success
- Moving in the right direction

These meanings highlight that effective leaders possess the following characteristics: ethical (practising truth), professional (achieving success and moving in the right direction) and personal skills (maturity and responsibility).

Leadership coaching is a vital development tool both for helping leaders achieve success in their careers and personal lives and working with those around them. In an Islamic context, leadership includes (1) the ethical dimension, (2) the behavioural dimension and (3) the leadership dimension (Figure 22.1).

Table 22.1 Islamic Leadership Traits.

Leadership Skills	Behavioural Skills	Ethical
Faith in ALLAH -GOD	Good role model	Piety
Knowledge and experience	Grit and determination	Empathy and compassion
Vision	Kindness to subordinates	Honesty
Ability	Involving others (consultation)	Integrity
Delegation	• Dialogue—persuasion • Communication (language compatibility, eloquence and statement) • Eloquence and politeness in oral and written communication • Use examples to illustrate the concept • Repetition • Detailing the possibilities in the orders (a clear plan of action) • Gentle reproach—benefit	Trust in God and trust in Him
Ability to organise	• Understand others • Listening • Understand people's problems, listen to their conversations	Tolerance and forgiveness
Selection and appointment of qualified people	Inspiring, arousing enthusiasm and motivation	Humility
Building role models	Sacrifice	Justice and Equality
Biography (reputation)	Initiative—seizing opportunities	Patience

(*Continued*)

Table 22.1 (Continued)

Leadership Skills	Behavioural Skills	Ethical
Clarity of decisions Amending orders and stating their reasons	Calling others by nicknames and descriptions that they like	• Compassion (appreciating the circumstances of subordinates) • Maintaining human dignity
Social intelligence (social and cultural compatibility with subordinates)	Optimism	Fulfilling obligations
The ability to change	Assertiveness	Generosity
Loyalty	Time management	Courage—admitting and admitting mistakes
Understanding of human nature	Monitoring and inspection	Overlooking
Benefit from experienced people	Evaluating the conditions of subordinates	
• The ability to manage conflict • Managing crises	Building trust	
Providing a healthy environment for competition (psychological safety)	Smoothing when unable to meet subordinates' desires	
Perfection and quality	Moderation and balance (moderation in punishment, reward and use of authority)	
Wisdom (getting right in words and deeds)—the ability to act appropriately at the appropriate time and in the appropriate manner	Cleanliness and care for appearance	
Taking into account priorities		

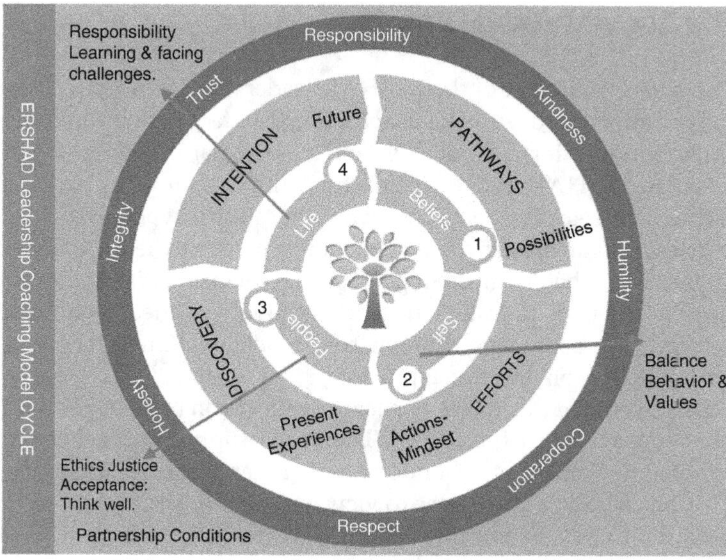

Figure 22.1 ERSHAD Leadership Coaching Model.

As illustrated above, the outer ring of the ERSHAD leadership framework is called the 'Partnership conditions.' These conditions emphasise the importance of establishing ethical, respectful and trusting relationships before and during coaching engagements. By focusing on Partnership conditions, positive, thoughtful relationships between coaches and leaders are sustained.

Ethics in Islam plays a vital role in defining what it means to be a true Muslim; it's the foundation that supports a decent life while strengthening social and professional relationships.

The partnership conditions are the cornerstone for building respectful and trusting relationships in the coaching process. This stage involves the coach and leader reflecting on the leader's ethical practices to ensure positive outcomes.

During this stage, the leader is coached, guided and trained to establish a moral foundation emphasising trust, respect, humility, honesty, cooperation and integrity. The focus is on how the leader and his team will work together effectively while considering ethical principles and how the leader practises these ethics in his daily personal and professional interactions.

The Conversational Process

The core component of the ERSHAD leadership framework is the conversational process. The coach's role is to facilitate meaningful conversation using a set of skills and a particular coaching way of being. In ERSHAD leadership coaching, the coaching way of being is characterised by patience, humanity, humility and positivity. The coach adopts an open, non-judgemental approach to help the leader understand what is most important and then identify the most appropriate path to follow. In this methodology, the coach must demonstrate alignment through role modelling. There are four phases of the conversational process:

Discovery: In this phase, the leader reflects on herself, her relationships and her experiences. The coach supports the client in appreciating and better understanding her existing resources. This phase allows the leader to view her current situation from a new or different perspective, gaining greater clarity about it. The goal is to ensure that the leader recognises her strengths and resources and carries forward what is most useful from her experiences.

Intention: This phase shifts the leader's focus to the future. The coach supports the leader in articulating her intention for the future, which goes beyond identifying *goals*. The purpose is for the leader to identify what is most meaningful for her, enabling her to set a direction. In ERSHAD coaching, this is a crucial phase, where the coach encourages the leader to clearly articulate her intention.

Pathways: Here, the leader is supported in exploring various ways to move closer to her intention. The coach encourages the leader to generate as many ideas as possible. Helping her to select one pathway to pursue.

Effort: In the final phase of the conversational process, the leader considers the effort required to follow the chosen pathway. The coach helps the leader align their effort with their intentions, guiding her to necessary behaviours where when applying will help the leader develop a new mindset. When successful, the leader integrates her intention into how she lives their life.

The Alignment Wheel is the most significant contribution of the ERSHAD leadership framework. Its purpose is to help leaders make decisions and choices aligned with their beliefs and values. Throughout the conversational process, the coach should prompt the leader to reflect on the alignment of her actions with her values and beliefs. For instance, how does her intention align with her values? The alignment wheel located at the heart of the framework should be referred to as needed throughout the conversation.

Applying the Framework

The ERSHAD leadership framework can be applied in various professional and personal contexts to help align a person's values with their practices. This alignment is achieved by raising the leader's self-awareness, encouraging self-reflection and fostering personal responsibility for investing effort in her intentions. By engaging in these practices and embracing themselves as they are, leaders can begin to make positive changes that enhance their psychological, physical and spiritual well-being.

Building a complete and well-rounded Muslim leader character requires continuous learning and development, and the ERSHAD leadership framework plays a crucial role in this journey. In other words, ERSHAD leadership can support leaders in achieving both personal and organisational goals while striving towards the 'fairest stature.'

Conclusion

The chapter explores the ERSHAD leadership framework, which is rooted in Islamic principles. It integrates ethical, behavioural and leadership dimensions. Leadership development can be supported through structured coaching conversations, which explore the four phases: discovery, intention, pathways and effort. It aims to guide leaders towards aligning their actions with their values and through this fostering integrity, empathy and personal responsibility. This model aids leaders in achieving both personal and organisational goals while cultivating ethical behaviour and fostering meaningful relationships.

References

bin Balqasim Albakri, A. (2020). *The Power of Leadership in the Holy Quran*, قوة القيادة في القرآن الكريم, AlNaba'a AlAzeam -Mekka – Saudi Arabia.

Kuklyte, J. (2017) Islamic leadership and workplace deviance, Balkan Journal of Social Science, Retrieved on 30 August 2024 from https://dergipark.org.tr/tr/download/article-file/399358.

23

Rahmah: Compassionate Leadership Development

Lyra Puspa

Vanaya & Companies, Jakarta, Indonesia

The Big Idea

This focus on compassion in leadership development aligns beautifully with a core principle in Islam: the all-encompassing mercy of Allah (God). The Quran, the holy book of Islam, resounds with this theme. This compassion is expressed abundantly through the words **Ar-Rahman** (رحمن—The Most Compassionate) and **Ar-Rahim** (رحيم—The Most Merciful). Both Rahman and Rahim stem from the root word **Rahmah** (رحمة) which signifies mercy in its most encompassing sense. It goes beyond simply showing kindness and extends to feelings of deep care, forgiveness and a desire to alleviate suffering. This term encompasses compassion, generosity, benevolence, forgiveness, nurturing, caring, love and kindness.

The presence of the phrase 'بِسْمِ اللَّهِ الرَّحْمَنِ الرَّحِيمِ' (Bismillah Ar-Rahman Ar-Rahim—In the name of Allah, The Most Compassionate, The Most Merciful) at the beginning of 113 out of 114 Quranic surahs (chapters) is ubiquitous (Taib, 2004). This recurring invocation merits attention, with 'Ar-Rahman' appearing a noteworthy 57 times and 'Ar-Rahim' mentioned a remarkable 114 times throughout the Quran (excluding the repeated opening verse). This statistical significance underscores the centrality of compassion (Rahmah) within Islamic values and ethical principles. This emphasis on compassion is further reflected in verses such as '*So let the believers who have wronged themselves not despair of Allah's mercy. Certainly, Allah is Forgiving, Most Merciful.*' (The Qur'an, 2004;

Mosaic Leadership: African, Asian, Middle Eastern and Indigenous Perspectives, First Edition. Edited by Jonathan Passmore, Badri Bajaj, and Mongezi C Makhalima.

Published 2026 by John Wiley & Sons Ltd.

Chapter: 24 Verse:22). Further emphasising compassion, the Qur'an exposes the emptiness of rituals without protecting the vulnerable (The Qur'an, 2004; Chapter: 107 Verse:1-7). It is upon this foundation of divine mercy that a powerful coaching approach can be constructed.

Although both denote God's mercy, a subtle distinction exists between Rahman and Rahim (Ibn Kathir, 2003). Rahman emphasises the universality of this divine attribute, encompassing all creation. Conversely, Rahim highlights the active and specific nature of this mercy, particularly directed towards believers. Within the Islamic tradition, the concept of Rahmah provides a powerful framework for understanding the compassionate mindset that underpins effective coaching. In this context, coaching can be viewed as an expression of the universal care and compassion inherent in Rahmah. This is reflected in the coach's focus on understanding, supporting and guiding leaders towards their goals, while maintaining a non-judgemental and neutral stance.

The concept of Rahman signifies God's all-encompassing compassion, a boundless force that empowers all creation to thrive (Ibn Kathir, 2003; Taib, 2004). A compassionate coach, drawing inspiration from this divine attribute of Rahmah, empowers leaders to cultivate and activate their own potential within a supportive and non-judgemental environment. This empowerment is facilitated through encouraging reflective thinking, a process that combines active exploration with focused reflection to cultivate deeper understanding and meaning. By fostering a safe space for exploration and reflection, a coach can empower leaders to unlock their potentials and become their best.

Islamic thought emphasises reflective thinking as a crucial tool for self-discovery and understanding the world around us. Within this framework, there are two key aspects: Tafakkur (تفكر) and Tadabbur (تدبر). Tafakkur and Tadabbur are not entirely separate ways of thinking but rather complementary aspects of Islamic reflective thinking (Ibn Kathir, 2003). They work together in a cyclical process:

- **Tafakkur (تفكر):** This term refers to active reasoning, using the mind's analytical and imaginative faculties. Tafakkur involves using logic, imagination and knowledge to explore possibilities, brainstorm solutions and envision goals. It promotes critical thinking, intellectual growth and understanding of complexities. A compassionate coach, mirroring the universality of mercy, creates a safe space for leaders to engage in this process regardless of background or beliefs.

- **Tadabbur (تدبر):** This term refers to deep contemplation, pondering the meaning and significance of something. It is a form of distancing oneself to gain a broader perspective and understand the 'why' behind things. It fosters spiritual development, ethical consciousness and a sense of spiritual fulfilment. The coach, guided by the spirit of benevolent mercy, asks thought-provoking questions that prompt leaders to explore their values, motivations and purpose.

By actively exploring possibilities through Tafakkur (reasoning) and then reflecting on their deeper meaning through Tadabbur (contemplating), leaders gain a more complete understanding of themselves and their goals. This integrated approach empowers them towards greater self-discovery and informed decision-making.

How to Apply It

Guided by the compassionate spirit of Rahmah, the CARE model (Puspa, 2022) provides a practical framework for implementing the principles of Tafakkur and Tadabbur in the leadership development processes such as coaching, ensuring the act of caring remains at the heart of the journey. This framework utilises four critical aspects of development (Clarity, Awakening, Resolution and Empowerment) to guide individuals through a reflective and exploratory process. The CARE model, when integrated with the Islamic concepts of Tafakkur (reasoning) and Tadabbur (contemplating), empowers the individual (Figure 23.1).

Clarity: Cultivating a Clear Vision With Compassionate Guidance

The initial stage of the CARE model, Clarity, focuses on establishing a clear vision for the future. Here, Tafakkur (reasoning) comes into play. This concept aligns with the Quranic perspective of inside-out change, *'Indeed, Allah will not change the condition of a people until they change what is in themselves.'* (The Qur'an, 2004; Chapter: 13 Verse:11). This verse emphasises that positive change begins within. Compassionate coaches guide

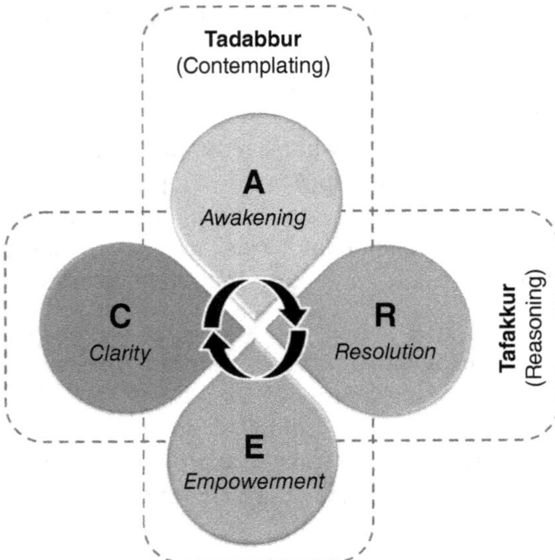

Figure 23.1 The CARE Model Framework of Rahmah-Inspired Coaching.

leaders through a process of visualisation, encouraging them to critically analyse and imaginatively envision their desired future state in detail. By reflecting on their current reality and ideal state (Tafakkur), leaders can identify areas for improvement and begin to shape their desired future in a safe and supportive environment. Through gentle open-ended questions, the coach encourages leaders to explore possibilities with a positive and hopeful outlook. This collaborative process, infused with compassionate care, ultimately leads to a clear understanding of the desired outcomes.

Awakening: Unveiling the Inner Compass With Compassionate Inquiry

The second stage, Awakening, delves into self-awareness. This phase aligns with Tadabbur (contemplating), where leaders are encouraged to reflect deeply on their values, motivations and purpose. The compassionate coach facilitates this process by asking thought-provoking questions that prompt leaders to explore their inner landscape. This aligns with the Quranic call for introspection: '*Do they not contemplate within themselves? Allah has not created the heavens and the earth and what is between them except in truth and for a specified term.'* (The Qur'an, 2004; Chapter: 30 Verse8). However, the coach's role extends beyond simply asking questions. The delivery of these inquiries requires empathy and understanding, fostering a sense of care and psychological safety. This compassionate inquiry empowers leaders to awaken to limiting beliefs and self-imposed obstacles, paving the way for positive change.

Resolution: Crafting a Path With Compassionate Co-Creation

The Resolution stage focuses on developing a concrete action plan to achieve the desired outcomes established in the Clarity stage. Here, Tafakkur (reasoning) is again crucial. With newfound clarity and self-awareness, leaders engage in critical thinking to analyse their strengths, potentials, opportunities and challenges. The compassionate coach fosters a safe space for this process, encouraging leaders to explore various possibilities and design a realistic action plan. This aligns with the Quranic emphasis on utilising one's intellect to explore resources and possibilities: *'Do you not see that Allah has made subject to you whatever is in the heavens and whatever is in the earth and amply bestowed upon you His favours, [both] apparent and unapparent?'* (The Qur'an, 2004; Chapter: 31 Verse:20). The coach demonstrates compassionate care by fostering a co-creation process to ensure leaders feel supported as they navigate their chosen path. This collaborative approach empowers leaders to take ownership of their action plan, fostering a sense of responsibility and agency.

Empowerment: Building Self-Reliance With Compassionate Support

The final stage, Empowerment, focuses on fostering self-reliance and accountability. Tadabbur (contemplating) plays a central role in this stage. Leaders are encouraged to reflect on their commitment level and capacity to achieve their goals. The compassionate coach empowers leaders to take ownership of their goals by supporting them in setting realistic milestones and accountability measures. This stage emphasises the leaders' agency, aligning with the Quranic emphasis on human striving: '*And that there is not for man except that [good] for which he strives.*' (The Qur'an, 2004; Chapter: 53 Verse:39). However, the coach's role is not to take control. Instead, the coach acts as a supportive guide, providing compassionate support and encouragement throughout the journey. Ultimately, the leaders takes ownership of their journey, empowering them to achieve their desired outcomes and cultivate self-reliance.

Conclusion

Infused with the spirit of Rahmah, the CARE model provides a practical framework, within Islamic thinking, for cultivating compassionate leadership through fostering a journey of self-discovery, goal achievement, and ultimately, empowering leaders to thrive.

References

Ibn Kathir, H. (2003). *Tafsir Ibn Kathir Volume 1: Parts 1 and 2.* Translated and abridged by a group of scholars under the supervision of Sheikh Safiur-Rahman Al-Mubarakpuri (2nd ed.). Riyadh: Darussalam Publications.

Puspa, L. (2022). Brain-focused coaching. In S. Greif, H. Möller, W. Scholl, J. Passmore, & F. Müller (Eds.), *International handbook of evidence-based coaching*. Cham: Springer.

Taib, M. I. M. (2004). *The central role of compassion in Muslim ethics. Muslim Reader*, 1–7.

The Qur'an (2004). *Translation of the meaning of the Qur'an.* Translated by Saheeh International. Riyadh: Abul-Qasim Publishing House, Al-Muntada Al-Islami.

African Perspectives

24

Ubuntu Intelligence

Dumisani Magadlela

Founder and CEO, Afrika Coaching, Johannesburg, South Africa

The Big Idea

Ubuntu is a global phenomenon that is best understood experientially. It is when we encounter it that we can fully grasp what it really is, or what it can be, and know what it is not. While Ubuntu means 'I am because we are.' Ubuntu means far more than this old and well-known cliché. Ubuntu is not simply about loving each other and singing kumbaya (freedom) while dancing in merriment to assumptions of collective understanding and attunement.

Ubuntu means that when I obstruct you or anyone else from becoming the best version of yourself or themselves, I directly or inadvertently rob and deny myself and the rest of humanity the gifts that can only come through and be expressed through your unique gifts and talents. I rob the world of your genius. Ubuntu helps us co-create sacred shared spaces where everyone can unleash their true brilliance.

When we embrace Ubuntu into coaching, we help unlock human greatness through a genuine connection which is often initiated through genuine rapport and contracting, what I have called *'conscious greetings'* (Magadlela, 2023, p. 72).

In isiZulu, the language of the Zulu people (called amaZulu), people greet each other by saying *'Sawubona'*. This literally translates to 'I see you.' It means that I see you as you are and not the story I have read somewhere or from some anthropological or National Geographic episode somewhere. Greeting others

Mosaic Leadership: African, Asian, Middle Eastern and Indigenous Perspectives, First Edition. Edited by Jonathan Passmore, Badri Bajaj, and Mongezi C Makhalima.

Published 2026 by John Wiley & Sons Ltd.

consciously is a gift we give ourselves and those we encounter. It is what sets the tone for genuine Ubuntu connection, engagement and relationship building.

When we meet, see, and consciously, intentionally and mindfully greet others as we encounter them—without for a moment referencing whatever we think we know about them—we give space and room for them to present themselves and for a new relationship to emerge based on a genuine 'mutual presentation' of each other to each other. What I have called the *'fore-story'* about others can easily be a misconstrued or edited version of who they are. The *'fore-story'* is often someone else's take, their perspective or narrative, and may lead us away from who the one we are meeting really is.

The magic of Ubuntu conscious greetings is in co-creating space to meet others where they are. When we put what we think we know about them aside (the *fore-story*), we give ourselves the opportunity to 'see' them as they see themselves. This is the affirming power of conscious greetings that Ubuntu values enable and unleash.

I believe that in a safer world, there is no harm in saying hello to a 'total stranger' and meaning it. Watch what happens within you when you seek to connect authentically. It helps to prepare to take some punches of rejection along the way in this disconnected world. It is worth it in the long term.

How to Apply It

While Ubuntu is the essence of being an interconnected human, Ubuntu Intelligence (UbuQ) is the ability and capacity to constantly live with and embody the qualities and values of Ubuntu in daily life and in everything we say, do and become. It is the living out of clear intention to actively help co-create spaces and opportunities for others (and myself) to become the best version of myself. The following is an excerpt from the Ubuntu Coaching and Connection Practices book on Ubuntu Intelligence (UbuQ):

> *'Ubuntu Intelligence is the ability to navigate social relationships in ways that benefit those involved in the relationships without conscious or unconscious prejudice or discrimination. Ubuntu Intelligence requires new mind-sets and especially new heart-sets that enable us to see the self in the other, and most importantly, to feel genuine empathy and connection with other beings. Ubuntu Intelligence equips us with*

> *"laser eyes" to see through the layers of taught (or learned, programmed and conditioned) narratives about others, to see them as they present themselves in shared (and sacred) safe spaces. Ubuntu intelligence ... frees us from the learned separating and programming, and from our smaller circles which are often laced with (sometimes unconsciously) taught biases and stereotypes*' (Magadlela, 2023: p. xiii).

Ubuntu coaching recognises that the ability to coach anyone is a gift to at least four parties engaged in any coaching engagement. It benefits the coaching client (coachee), the coach, the coaching relationship as an entity, the coaching client's relationships such as team members or direct reports of a leader or manager and the organisation that they are part of. Ubuntu coaching heightens systemic awareness of the need to 'see the systems' at play.

I have argued many times that coaching is little else if it is not one of the 'most sacred human endeavours'. I believe that coaching is a sacred engagement where one serves to co-create and hold the space for another to work on becoming the best version of themselves and doing so non-judgementally and confidentially. With Ubuntu and Ubuntu intelligence in coaching, the sacredness takes on another character and steps up to another level. It becomes a collective gift to whoever is involved in ways that can shape whole organisations, societies and the world at large.

In some parts of the world, coaching is still not well-known as a way of managing, leading or supporting others to become their best selves. Sometimes mentoring is used interchangeably with coaching as if they are one and the same thing. They are different.

There is an intersection between Ubuntu Intelligence coaching and some forms of mentoring in indigenous communities. Malidoma Some (1999) describes the great role and immeasurably powerful value of mentoring in Indigenous communities and suggests that the rest of the world, and especially the Western world, could draw valuable lessons by learning from how mentoring is practiced in some communities.

Conclusions

This chapter discusses Ubuntu as a global philosophy centred on interconnectedness, co-creation and self-realisation through others. It emphasises Ubuntu's application in coaching, where conscious greetings and mutual respect foster genuine connections, shaping individual and collective growth. Ubuntu Intelligence embodies these values, encouraging empathetic relationships free of prejudice, benefiting individuals, teams and organisations and can serve as a model for leaders and leadership development across the world.

References

Magadlela, D. (2023). *Ubuntu coaching and connection practices for leader-managers: Selected practices to grow your team in a fast-changing world.* In S. Stout Rostron (Ed.), *The management mastery and practice.* Johannesburg: Knowledge Resources.

Malidoma Some, M. P. (1999). *The healing wisdom of africa: Finding life purpose through nature, ritual, and community.* New York: Jeremy P. Tarcher-Putnam, Penguin Putnam Inc.

25

Leadership Rooted in Community and Mentorship

Ekhoe Ame-Ogie

HR Leader, Deloitte, Lagos, Nigeria

The Big Idea

When we talk about leadership, especially in today's world, it's easy to focus on individual success stories—those charismatic leaders who seem to have all the answers. But what if leadership was less about the individual and more about the community? The Igbo people of southeastern Nigeria offer us a powerful model that intertwines mentorship and communal responsibility.

Through their practices of apprenticeship and the umunna (extended family structure), the Igbo show us that true leadership is about uplifting others, sharing wisdom and ensuring that everyone moves forward together.

The Igbo Leadership Model: Where Apprenticeship Meets Community

At the heart of Igbo society lies a deep commitment to community. The umunna, an extended family unit, is the bedrock of this commitment. It's not just a family in the narrow sense; it's a collective of people bound by blood, but more importantly, by shared responsibilities and values. Leadership within the umunna isn't about one person holding power; it's about the entire group working together to ensure the well-being of all its members.

Mosaic Leadership: African, Asian, Middle Eastern and Indigenous Perspectives, First Edition. Edited by Jonathan Passmore, Badri Bajaj, and Mongezi C Makhalima.

Published 2026 by John Wiley & Sons Ltd.

Connected to this idea of communal leadership is the Igbo apprenticeship system, known as 'Igba boi'. This system is a brilliant example of how leadership through mentorship can create a cycle of growth and prosperity. In Igba boi, a young person, or apprentice, lives and works with an experienced master who teaches them the ropes of a trade. But this isn't just job training. It's a holistic education where the apprentice learns about integrity, hard work and the importance of giving back to the community.

When the apprenticeship is over, the master typically helps the apprentice set up their own business, often providing seed money or resources. This ensures that the apprentice isn't just left to fend for themselves but is supported in becoming an independent and successful member of the community. This transition from apprentice to business owner is also a transition into becoming a leader within the umunna.

This system reflects several key principles:

- **Shared Growth:** Success is not an individual pursuit; it's a collective one. The master's success is reflected in the apprentice's growth, and the community benefits from the prosperity of both.
- **Long-Term Vision:** Both the apprenticeship and the umunna emphasise patience and long-term thinking. Whether it's the years spent in training or the collective decision-making within the umunna, the focus is always on sustainable, lasting success.
- **Mutual Responsibility:** In Igbo culture, leadership is a responsibility to others. The master is responsible for the apprentice, just as the leaders of the umunna are responsible for the well-being of all its members.

Umunna and the Apprenticeship Concept in the Igbo Culture at Play

Igbo culture is rich with stories that highlight the values embedded in their leadership models. One such story is the legend of Eze Nri, a mythical king who is celebrated not for his military conquests, but for his wisdom, justice and ability to unite the people. Eze Nri's leadership was built on spiritual authority and a deep commitment to the common good—principles that continue to guide Igbo leaders today.

Another popular story is that of Chukwuemeka, a young boy who started with nothing but became a wealthy and respected merchant through the apprenticeship system. His story isn't just about financial success; it's about humility, hard work and the importance of giving back. After achieving success, Chukwuemeka returned to his village to mentor other young boys, ensuring that the cycle of growth continued.

These stories serve as moral guideposts, reminding leaders that true leadership is about serving others, acting with integrity and fostering unity.

Like many other tales in Igbo culture, the reinforcing idea that leadership isn't about holding power over others—it's about empowering others. It's about using your success to lift others up, creating a ripple effect that benefits the entire community. The umunna and apprenticeship system work together to make this possible. The umunna provides the support system, while the apprenticeship provides the skills and knowledge. Together, they create a leadership model that is as much about giving back as it is about personal achievement.

How to Apply It

The Igbo model of leadership—where apprenticeship meets communal responsibility—offers a powerful blueprint for modern leaders. Here's how you can apply these lessons in today's world.

Mentorship with a Purpose

Incorporate the mentorship model of the Igbo apprenticeship into your leadership style. Mentorship shouldn't just be about teaching skills; it should be about nurturing values, building character and ensuring that those you mentor are set up for long-term success.

How to Apply: Create a mentorship program in your organisation that goes beyond the basics. Focus on long-term development, provide ongoing support and encourage your mentees to become mentors themselves, creating a cycle of growth and leadership.

Emphasise Collective Success

The umunna teaches us that leadership is about shared responsibility and collective success. Modern leaders can take this to heart by fostering an environment where everyone feels responsible for the organisation's achievements.

How to Apply: Build teams that operate with a collective mindset. Encourage collaboration, celebrate team successes and make sure that everyone feels their contributions are valued and recognised.

Lead with Integrity and Community Focus

Leadership, as demonstrated by the Igbo, is not just about being in charge; it's about leading with integrity and a commitment to the community. Whether in business, politics or any other field, leaders should prioritise the well-being of those they serve.

How to Apply: Make ethical leadership a cornerstone of your approach. Lead by example, be transparent in your decision-making and always consider the broader impact of your actions on the community.

The Igbo tradition of intertwining mentorship with communal responsibility offers timeless lessons for today's leaders. By focusing on shared growth, long-term thinking and mutual responsibility, we can create leadership models that not only drive individual success but also uplift entire communities. In a world that often prioritises the individual, the Igbo remind us that true leadership is about the collective—about lifting each other up and ensuring that everyone has the opportunity to succeed.

Conclusion

The chapter explores the Igbo model of leadership, which intertwines mentorship through the apprenticeship system and communal responsibility via the *umunna* structure. Leadership in this context is about uplifting others, fostering shared growth and ensuring collective success. This approach emphasises integrity, mutual responsibility and long-term community well-being over individual power.

26

Igwebuike (Strength in Unity)

Ugochi Ossai

Business Management, University of Lagos, Lagos, Nigeria

The Big Idea

The Igbo tribe, native to the southern part of Nigeria, is one of the largest ethnic groups in Africa. The tribe claims a heritage dating back to 2000 BC. Igbos have a distinctive approach to leadership that is deeply rooted in their cultural values and communal philosophy (Ezenagu, 2017).

Igbos seek to delve into the principles guiding Igbo leadership, highlighting the integral role of community, the sanctity of life, respect for authority and elders, the place of proverbs and folklore, and above all, the overarching belief in a righteous God ('Chi or Chineke') who oversees human affairs.

A defining feature of Igbo leadership is its decentralised nature, encapsulated in the saying, 'Igbo enweighi EZE' (Igbos have no king). Igbo society operates through a system of collective leadership. Leaders emerge not as absolute rulers but as first among equals, often chosen based on their wisdom, integrity, and service to the community.

This collective leadership is typically exercised through a council of elders. These councils, composed of respected and experienced community members, play a crucial role in decision-making. The elders deliberate on issues concerning the tribe and reach a consensus, while the leader, acting as a spokesperson, implements and communicates these decisions. This participative leadership style ensures that leadership is a shared responsibility and that decisions

Mosaic Leadership: African, Asian, Middle Eastern and Indigenous Perspectives, First Edition. Edited by Jonathan Passmore, Badri Bajaj, and Mongezi C Makhalima.

Published 2026 by John Wiley & Sons Ltd.

reflect the collective will and wisdom of the community. Their main focus, especially in the pre-colonial era, was the longevity of the Igbo cultural heritage and identity.

The Role of Proverbs and Oral Tradition

Proverbs are an intrinsic part of Igbo culture and serve as a tool for communication and instruction in leadership, and are known as "the palm oil with which words are eaten". They make language richer, helping the elders 'oil' their words to glide into the hearts and minds of the people. According to famous Igbo author Chinua Achebe (1958, 1964), proverbs are interwoven into the fabric of speeches, deliberations and everyday conversation, and are a key component of leadership, persuading others of complex ideas.

For instance, the proverb 'anyuko mamiri ya gba ufufu' (if we 'pee' together, it foams and creates a stronger force) underscores the power of unity and collaboration to produce results. Leaders use such proverbs to inspire collective action and emphasise the importance of working together for the common good.

These serve as a moral compass, guiding leaders and community members alike toward righteous and just actions. This proverb aligns with the Igbo principle of IGWEBUIKE, which may be translated as strength in unity.

Values Guiding Igbo Leadership

Several core values underpin Igbo leadership principles, shaping how leaders are chosen and how they govern (Isidienu, 2014). These values include:

1. **Communality:** A strong sense of belonging and interconnectedness is paramount in Igbo society. Leaders are expected to prioritise the community's interests over personal gain. This communal ethos ensures that decisions are made with the welfare of the community in mind.

2. **Sanctity of Life:** Respect for human life is fundamental. Leaders are charged with the responsibility of protecting their people and ensuring their well-being and growth. Any form of leadership that endangers lives is considered illegitimate. The sense of the sacredness of life to Igbos is captured in the adage: 'Don't laugh at a distant boat being tossed by the waves because your brother may be in it'.

3. **Respect for Authority and Elders:** Elders (Ndi Ichie') are revered in Igbo culture for their wisdom and experience they can offer. Respect for their authority is a cornerstone of Igbo leadership. Elders provide counsel and guidance, much like a mentor, ensuring that leadership decisions are grounded in communal wisdom.
4. **Promotion of Peace and Unity:** Leaders are seen as custodians of peace. They are expected to mediate conflicts, foster unity, and promote harmonious coexistence within the community. The Igbo belief in 'Chi', a divine force watching over human affairs, reinforces this responsibility, as leaders are seen as chosen by a higher power to guide and protect their people.

Leadership Selection and Accountability

In Igbo society, leadership is not inherited but earned. Individuals who aspire to leadership positions must demonstrate exceptional qualities: honesty, wisdom, courage, and integrity. The selection process involves scrutiny by a council of elders as well as the community at large. This approach ensures that leaders are chosen based on their abilities and contributions to the community, not on their personal pride or desire.

Such processes enhance accountability. With leaders accountable to the community and the law. They are subject to the same (or higher) moral and ethical standards as any other community member, and a failure to rule justly will invoke not only community disapproval but also divine retribution.

The Spiritual Dimension of Leadership

A unique aspect of Igbo leadership is the intertwining of spirituality with governance. The Igbos believe in a righteous God ('Chi') who watches over human actions and rewards just behaviour. Leaders are seen as chosen by this divine force to serve the community. This belief instils a sense of higher purpose and moral duty in leaders, motivating them to govern with integrity and justice. 'Ndu bu isi' (life is the head).

Folklore, legends, and myths, such as tales of the wise tortoise, reinforce these spiritual values. The tortoise, a prominent character in Igbo folklore, symbolises wisdom and strategic thinking. Such stories serve as moral lessons, guiding both old and young in the virtues of prudence, cunning, and ethical behaviour.

One of such well-known stories is that of the tortoise and the birds. In this tale, the tortoise, known for his cunning and wisdom, convinces the birds to lend him some feathers and permit him to join them in a feast in the sky. The tortoise tells the birds to adopt new names for the event, and he chooses the name 'All of You.' When the food is presented at the feast, the birds are informed that the food is for 'All of You.' The tortoise rose, saying that was his name and proceeded to eat all the food. The birds in anger took back the feathers they had lent to the tortoise to enable him to fly to the skies, leaving it stranded. With no option, the tortoise suffered a painful fall from the sky. That fall is responsible for the cracked shell of the tortoise today. This tale highlights the importance of honesty and the consequences of deceit.

In a world often characterised by individualism and centralisation of power, where African society is perceived as primitive, simple and backwards, the Igbo leadership model offers valuable lessons for modern governance. As the modern world grapples with issues of leadership and governance, the timeless principles of Igbo leadership offer enduring wisdom and inspiration.

Core Principles—Igbo Model

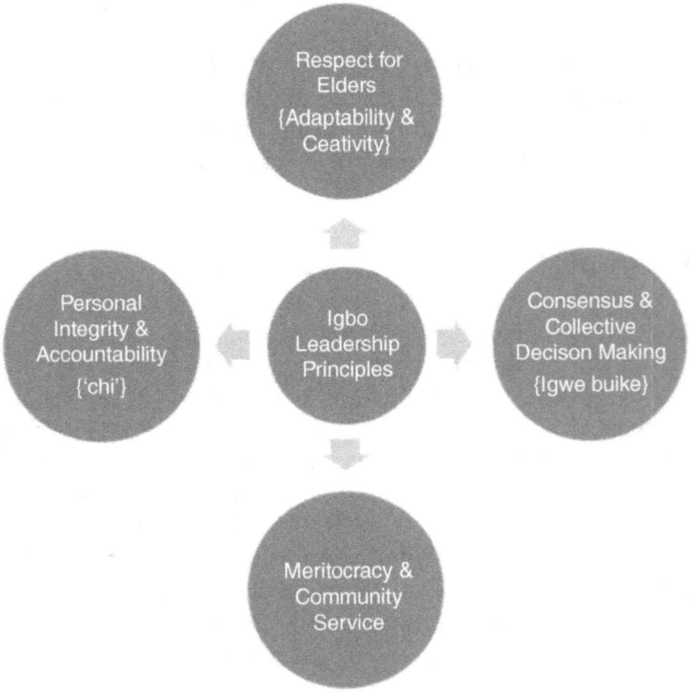

How to Apply It

In applying these ideas, leaders may consider these features in their own leadership:

- **Consensus and Collective Decision-Making:** A strong focus on facilitating group discussions with the aim of enhancing teamwork, encouraging participation and guiding the leader through paying attention to diverse perspectives.
- **Meritocracy and Community Service:** A focus on personal development plans, goal-setting and recognition systems to reinforce the meritocratic values in leadership, which benefits all in the community.
- **Respect for Elders:** Paying attention to elders whose experience can inform and guide the leader. To do this, the leader needs to both listen and be open to communications from others and avoid assuming they know best.
- **Personal Integrity and Accountability:** Setting the highest standards of personal integrity, at or above others in the community, and demonstrating this through both word and personal deeds.

Conclusions

This chapter explores the Igbo leadership model, characterised by decentralisation, communal decision-making, respect for elders and meritocracy. Grounded in proverbs and oral traditions, the Igbo model emphasises accountability, integrity, and spiritual duty, offering timeless wisdom for modern governance. Leaders are expected to prioritise community welfare and uphold moral standards through collective leadership and spiritual guidance.

References

Achebe, C. (1958). *Things fall apart.* London: William Heinemann.

Achebe, C. (1964). *Arrow of God.* London: William Heinemann.

Ezenagu, N. (2017). *Leadership styles in the management of Igbo cultural heritage in pre-european era. OGIRISI: A New Journal of African Studies, 13*(1), 22. https://doi.org/10.4314/og.v13i1.2

Isidienu, I.C (2014) *A symbol of leadership and authority: Igbo Scholars International Journal 1*(1) Suleija Niger Basing Books

27

Omoluabi Leadership

Ify Nonyelu

Geneva Business School, Geneva, Switzerland

The Big Idea

In the ever-evolving global business landscape, one constant remains: the most impactful leaders are those who lead with character and conviction. Leadership involves creating new solutions and motivating others towards shared goals. In Africa, corporate leadership development has often been influenced by external Western models. Bukusi et al. (2023) argue that supporting African leaders requires developing Afrocentric frameworks that leverage indigenous wisdom, such as the Omoluabi leadership framework.

Omoluabi is rooted in the rich cultural traditions of the Yoruba people of West Africa and embodies the highest ideals of personal character, integrity and social responsibility. It challenges leaders to lead with wisdom, empathy and a deep commitment to their community. This framework offers timeless lessons that have shaped Yoruba leadership and presents a universal guide for developing leaders who inspire, serve and transform their environments.

The Omoluabi title is accorded to a person of great character, a role model, an individual who stands out for their excellence and embodies values that are respected/admired by all in their society. An Omoluabi is a relentless go-getter who does not accept 'no' as an answer. A 'no' is never an obstacle; it's simply a signal that a different approach is needed. Even when faced with setbacks, they persist, finding alternative paths until they achieve a 'yes.'

Mosaic Leadership: African, Asian, Middle Eastern and Indigenous Perspectives, First Edition. Edited by Jonathan Passmore, Badri Bajaj, and Mongezi C Makhalima.

Published 2026 by John Wiley & Sons Ltd.

An Omoluabi does not shy away from responsibilities—they embrace them wholeheartedly. They understand that being entrusted with responsibilities reflects a deep sense of trust, and they honour that trust by carrying out their duties with dedication and integrity. Trust is highly valued by an Omoluabi because it signifies that those around them (i.e. colleagues, family, elders or respected figures) believe in their ability to uphold important values. Carrying this banner of trust is not just a responsibility; it is the essence that sustains the family's legacy. In fact, their family members would often not hold meetings without them. An Omoluabi isn't necessarily the firstborn, middle child or lastborn; it's about being seen as the one who carries the family's legacy, projecting the family name with pride and integrity wherever it matters.

In the corporate space, the traits of an Omoluabi extend beyond personal or familial obligations and become crucial assets in professional settings. An Omoluabi in the workplace embodies reliability, accountability and a strong ethical compass. They are often the go-to individuals for leadership roles and high-stakes projects because they consistently demonstrate their commitment to excellence and the collective good of the organisation.

Their respect for trust translates into a leadership style that values transparency and open communication. An Omoluabi leader fosters a culture of mutual respect and collaboration, ensuring that every team member feels heard and valued. They don't just meet expectations—they exceed them, setting a standard for others to follow.

In decision-making, an Omoluabi applies a balanced approach, considering not only the immediate outcomes but also the long-term impact on stakeholders, colleagues and the company's reputation. They understand that their actions reflect not just on themselves, but on the larger entity they represent, much like how their actions uphold the family name in their personal life.

An Omoluabi's approach to challenges in the corporate environment mirrors their personal philosophy: a setback is not a defeat but an opportunity to find a better way forward. They demonstrate resilience and adaptability, continually seeking solutions rather than dwelling on obstacles. This mindset not only drives personal success but also inspires those around them to adopt a similar perseverance and positive outlook.

Ultimately, the traits of an Omoluabi make them invaluable in any professional context. Their integrity, dedication and commitment to upholding trust/excellence create a positive ripple effect that can transform teams, shape company cultures and drive organisations towards greater achievements. In every aspect of their professional journey, an Omoluabi carries the same principles that define their personal life, making them not just leaders but role models who set a high bar for what it means to be both capable and principled in the corporate world.

The word Omoluabi is derived from several Yoruba words: 'Omo' (child), 'ti' (that or which), 'Olu-iwa' (chief or master of 'iwa', meaning character) and 'bi' (born). Together, they convey the meaning 'a child born of good character'. In Yoruba culture, being called an Omoluabi signifies exceptional qualities in both personal and professional life. It also reflects the idea of a child nurtured by the community, emphasising how communal values shape individuals who contribute positively to society.

Conversely, Agbaya represents the opposite of Omoluabi. It describes someone who, despite being old enough to know better, behaves in a disgraceful or immature manner.

The primary traits of an Omoluabi include wisdom in speech (Oro Siso), good character (Iwa), hard work (Ise), goodwill (Inu Rere), respect for self and others (Iteriba) and truth and integrity (Otito).

Applying Omoluabi as a leadership model focuses on these qualities as the foundation for growth and inspiring others. Onamusi (2020) characterises an Omoluabi as someone who exemplifies hard work, transparency, accountability, respect and good judgement—essential traits for handling challenges. In the Yoruba worldview, individuals who embody these values can drive positive change in their communities.

Core Principles

The core principles of Omoluabi are informed by values and moral codes of the Yoruba culture, namely:

***Iwa* (Character)**: Iwa translates to good character. This involves honesty, patience and humility. Leaders who exhibit this trait build trust and credibility within their environment.

***Èṣìṣẹ́* (Hard Work and Industry)**: Omoluabi values hard work, dedication, a strong work ethic and motivating others through example.

Respect and Integrity: Respect for others and maintaining integrity are crucial traits of an Omoluabi, thus fostering a positive and inclusive work environment.

Community and Cooperation: A sense of community, working collaboratively, raising others and thus teamwork are key to an Omoluabi's conduct and practice.

Accountability: Taking ownership of one's actions is a key aspect of Omoluabi—i.e. being accountable for their decisions and actions.

How to Apply It

Omoluabi leadership can be brought to life using the Omoluabi coaching framework. The framework is designed to aid leaders in developing ethical and effective leadership skills based on the principles of integrity, responsibility, wisdom, empathy, community service and cultural respect. Leaders who adopt the framework in their growth journey are expected to:

- Show strong ethical behaviour in all areas of their leadership
- Take responsibility and be accountable for their actions and decisions
- Make wise and thoughtful decisions
- Lead with empathy and compassion, creating supportive and strong teams
- Actively give back to the community and encourage a culture of service
- Respect cultural traditions while also promoting innovation and growth

The process is based on the C-CHAIR model. This stands for:

- **C—Character and Self-Reflection**: encourages leaders to reflect on their values and behaviours, promoting ethical conduct.
- **C—Commitment**: stresses perseverance and dedication, with a focus on setting and achieving strategic goals.
- **H—Hard Work and Positive Mindset**: highlights the importance of diligence, optimism and resilience, inspiring others through a strong work ethic.

- **A—Accountability and Strategic Vision**: focuses on responsibility, ethical standards and creating a strategic vision aligned with core values.
- **I—Innovation and Adaptability**: guides leaders to be adaptable, creative and resilient in overcoming challenges.
- **R—Respect and Community**: emphasises respect, empathy and fostering a sense of unity and community.

The C-CHAIR leadership framework emphasises the inherent virtues of individuals, positioning them to act with integrity and make transformative contributions in their environment. Leaders are expected to combine technical skills with strong moral principles and the capacity to uplift their communities.

The C-CHAIR framework encourages leaders through a journey of building exceptional character by affecting:

1. **Self-reflection and character**: encourage leaders to reflect on their character and identify areas for improvement.
2. **Developing a strong work ethic**: focuses on developing perseverance dedication and a robust work ethic.
3. **Building respectful relationships**: challenges leaders to establish trust and connection through active listening and empathy.
4. **Fostering collaboration and community**: promotes teamwork, open communication and collective problem-solving.
5. **Promoting accountability**: emphasises transparency and responsibility, and creates an environment of trust.

Observation: coaches collaborate with leaders to observe how their actions, decisions and interactions reveal their character and personality.

Feedback: gather input from leaders, their peers, superiors and subordinates about their character, personality and its impact on perceptions of their leadership and expertise.

Reflection: Coaches encourage leaders to engage in intentional self-reflection to assess how their personalities and character align with the ideals of their roles and organisations.

Improvement: The leaders are guided to identify their strengths and areas for growth, fostering a commitment to continuous self-reflection and development.

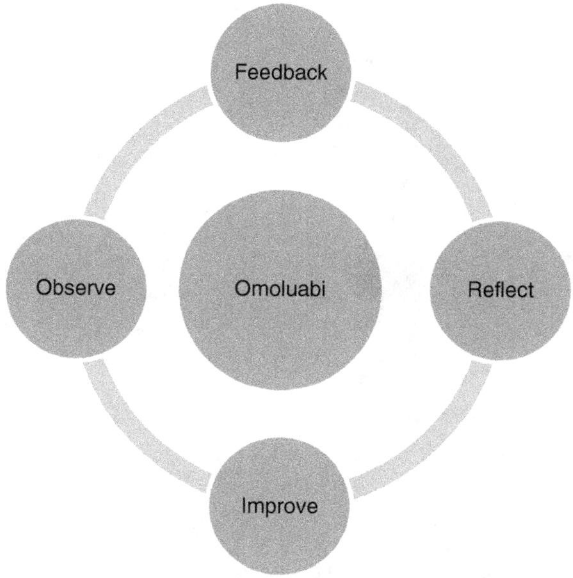

Figure 27.1 C-CHAIR Leadership Assessment Framework.

Conclusion

This chapter explores the Omoluabi leadership framework, rooted in Yoruba culture. It emphasises integrity, accountability and community service as essential leadership traits. Through the C-CHAIR model, leaders can cultivate ethical, empathetic leadership, inspire collective success and maintain strong moral principles. This Afrocentric framework provides a holistic approach to effective leadership development.

References

Bukusi, A. D. M., Korir, A. J., & Musya, J. K. (2023). How indigenous leadership research in Africa can inspire national prosperity. *Open Journal of Social Sciences, 11*, 134–155. https://doi.org/10.4236/jss.2023.117010

Onamusi, A. B. (2020). Strategic response capability and firm competitiveness: How Omoluabi leadership makes a difference. *Business Excellence and Management, 10*(4), 23–27.

28

Indaba

Decimar Ogutu

Nairobi, Kenya

The Big Idea

The Baobab tree represents unity and sagacity in numerous African cultures. An Indaba, literally 'a matter for discussion' (Edwards et al., 2020), is a traditional way of addressing problems and making decisions among the Zulu people of South Africa. Under the shade of the Baobab tree, members of the community meet for the Indaba to discuss and find solutions to problems. Other African traditions that share this approach include the Harambee of Kenya and the Bantaba of Gambia, both of which place an emphasis on collective wisdom and collaborative action to resolve conflicts.

There are numerous metaphorical meanings associated with the Baobab tree, and everyone from humans to animals can find what they need in this 'tree of life', which serves as a source of nourishment. A solid foundation of deep, sturdy roots holds it firmly in place, while a canopy of spreading branches provides welcome shade and shelter. Because of these qualities, it is a fitting emblem for the community, which ought to be inclusive and firmly grounded in common principles.

The Baobab tree offers a safe, sacred gathering spot because of its large canopy and sturdy trunk. Everyone in the community can contribute guidance and share stories, helping to find solutions to issues. In and of itself, the tree represents the community's fortitude and interdependence. There is an atmosphere of mutual respect and

Mosaic Leadership: African, Asian, Middle Eastern and Indigenous Perspectives, First Edition. Edited by Jonathan Passmore, Badri Bajaj, and Mongezi C Makhalima.

Published 2026 by John Wiley & Sons Ltd.

understanding beneath the Baobab tree, where everyone's opinions are valued equally and the group's common knowledge is used.

The Indaba beneath the Baobab tree represents leadership and the essence of community building, at least in a metaphorical sense. Leadership concerns are analogous to those debated in the Indaba, and the Baobab tree stands for the community's accumulated knowledge and lived experiences. Here, tales take on a more potent role. The stories told beneath the Baobab tree are more than simply anecdotes; they include wisdom, caution and ideas for what lies ahead. Wisdom and experiences are passed down over the ages through these stories. They help guide young people and facilitate the community in navigating difficult situations.

The foundation of the Indaba under the Baobab tree is premised on the practice that there is no single person who holds monopoly to knowledge. For a community to thrive and stay together, its members must feel welcome and accepted, and this belief helps to create such an environment. It also makes sure that diverse viewpoints are taken into account.

The Indaba places a premium on deep listening (listening with an empty mind and a heart of empathy). Deep listening is of utmost importance in this context. Everyone is expected to listen respectfully. This method guarantees that everyone's perspective is included and that the end result accurately reflects the group's desire.

Outside of its conventional African setting, the idea of the Indaba beneath the Baobab tree retains significance. Leadership development in the present era can learn a lot from it. The capacity to tap into collective intelligence and make decisions and seek guidance that are considerate of varied viewpoints is more crucial than ever in today's complicated and interdependent society.

Boardrooms in corporations and non-profits alike can benefit from this idea. The Indaba teaches leadership and those concerned with leadership development that deep listening is key, and that everyone should feel welcome. Communities and organisations may be built stronger and more robust when leaders provide spaces, both literal and metaphorical, where people can gather to share their experiences and perspectives.

Collective wisdom, inclusivity and community are powerfully symbolised by the Indaba under the Baobab tree. The greatest solutions are those that are influenced by the viewpoints and experiences of many, and no one individual has all the answers.

How To Apply It

A number of leadership development and coaching strategies can be derived from the Indaba that takes place under the Baobab tree. Fundamental to this idea is the concept that problem-solving and guiding a new generation of young leadership are best accomplished via the use of collective wisdom. Where everyone can feel they can stand up and take the lead. Leaders and coaches alike may encourage an Indaba mindset that is collaborative and open.

One of the most important takeaways from the Indaba is the significance of embracing communal wisdom. What this means in practice is that we should not expect any one person to know everything, and that the greatest solutions are usually the result of a combination of different perspectives and experiences. Leaders can put this notion into practice by making an effort to hear everyone out, particularly those with different backgrounds or points of view.

For instance, in a business context, leaders can arrange Town Halls or forums that resemble the Indaba beneath the Baobab tree, for discussion without 'filters'. This can allow team members to offer their authentic perspectives and help them bring their talents to the task.

Specially:

i) **Making Inclusivity a Priority**: The Indaba places a premium on inclusivity. Everyone in the community is welcome to join in the gatherings, no matter what their rank or position is. To put this theory into practice, leaders should make sure that everyone's perspective is heard, particularly those from junior positions.

   Methods like anonymous feedback, roundtable conversations or frequent check-ins with team members at every level of the company can help accomplish this. To succeed in the long run, a team needs people who feel like they belong and who are willing to put in the effort to keep the engagement authentic.

ii) **The Influence of Narratives**: The Indaba held beneath the Baobab tree revolves around narratives. We learn from stories, we share our experiences, and we are inspired to take action. To tap into the power of storytelling, coaches and leaders hold a safe space to inspire the sharing of 'on top of the mind' ideas, concerns and imaginations.

Coaching from this perspective invites an individual's narrative to serve as a springboard for introspection and development in the context of personal development. A person's ideals, goals, and struggles can be better understood by reading about their own life experiences. Individuals can benefit from making better judgements regarding their future when they cultivate this level of self-awareness, which is crucial for personal growth.

iii) **Promoting an Attitude of Deep Listening**: The Indaba emphasises the need of deep listening for the purpose of understanding, not only responding. One way leaders can put this into practice is by encouraging their teams to listen with an empty mind and a heart of empathy.

Individuals can work on their interpersonal and professional listening skills by making active listening a regular part of their self-development routine. The ability to listen deeply and understand another person's perspective is a key component of healthy relationships, which are necessary for success in the Indaba gathering.

iv) **The Significance of Community in Overcoming Adversity**: The Baobab tree, a symbol of resilience and strength, serves as a reminder of this. An effective way for leaders to put this into practice is by creating an environment where team members feel comfortable talking with one another, sharing ideas and working together towards a common goal.

Building resilient relationships with loved ones, acquaintances and co-workers is an important part of self-improvement. With the support of these networks, people are better able to face obstacles and realise their dreams.

In summary, the Indaba under the Baobab tree teaches us important lessons about leadership and coaching. Leaders and individuals can cultivate communities that promote resilience, encourage deep listening, embrace collective wisdom and use storytelling to reach out to everyone. These qualities create conditions that are favourable to growth, creativity and success.

These concepts, which have their origins in African tradition, can be used in any situation and can be adjusted accordingly. Lessons learnt at the Indaba under the Baobab tree offer a timeless roadmap for overcoming obstacles and creating a better future, whether one is in a corporate boardroom, a community organisation or just living life on one's own.

Conclusion

The chapter highlights the significance of the Indaba under the Baobab tree, emphasising collective wisdom, inclusivity and storytelling as essential tools for leadership and coaching. These African traditions foster resilience, deep listening and collaboration, offering valuable lessons for building stronger communities and organisations. Leaders can apply these principles to create inclusive environments where diverse perspectives shape decision-making and foster growth.

Reference

Edwards, S. D., Holdstock, T. L., Nzima, D. R., & Edwards, D. (2020). Indaba: Towards an African psychology of education founded on Indigenous knowledge systems. *African Journal of Indigenous Knowledge systems, 19*(2), 155–164.

29

Kundavai's Wisdom

Thulasi Mohanadas

Thulasi Mohanadas Ltd., London, UK

The Big Idea

When we think about leadership, especially in the Western world, certain images often come to mind: a charismatic figure at the helm of an organisation, making bold decisions and giving rousing speeches. Hierarchical structures, titles, frontstage visibility and decision-making authority often characterise assigned, formal positions of leadership. And all too often, we associate this image with the agentic qualities of men in formal leader roles: dominant, aggressive, decisive and strong.

Ponniyin Selvan is a fictional story depicting the ascent of Raja Raja I (Kalki, 1955), the most powerful Chola emperor of the 10th–11th century who ruled over much of South India, Sri Lanka and the Maldives Islands. Many of the women of the Chola Dynasty are portrayed as strong, decisive and influential and challenge modern-day gender stereotypes and perceptions of women in leadership and leadership in general. Our story here focuses on the impact of Princess Kundavai, Raja Raja's elder sister. Instead of holding the highest office, Kundavai worked behind the scenes, using her intelligence, diplomatic skills and deep understanding of politics to guide the empire and shape its destiny in profound ways. Her story illustrates how influence can be effectively wielded without formal power, challenging stereotypes and perceptions of women leaders and Western notions of leadership hierarchy.

Mosaic Leadership: African, Asian, Middle Eastern and Indigenous Perspectives, First Edition. Edited by Jonathan Passmore, Badri Bajaj, and Mongezi C Makhalima.

Published 2026 by John Wiley & Sons Ltd.

Kundavai was a master of soft power. Whilst she did not hold the authority to issue royal decrees or command the royal armies, her words carried weight. She was known for her wisdom and ability to negotiate complex political situations. Rather than trying to dominate others, she worked to build consensus and create win-win situations. This approach stands in contrast to more competitive models of leadership in Western cultures. During the time her brothers were away looking to expand the Chola empire, and her father was bedridden, she was the only person closely associated with the administration of the kingdom and keeping civil order in their society. Historical accounts of Kundavai do not mention a single instance of violence or threats to ministers or the people to achieve these aims. Coupled with her compassionate and just nature, her influence and effectiveness relied on persuasion, building relationships and having a deep understanding of human nature.

This deep understanding of human nature was what enabled her to focus on the strategic long game. She is cited as being an influential mentor, guide and confidante to her brother Raja Raja Chola I since a young age. Her actions focused on ensuring the long-term stability and prosperity of the Chola Empire, and she herself resolved to stay in the Chola Kingdom for the rest of her life to serve its people. She was a stabilising force in the kingdom during a time of chaos and treachery, when people both internally and externally to the kingdom were vying for the throne. Following the death of their father, Sundara Chola, Kundavai uses her diplomatic skills to arrange the ascension of their uncle, Uttama, to the throne. Knowing he had missed the throne three times, this was a strategic move to quash discontent that had the potential to boil over. A deal was brokered where Uttama's children would have no claim to the throne following his death, and the reigns would be handed to Raja Raja Chola I, as it was 15 years later, allowing him to have matured from a young prince into a dynamic leader. Kundavai knew how to play the long game and wield power in the interest of her brother and the kingdom.

These examples of Kundavai's impact also challenge our ideas about visibility in leadership. In the age of personal branding and social media, we often think leaders need to be constantly in the spotlight. In fact, this can be especially off-putting for those individuals who feel they do not necessarily 'fit' into the front and centre leadership prototype and question whether they should be in leadership roles. But Kundavai's influence was often subtle and

Table 1 Kundavai's Leadership Approach.

Kundavai's Leadership Approach	Agentic, Hierarchical Leadership Models
Influence (soft power)	Direct power
Collaboration	Competition
Long-term thinking	Quick wins
Behind-the-scenes	Front and centre
Wisdom	Authority

behind the scenes. This is seen in how she built the reputation of the Cholas through the commissioning of architecture. Kundavai sponsored the building of hospitals, the construction of irrigation tanks and the building of temples for the Hindu, Jain and Buddhist communities. Her desire was to ensure the success of the Chola empire, and no doubt, the reputation and legacy of the Cholas live on. Kundavai's approach reminds us that sometimes, the most effective leadership happens quietly, behind the scenes.

Kundavai also exemplifies the power of knowledge and continuous learning in leadership. She was renowned for her education and wisdom, which formed the basis of her influence. This reminds us that true leadership is not just about charisma or decisiveness, but about having the depth of understanding to make wise decisions. We can see this in how her leadership style was deeply rooted in her cultural context. She didn't try to break all the rules of her society, but rather worked within existing structures to effect change. This nuanced approach to leadership—understanding when to push boundaries and when to work within them—is a valuable lesson for leaders in any context.

In essence, Kundavai represents a leadership paradigm that values influence over direct power, collaboration over competition, long-term thinking over quick wins, behind-the-scenes over front and centre and wisdom over mere authority.

How to Apply It

Kundavai's most striking quality was her ability to influence without formal authority. Instead of relying on your title to get things done or feeling the need to resort to 'hard' power, focus on building relationships and trust and understanding motivations and different cultural perspectives. Be the go-to person for advice. You can shape outcomes without necessarily being assigned a formal leadership title. This could mean mentoring junior colleagues, breaking down silos and facilitating connections between departments or being the voice of reason in heated discussions.

Kundavai's approach was inherently collaborative, focusing on building consensus rather than imposing her will. In some competitive organisational cultures and industries, this can seem counter-intuitive. But in our multinational and global organisations, this approach is more needed than ever. When we collaborate, we tap into diverse perspectives and create innovative solutions. Try fostering a team culture where sharing diverse ideas is celebrated, not seen as giving away your competitive edge. Organise cross-departmental projects, or even look for collaborative opportunities with other companies in your industry. Kundavai was known for transforming potential threats outside of the kingdom into strategic alliances, leading to more stable, long-lasting international partnerships. Finding ways to collaborate with externals can generate unique opportunities.

Like Kundavai, who worked to ensure the long-term stability of her empire, we need to look beyond immediate results. Certainly, a challenge in an age of immediacy and instant gratification. Leaders experiencing a transition, new to a role, or trying to move to the next step often find it hard to let go of the day-to-day operations and people management and focus on strategy and capability building. The aim here is to invest in employee development and developing a strong leadership pipeline, even if it doesn't show immediate returns. Or develop sustainable business practices that might hit profits and deliverables in the short term but ensure your company's longevity.

Kundavai's influence often operated behind the scenes. This approach can be particularly effective in situations where visible leadership might face resistance. This doesn't mean becoming invisible; rather, it's about enabling others. For example, in delivering change initiatives, instead of pushing for changes from the top down, it may be more effective to work with influential employees at various levels. Helping them to understand the benefits of the change and empowering them to become advocates. Like Kundavai, who shaped events without always being at the forefront, you can lead by empowering others and catalyse change without being in the spotlight.

Finally, there's Kundavai's emphasis on wisdom over mere authority. In today's knowledge economy, this is more important than ever. Cultivate a learning and growth mindset. Stay curious. Be the leader who asks thoughtful questions rather than always having the answers. Learn to become comfortable with not knowing and the discomfort we can feel with this. Encourage your team to challenge ideas—even yours. Create an environment where knowledge is shared freely, not hoarded as a source of power.

Of course, applying these principles isn't always easy. But leadership à la Kundavai isn't about quick fixes or flashy moves. Kundavai reminds us that leadership is not just about position or authority. It is about how we influence, support and guide others towards a better future. By bringing a touch of ancient Indian wisdom to our modern Western workplaces, we might just find ourselves creating more resilient, innovative and harmonious organisations. Like Kundavai, we might end up shaping something that lasts long after we're gone.

Conclusion

The chapter highlights the leadership of Princess Kundavai from the Chola dynasty, who demonstrated soft power, wisdom and collaboration, challenging traditional Western leadership models. Her influence behind the scenes through diplomacy, long-term thinking and community-building offers valuable lessons for modern leadership, emphasising the importance of fostering relationships, inclusivity and wisdom over direct authority.

Reference

Kalki, K. (1955). *Ponniyin Selvan* பொன்னியின் செல்வன் (in Tamil). Madras: Mangala Noolagam. Ponniyin Selvan.

30

Wisdom from Proverbs

Mavuto Kapyepye

Mlambe Consulting Africa, Blantyre City, Malawi

The Big Idea

Proverbs, or sayings, have been part of people's traditions for the whole of human history. Proverbs are used to summarise complex ideas and capture people's lived experience, which they wish to both share and also to pass on to the next generation. Despite the localised touch to the vocabulary expressed, some proverbs have been known to communicate concepts that have global relevance, including leadership.

The Lhomwe Ethnic group in Malawi, Southern Africa, is common among thousands of tribal peoples in using proverbs as a shorthand to pass on wisdom. This chapter contains four examples selected from Lhomwe proverbs, using the original form, alongside the translated English version in brackets, which can inform leaders in their developmental journeys.

Proverb 1: Khomalhe dhamuwano (Mind your tongue)

In the African traditional thought system, the wisdom of minding one's tongue is a well-established imperative. A member of the community, young or old is expected to speak respectfully. The words of an organisational leader similarly can impact a team's morale and productivity and contribute to an organisation's culture.

Mosaic Leadership: African, Asian, Middle Eastern and Indigenous Perspectives, First Edition. Edited by Jonathan Passmore, Badri Bajaj, and Mongezi C Makhalima.

Published 2026 by John Wiley & Sons Ltd.

How to Apply It?

Tone: Using a positive tone facilitates motivation and can inspire a team. Even when addressing challenges or mistakes, frame your language in a way that encourages improvement and learning.

Respect: Speaking with respect and courtesy, regardless of the situation. Avoid language that could be perceived as demeaning or dismissive.

Inclusivity: Using inclusive language that makes everyone feel valued and respected. Avoid jargon, slang or terms that might exclude or alienate any team members.

Balanced feedback: Provide balanced feedback that highlights both strengths and areas for improvement. Ensure your feedback is constructive and aimed at fostering growth.

Proverb 2: Khunyambuse avathi, wiikuha anutote pani (Respect the people below you. You may need them one day)

In the African traditional set-up, humility is emphasised. Let us put this proverb into context with the scenario of a funeral ceremony. In Malawi, during funerals, there is a strong sense of community. The ones who dig the grave hole are members of the community (commonly called *adzukulu*). Adzukulu are members of the community, male and without a reliable source of income and can sadly be unnoticeable due to their low economic status. However, during funerals, they play a pivotal role at the burial site where they dig the burial pit. Although they get compensated for the work they do, it is important to acknowledge that they do a noble job in preparing the ground for the deceased. The proverb has a deeper meaning that although during sunny days some members of society may look down upon these people because of their economic status, they are needed at important times, such as during a burial.

How to Apply It?

Respecting those below us in the organisational hierarchy is a fundamental principle that underscores the importance of humility, interconnectedness and the unpredictable nature of life's circumstances. Here's an expanded perspective on why it's important to respect the people below you, illustrated through African wisdom and general principles of leadership:

Ubuntu Philosophy: 'I am because we are'. This African philosophy teaches that our humanity is interconnected. By respecting and supporting those below you, you are contributing to the well-being and strength of the entire community.

Life's Unpredictability: 'The one who is down today may rise tomorrow'. Respecting everyone acknowledges the reality that circumstances can change. Someone you helped when they were down might be in a position to help you in the future.

Responsibility: True leadership is about serving others. Treating those below you with respect is an ethical obligation that reflects your integrity and moral values.

Role Modelling: Leaders who respect everyone set a positive example for others to follow, fostering a culture of respect and kindness within the organisation or community.

Proverb 3: Malhavi khem'thurumelhiwa (Do not test trouble deliberately)

This proverb touches on the dangers of not taking precautions on potential risks that one may face, especially in situations where it is obvious.

How to Apply It?

Risk Management: Leaders should be prudent in their decisions, avoiding actions that unnecessarily introduce significant risks to the organisation. This means thoroughly evaluating potential consequences before making decisions that could lead to trouble.

Calculated Decisions: While taking risks is sometimes necessary for growth and innovation, these should be calculated and well-considered rather than impulsive or reckless.

Integrity and Honesty: Leaders should act with integrity and honesty, avoiding actions that could be perceived as manipulative or deceitful. Ethical lapses can lead to significant trouble, both legally and reputationally.

Transparency: Being transparent in decision-making and communication helps build trust and prevents misunderstandings that could lead to trouble.

Well-being of Team Members: Leaders should be mindful of the well-being of their team members. Actions that deliberately cause stress or hardship can lead to burnout, decreased morale and a high turnover.

Supportive Environment: Creating a supportive and positive work environment helps foster trust and loyalty among team members.

Proverb 4: Msilhu nakhalha mpa mwao weyano kohelha enumba mwaha wa msilu (No matter how annoying a rat can be in a house, the owner will not set ablaze the roof to hunt for it)

This proverb presents the context of a household that is infested by a mischievous rat. It causes a lot disruption in the home and naturally the occupants would like to get rid of the nuisance caused by the rat. But is it worth burning the house in order to get rid of the rat?

How to Apply It?

This is a principle advocating for proportional and measured responses to problems. It highlights the importance of addressing issues without causing excessive or unnecessary damage.

Avoid Overreactions: Leaders should respond to problems in a way that is proportionate to their severity. Overreacting to minor issues can cause more harm than good, much like setting a fire to drive out a rat.

Calm and Rational Decision-Making: Maintaining composure and rationality in the face of challenges ensures that solutions are effective without causing collateral damage.

Effective Problem-Solving: Address issues directly and efficiently, using appropriate strategies that solve the problem without creating larger issues. This means identifying the root cause and dealing with it in a focused manner.

Minimising Disruption: Aim to resolve problems with minimal disruption to the team or organisation. This involves finding solutions that maintain stability and continuity.

Resolve Conflicts Peacefully: In dealing with conflicts or difficult individuals, leaders should seek peaceful and constructive resolutions rather than drastic measures that escalate the situation.

Mediation and Negotiation: Employ mediation and negotiation to handle disputes. These approaches are often more effective and less damaging than confrontational methods.

Ethical Decision-Making: Ensure that all decisions are ethical and just. Avoid actions that might seem like an easy fix but are ethically questionable or harmful in the long run.

Integrity and Trust: Maintain integrity and build trust by handling problems transparently and responsibly.

Conclusions

In this chapter, I have explored the concept of proverbs as a tool for supporting leaders to developer greater awareness of themselves and others within the Lhomwe Ethnic tradition.

31

Gacaca Leadership

Jean Nyiramasuhuko

Catholic University of Rwanda, Rwanda

The Big Idea

In the wake of the Rwandan genocide in 1994, the country faced an unimaginable challenge: rebuilding trust, justice and cohesion within a fractured society. Over a million people had been killed in a few short months, leaving communities broken, families torn apart and social structures in disarray (Klein, 2012). Among the many responses to this crisis was the revival of an ancient form of justice known as the Gacaca courts (Nyseth Brehm et al., 2014). These community-based courts played a pivotal role in Rwanda's reconciliation and recovery, demonstrating a unique model of leadership focused on healing, accountability and unity.

The Gacaca system, which originates from traditional Rwandan practices, translates roughly to 'justice on the grass'. For centuries, it served as a customary method for resolving conflicts and disputes within communities. The practice involved gathering villagers in an open space, often a grassy area, where they would discuss grievances, hear from witnesses and work towards collective resolutions. Unlike Western legal systems, Gacaca did not depend on professional judges or lawyers; instead, it involved community elders or respected individuals who were chosen to lead these gatherings. Their role was not only to judge but to facilitate a process that would encourage understanding, restitution and forgiveness (UN, n.d.)

Mosaic Leadership: African, Asian, Middle Eastern and Indigenous Perspectives, First Edition. Edited by Jonathan Passmore, Badri Bajaj, and Mongezi C Makhalima.

Published 2026 by John Wiley & Sons Ltd.

In the aftermath of the genocide, Rwanda's government, working with the UN, saw potential in Gacaca's model of communal justice as a way to address the overwhelming backlog of cases. Given the vast number of suspects, the formal justice system was insufficient for processing the sheer volume of crimes. Gacaca was revived as a means to expedite justice but also as a way to foster national healing and reconciliation. Over the course of a decade, Gacaca courts addressed nearly two million cases, providing an opportunity for survivors and perpetrators to confront the past together in a framework grounded in dialogue and restorative justice.

The success of Gacaca lies in its core principles, which reflect a profound approach to leadership—one that prioritises the well-being of the community over retributive justice. Unlike typical court systems, which focus on punishment, Gacaca sought to repair the social fabric. This approach requires an understanding of justice that is not merely about assigning blame but about rebuilding relationships, cultivating empathy and creating a path for reconciliation. This model challenges conventional Western concepts of leadership by emphasising the leader's role in restoring trust and unity rather than asserting authority or power.

One of the key tenets of Gacaca is inclusivity. Every member of the community had a stake in the process, with survivors, perpetrators and their families all involved. By participating in the proceedings, community members were given a voice, a chance to tell their stories and an opportunity to contribute to the healing process. The structure of Gacaca required leaders to be attuned to each individual's story, recognising the suffering on all sides and acknowledging the pain caused by both acts of violence and subsequent judgements. This inclusivity promoted transparency and allowed for shared responsibility, where community members bore witness to each other's trauma and collectively sought ways to move forward (Rettig, 2008).

Gacaca leaders played a pivotal role in moderating these gatherings, requiring them to embody values of patience, fairness and empathy. They were not there to exercise dominance but to foster an environment where all voices could be heard. By guiding the discussions and ensuring that everyone had a chance to participate, these leaders modelled a form of justice that went beyond the individual to address the needs of the entire community. Their role was to bridge divides, create safe spaces for open dialogue and cultivate an environment where empathy could emerge even in the face of immense pain.

The emphasis on empathy is another fundamental aspect of Gacaca leadership. The process was not only about facing legal consequences but about understanding and acknowledging the human toll of one's actions. For the perpetrators, Gacaca offered a chance to confront their actions in the presence of those they had harmed. For the survivors, it was an opportunity to voice their suffering and receive acknowledgement. This dynamic fostered a mutual awareness that transcended mere punishment and led towards personal and collective accountability. This sense of empathy was crucial in rebuilding trust within communities, as it emphasised shared humanity over retribution.

Accountability is also central to Gacaca's model of leadership. While the courts did offer forgiveness and opportunities for reconciliation, they did not ignore the importance of facing consequences. Gacaca leaders ensured that those who admitted guilt and demonstrated genuine remorse were given an opportunity to make amends through community service or reparations. This approach balanced forgiveness with accountability, reinforcing the notion that justice could be both compassionate and firm. This balance is critical to understanding Gacaca's impact on Rwandan society, as it provided a framework in which people could be held accountable without erasing the possibility of redemption.

One of the most profound aspects of Gacaca leadership is the commitment to a shared future. By fostering reconciliation, Gacaca leaders were not just settling disputes but actively working to rebuild a unified society. This focus on collective healing underscores a leadership model grounded in vision—a vision of peace, coexistence and a Rwanda free from division. Gacaca leaders were called to transcend individual grievances and to look beyond immediate judgements towards a broader goal of national harmony. This required a deep sense of purpose, resilience and the ability to inspire others to work together despite painful histories.

The Gacaca courts ultimately teach us that leadership can be transformative when it prioritises healing and inclusion over punishment. It demonstrates that true leadership often means guiding people through processes that are difficult, uncomfortable and deeply emotional. By focusing on relationships and a shared vision of peace, the Gacaca courts offer a powerful model of restorative leadership. This model is one in which leaders view justice as a means of building community and compassion, rather than dividing or isolating individuals.

How to Apply It

For leaders today, the principles of Gacaca courts offer a unique approach to managing conflict, fostering inclusion, and driving organisational culture to create psychological safety (Edmondson, 2018). The model teaches us that effective leadership is not about asserting power but about creating space for open dialogue, understanding and shared accountability. Leaders can apply the essence of Gacaca by embracing inclusivity and ensuring that all stakeholders have a voice. This can mean incorporating collaborative approaches to decision-making, where people across all levels feel their input matters, fostering a culture of transparency and respect.

Empathy is another crucial element that leaders can adopt from Gacaca. Empathy goes beyond listening—it requires leaders to truly understand the concerns, challenges and emotions of their teams. Leaders can apply this by spending time with team members, observing their work environments, and engaging in one-on-one conversations that allow them to connect on a deeper level. In moments of conflict or disagreement, leaders who prioritise empathy can facilitate resolutions that go beyond surface-level solutions, building bridges that strengthen relationships within the team.

Accountability is also essential. Gacaca reminds us that accountability doesn't have to be punitive; it can be restorative. In organisational settings, this translates to fostering a culture where mistakes are addressed and employees are encouraged to take ownership of their actions. Leaders can cultivate this environment by encouraging feedback, acknowledging both successes and failures and implementing systems where corrective actions are seen as opportunities for growth rather than blame.

Finally, the concept of a shared future is fundamental to applying Gacaca principles in leadership. Leaders should inspire their teams by connecting their work to a larger mission or vision, fostering a sense of shared purpose. In times of change, leaders can remind employees of the collective journey, reinforcing the importance of working together to achieve common goals. This vision-oriented approach creates a foundation for unity, resilience and a commitment to long-term success.

Conclusion

By embracing these principles, leaders can foster environments where reconciliation, trust and accountability thrive. A Gacaca style teaches us that leadership rooted in empathy, inclusivity and a vision for collective well-being can create profound, lasting change, which strengthens teams and communities. This model not only helps resolve immediate issues but also fosters a culture of collaboration, unity and shared understanding.

References

Edmondson, A. (2018). *The fearless organization.* New York: Wiley.

Klein, K. (2012) The secrets of Rwanda. Retrieved on 21 October 2024 from: https://knowledge.wharton.upenn.edu/article/the-secret-of-rwanda-pushing-leadership-down-the-line/

Nyseth Brehm, H., Uggen, C., & Gasanabo, J.-D. (2014). Genocide, Justice, and Rwanda's Gacaca Courts. *Journal of Contemporary Criminal Justice, 30*(3), 333–352. https://doi.org/10.1177/1043986214536660

Rettig, M. (2008). Truth, Justice and Reconciliation in post-conflict Rwanda. *African Studies Review, 51*(3), 25–50. https://doi.org/10.1353/arw.0.0091

United Nations. (n.d.) Prevent Genocide. Retrieved on 21 October 2024 from: https://www.un.org/en/preventgenocide/rwanda/assets/pdf/Backgrounder%20Justice%202014.pdf

32

Yoruba Leadership

Frans van der Colff

Henley Business School, Johannesburg, South Africa

The Big Idea

The Yoruba are the second-largest ethnic group of Nigeria, mostly located in the southern part of the country, with smaller groups found in Benin and Northern Togo. They have shared a common language and culture for centuries and are among the most urbanised Africans with many living in large communities.

The Yoruba value system is community-oriented, eco-friendly and geared towards sustainable human habitation of the continent. The colonisers misunderstood and often exploited the generosity and humility of the Yoruba people, responding with hostility, enslavement and cultural suppression.

The Yoruba never claimed to be the only civilisation on earth and were ever eager to interact and exchange ideas with people from other places and lands. They have always displayed a holistic view of the universe that requires respect for all things, and this view encompasses a sophisticated understanding of the environment and its interconnections. The environment is understood as everything that surrounds us, material and non-material, involving individual resources that relate to each other. It is believed that maintaining an equilibrium among all elements fosters peace and harmony; it is the balance that is necessary for living a fulfilled life.

The values of respect, truthfulness, honesty and accountability are always present in interactions with others, human or not human. It is believed that all entities in nature deserve respect,

Mosaic Leadership: African, Asian, Middle Eastern and Indigenous Perspectives, First Edition. Edited by Jonathan Passmore, Badri Bajaj, and Mongezi C Makhalima.

Published 2026 by John Wiley & Sons Ltd.

including things such as trees and rivers. Trees offer shade, while rivers provide water and food, all necessary for living, and these resources are often the reasons why communities thrive. The Yoruba society strives towards sustainable survival, recognising that the balance in nature is crucial for long-term well-being. This perspective could be described as a form of ecological intelligence, demonstrating a deep understanding of environmental interdependence.

Ori, or purpose, fits into the framework of self-determination in Yoruba philosophy. It consists of three elements: ara (the body), emi (the life-giving element or breath) and ori (the spiritual head responsible for human destiny). The Yoruba concept of ori exists in two interconnected senses: it is both the unconscious self that makes choices about the course of life and the chosen individual destiny.

There are avenues open to shape and influence this destiny, including sacrifice, hard work and character development. One is held responsible for the actions performed by oneself. The Yoruba belief system emphasises relatedness, interconnectedness and interdependence between the physical and spiritual worlds. These two realms operate in harmony, each influencing the other.

Yoruba belief about Ori and Life

Ori controls and guides the life and actions of a person, serving as a personal deity or higher self. One must achieve alignment with one's Ori before death or face consequences in their next life, as death is not the end but part of the cycle of reincarnation. Having a good and happy life is an integral part of Yoruba culture.

Guidelines from the Yoruba beliefs include that one can change one's destiny, except for the days of birth and death, and that everyone is part of the universe. They advocate that everyone should strive for a successful, fruitful and a happy life; acquire knowledge and wisdom at all times during life; and that nature should be respected at all times. Others should never be harmed, one should not fear and respect the spirits of the ancestors.

It is important to remember that everyone is born with a destiny and that you fulfil your Ori through integration of the heart and mind by using established values to align yourself with your purpose. Spiritual growth is important; every person has the right to grow and to be fulfilled, and is valuable in their own way and should be respected for what they contribute. The Yoruba say that no one is better than others and that your character determines your fate. Diversity should be celebrated, as it brings people together, and all experiences serve to improve character.

The Yoruba leadership principles embody a comprehensive approach to governance that prioritises the collective well-being of society. At its core, this leadership philosophy emphasises a strong commitment to societal goals, ensuring that leaders work towards the betterment of the community rather than for personal gain. This is coupled with a focus on equitable wealth distribution and sustainable resource management, reflecting a long-term vision for societal prosperity and environmental stewardship.

The principles of accountability, transparency and commitment to justice form the ethical backbone of Yoruba leadership, ensuring that those in power remain answerable to their people and uphold fairness in their actions. Equality and good character conclude these principles, underscoring the Yoruba belief that effective leadership stems not just from authority but from moral integrity and the recognition of every individual's inherent worth.

These leadership principles are deeply intertwined with the Yoruba approach to education and personal development. In Yoruba society, education transcends mere academic or technical skills, encompassing a broader spectrum of values, wisdom and character development crucial for maintaining social harmony. Leaders are expected to embody this holistic education, possessing not only the knowledge and skills to govern effectively but also the moral character to prioritise the greater good over personal interests. This perspective views leadership as a form of community service, with decision-making processes often involving consultation with elders and consideration of traditional wisdom. Such an approach ensures a balance between innovation and cultural heritage, fostering leadership that is both progressive and rooted in time-honoured values. Ultimately, Yoruba leadership principles create a framework for governance that is ethical, inclusive and deeply committed to the sustainable development of both the community and the individual.

How to Apply It

The Yoruba leadership principles can be summarised as follows (Table 32.1):

Table 32.1 Yoruba Leadership Principles Diagram.

1. Commitment to societal goals
2. Equitable distribution of wealth
3. Sustainable management of resources and the environment
4. Accountability
5. Transparency
6. Commitment to justice
7. Equality
8. Good character

One of the key aspects of Yoruba leadership is education, and it is important to understand that formal skills are not enough and that education needs to include values and wisdom that will assist in maintaining communal order. Leaders should possess not only the necessary knowledge and skills to lead but also the character to make decisions that serve the greater good. The Yoruba approach to education is holistic, recognising that learning extends well beyond the mere acquisition of knowledge. By placing great emphasis on developing good character, the approach ensures that leaders make thoughtful and ethical decisions that benefit the entire community.

The Yoruba view leadership as a service to communities, fundamentally prioritising the well-being of people over personal gain. Decision-making is deeply collaborative and involves consultation with elders and careful consideration of traditional wisdom. This approach creates a balanced leadership model that respects cultural heritage while remaining open to innovation. By valuing both established traditions and new ideas, Yoruba leadership principles create a dynamic and responsive governance framework.

In today's complex global environment, the Yoruba approach to leadership offers remarkable relevance. It provides a comprehensive framework that enables leaders to align organisational goals with broader societal objectives. The approach has the potential to enhance shared value creation and work towards building more equitable societies. By prioritising collective well-being over individual interests, this leadership model addresses many of the systemic challenges that plague contemporary social and organisational structures.

The principles of Yoruba leadership promise a more equitable distribution of wealth, which is critically important in the many unequal societies across our world. Moreover, this approach inherently supports environmentally friendly practices, contributing to the long-term health of our planet and its inhabitants. By addressing climate change through a holistic lens, Yoruba leadership principles offer a sustainable approach to development that meets both human and ecological needs.

Good character stands as a fundamental element that encourages ethical leadership and integrity. In an era marked by increasing corruption and ethical challenges across various aspects of life, this approach provides a much-needed solution. The concept of holistic education is equally transformative, extending beyond professional development to encompass personal growth. It assists individuals in discovering their purpose and living a more meaningful life, creating a sense of fulfilment that transcends mere professional achievement.

Ultimately, Yoruba leadership prioritises the well-being of teams and communities. Decision-making is consultative and inclusive, creating a sense of belonging, and it emphasises the interconnectedness of individual and collective well-being.

Conclusion

The Yoruba concept of Ori emphasises the importance of purpose in leadership, asserting that one should lead with good character and ensure that the purpose is realised. By integrating Yoruba leadership principles into contemporary leadership practices, leaders will not only be more effective, but more committed to the well-being of their communities and the sustainability of their practices. This is a leadership approach that respects both people and the environment, recognising the intrinsic connection between human potential, community welfare and ecological balance.

33

African Stool

Mbithe Anzaya

Kaskazini Coaching-Africa, Nairobi, Kenya

The Big Idea

The three-legged stool is common across many parts of Africa. It is used at night when groups gather to talk about the day or share stories. Stools are often passed down from one generation to the next. As a result, it has a special place in the hearts of many African people who remember their own experiences as little children and return to these experiences as they become leaders.

The three-legged African stool can be used as both a connection with evocative memories and as a metaphor; as the seat of the stool is circular, it symbolises that we are whole people; we are not broken. As a three-legged object, it can be used to represent the present, past and future.

It can also be used to connect individuals with their past, the values which surrounded them as a child and those they wish to carry forward into new roles and identities.

How It Works

The metaphor can be used in a variety of ways in leadership development. One common use is to explore timelines: present, past and future. For example:

Mosaic Leadership: African, Asian, Middle Eastern and Indigenous Perspectives, First Edition. Edited by Jonathan Passmore, Badri Bajaj, and Mongezi C Makhalima.

Published 2026 by John Wiley & Sons Ltd.

i) **Exploring present circumstances:**
What are the challenges of your present situation?

ii) **Reviewing the past:**
What have you experienced in the past that you could leverage on your current situation?

iii) **Addressing future fears:**
If you were not afraid, what would you do to influence your desired outcomes in the future?

It also has value in helping leaders recognise the different roles people play over time as their wisdom and maturity develops.

A variation on this is the four-legged stool. This can be used by drawing on the notion of community. The additional fourth leg represents the communities in which we live—in many cases, we live in more than one village and are part of more than one community.

Community and relationships are an important feature in many leadership models, and this tool offers a way to draw upon this aspect and incorporate it into the reflective discussions about one's own development as a leader.

iv) **Exploring definitions of community**
What obligations do you have towards the communities that see you as their member?

What impact would you like to have on these communities?

Conclusion

The stool is a metaphor which, for many African peoples, has a particular significance. While simple, it can be a powerful tool to think about how people develop over time. The interconnection between past, present, future, and the community is the foundation for lasting growth and, therefore, must be factored into our conversations about true and lasting growth.

First Nation Perspectives

34

Deep Listening

Laura Brearley[1,2]

[1] *Monash University, Melbourne, Victoria, Australia*
[2] *The Living Circle 21 Creative Research Consultancy, Melbourne, Victoria, Australia*

The Big Idea

Listening lies at the heart of leadership. Listening is central to making connections, building trust and understanding changing contexts. The practice of Deep Listening takes it to another level and has profound relevance to current leadership practice, particularly in the context of the Earth's fragile future.

Central to Deep Listening is respect, reciprocity and the building of community. It incorporates multiple ways of knowing and opens up ways in which knowledge is shared and wisdom is passed on across generations. Deep Listening invites us into more generative ways of being together in community.

Australia has the oldest living continuous culture on the planet. Australia's First Nations people have passed on this approach to living and working together for tens of thousands of years. People who have suffered and survived extraordinary losses through colonisation and yet continue to pass on their wisdom may be our greatest teachers.

It has been my great privilege to work with First Nations artists, cultural educators and community leaders over the last 25 years. We have worked together inside the university system and beyond it, in collaborative environmental arts and education projects. We have co-authored books and publications together, produced music albums, made films and coordinated intercultural Eco Arts events. We have facilitated a cross-cultural exchange between

Mosaic Leadership: African, Asian, Middle Eastern and Indigenous Perspectives, First Edition. Edited by Jonathan Passmore, Badri Bajaj, and Mongezi C Makhalima.

Published 2026 by John Wiley & Sons Ltd.

Australia and Turtle Island (Canada and USA) since 2008 (Brearley, 2014).

With their permission, I am sharing the voices of two Aboriginal women, Lisa Kennedy and Aunty Fay Stewart-Muir, with whom I have collaborated for many years on a range of intercultural Eco Arts projects. Our work emerges from the spaces that lie between. Lisa is a descendant of the Pairrebeene/Trawlwoolway Clans of North-East Tasmania. She is an artist and storyteller who has illustrated a number of award-winning books, including 'Welcome to Country', 'Sea Country', 'Sky Country' and 'Wilam: A Birrarung Story' about the Yarra River that flows through Melbourne.

Aunty Fay Stewart-Muir is an Aboriginal Elder, author and community leader with Boon Wurrung and Wamba Wamba heritage in Victoria. Aunty Fay is a highly respected saltwater and freshwater woman who has lived a life of service, providing leadership in the fields of language revival, health, education, prisoner programmes and cultural advocacy. She has co-authored books for adults and children including 'Always Was, Always Will Be', 'Respect', 'Sharing', 'Family' and 'Country'.

Both Lisa and Aunty Fay celebrate multiple ways of knowing and the ancient and contemporary practice of deepening connections through Deep Listening.

This is how Lisa Kennedy describes it:

> *'Deep Listening' is an Aboriginal way of listening and learning. I use Deep Listening to guide me in hearing the voices of my Ancestors, listening to the land, the sea, the stars and hearing the stories that want to be told. Deep Listening allows me to hear the voices within that need to speak.'* (Lisa Kennedy, Personal Communication, 10/12/2013)
>
> *'Our work is about message making, about finding ways of bringing things forward that have been hidden. We need to find languages and forms to tell the stories that need to be told, that connect us and take us into the future. Our stories show us where we have come from, what has been passed down, what is still with us, and how we can go forward with it. The voice that the Earth speaks, comes through in many different ways. It comes through in strong feelings and it can also be subtle.*
>
> *We need to understand and relate to places in a deep way. We need to see Country as a whole. Everything is connected. The city has fragmented the cohesive way of understanding Country. If we pull the veil aside, we see the life that is flowing. It's an old way of being, a seasonal way of life. There is*

continuity from the past and a way of continually renewing going forward.

Deep Listening to Country is something beyond words. It requires open-heartedness, and some vulnerability. Sometimes we're defended against ideas that we get stuck on. Vulnerability cracks us open and helps us connect with our heart. Something in our consciousness cracks open into a heightened state of awareness. We become more sensitised.

We find our own meaning when we are ready to receive it. I am exploring how stories change and become contemporary and why we need to let go of old stories that are limiting and no longer serve. I am committed to creating a new ending. Our people have experienced enormous losses and that is still going on. Our generation has been very much supported by older people in retelling stories in different ways. I have been very lucky to be part of that generation. Those Old People did not want us to be stuck in that place of sorrow. I want our stories to bridge the past, present and the future. I want them to be healing and transformative.

Our stories are not lost. Nothing is lost. There is still hope. There is always hope. Never think it's too late. Life is supporting the process. It is present and we can learn. It is all there within us, in relationship and in connection with others and with Mother Earth.' (Lisa Kennedy, Personal Communication, 10/01/2025)

Aunty Fay Stewart-Muir also has a deep appreciation of the importance of connection through the practice of Deep Listening. She listens to country and to community, to her Ancestors and to what is emerging. Her creative practice and her leadership are profoundly relational and are underpinned by a quality of care. In her book 'Country', which Aunty Fay co-authored with Sue Lawson, she writes, 'Country is past, present, future. Country is songs, stories, art and ceremony ... Country is all of us. Country is how we behave, how we care for each other.'

In conversation, this is how Aunty Fay describes it:

'We need to listen and look and communicate with Country. If we don't look after Country, it's not going to look after us. It won't be around for our next generation to come. Take your time go for a walk. Sit on Country and let it commune with you. It speaks so much. It speaks from the heart. It's in our mother tongue. It's talking to us and our Ancestors are needing us to listen.

We are missing a lot of what is being communicated because we are not attuned. We need to feel Country speaking to us, hearing the sounds of Mother Nature and the reverberation of this land. Listening deeply in this way comes with a sense of care and responsibility. The past is still very much alive. It's not dead. It's a living thing and it's ongoing.

Different parts of the future are already with us. Children have foresight and they can see. They ask deep questions these days and they are not being held back. They want to know what's going on. They are listening to what is emerging.' (Aunty Fay Stewart-Muir, Personal Communication, 10/01/2025)

How to Apply It

Deep Listening is an ancient concept with relevance to contemporary leadership. It has much to teach us about effective leadership, particularly in the context of inspiring environmental stewardship. Listening deeply is a process of presencing, of becoming present to ourselves, to each other and to our ever-changing contexts. Three core ways in which Deep Listening can be applied in our leadership practice are the strengthening of a community, the incorporation of multiple ways of knowing and the fostering of a quality of care.

1. **Community Strengthening**
   Deep Listening is underpinned by respect and reciprocity and an appreciation of the significance of relationality. It fosters a sense of belonging, moving across time and between generations. It invites us to learn from the wisdom of Ancestors and Elders and to consider future generations in all of our life choices.
2. **Multiple Ways of Knowing**
   The practice of Deep Listening broadens and deepens how we learn and how we teach. Knowledge is passed on through multiple ways of knowing, with an appreciation of the different perspectives embedded in stories, art, music, ceremony, science and silence.
3. **Quality of Care**
   Deep Listening creates connections between people and place. It comes with responsibility. Caring for Country has been practiced by First Nations people for 2,400 generations in Australia. Given the ecological crisis facing the planet, it is a practice that

has never been more crucial to the future of all living beings and the health of our planet.

In Lisa Kennedy's words,

> *'Our work is about being, doing and connecting. It helps us to connect to Country in different ways, so we can feel things. We can feel our relationship with other sentient beings. We are part of the community of living beings of Mother Earth - the trees, insects, animals, and the rocks that contain histories, the millions of years of stories, emotions and transformations. Through Deep Listening, we become open to seeing beyond the senses. We are able to be in the world in a different way, open to Ancestors and to Country.*
>
> *When we talk about climate change and the planetary crisis, we have to hold that there is a bigger creative spirit at work. It is bigger than us. Many people have forgotten what they could be tuned into. The Old People are saying 'Remember to listen.''* (Lisa Kennedy, Personal Communication, 10/01/2025)

And some final words from Aunty Fay Stewart-Muir:

'On Country, you feel home.
When you're walking on Country,
You feel the heartbeat of the Land
And you belong.
You need to take off your shoes and socks
And feel that connection.
Just sit and listen to the birds speak
And let the Country speak to you.
Once you hear it
It's there all the time.
You understand who you truly are
And you are transformed.'

(Aunty Fay Stewart-Muir, Personal Communication, 19/11/2013)

Conclusion

Leadership underpinned by the practice of Deep Listening reveals our interconnectedness. The issues we face today are too complex and multi-layered for any individual to solve. There is a generosity and spaciousness in the practice of Deep Listening. We need to embed leadership practice in relationships, respect and reciprocity. We need each other as we listen deeply together to what is emerging. As Lisa Kennedy says, 'It is all about connection'. (Lisa Kennedy, Personal Communication, 10/01/2025)

Acknowledgement

I would like to express my profound appreciation to my First Nation friends and collaborators who have generously shared their insights, stories and artworks to inform and enrich a broader understanding of the practice of Deep Listening. Special thanks to Lisa Kennedy (Trawlwoolway/Pairrebeene) and Aunty Fay Stewart-Muir (Boon Wurrung/Wamba Wamba), whose words appear in this chapter. I also acknowledge the Ancestors, Elders and current and future leaders of Boon Wurrung/Bunurong Country on which I live and work.

Reference

Brearley, L. (2014). Deep listening and leadership: An Indigenous model of leadership and community development in Australia. In C. Voyageur, C. L. Brearley, & B. Calliou (Eds.), *Restorying Indigenous Leadership: Wise Practices in Community Development* (pp. 91–128). *Banff, Alberta: Banff Centre Press. Retrieved on 29th January 2025 from:* https://www.banffcentre.ca/sites/default/files/Lougheed%20Leadership/Research/Indigenous/4_Chapter_3.pdf

35

Strong Like Two People

Lisa Mantla

LM Consulting, Toronto, Canada

The Big Idea

The concept of 'Strong Like Two People' is deeply rooted in the lived experience and wisdom of Tłı̨chǫ̀ elders, the work of Chief Jimmy Bruneau (2018) and Elizabeth Mackenzie (2019), whose insights continue to shape Indigenous leadership models in the Northwest Territories and beyond. At its core, this philosophy embodies the ability to navigate two distinct but interconnected worlds: the traditional knowledge systems of the Tłı̨chǫ̀ people and the structures of Western education, governance and economic systems. It is not merely a theoretical construct but a lived reality for Indigenous communities who have had to balance cultural survival with participation in the contemporary world. 'Strong Like Two People' emerges as both a response to historical disruption and a vision for the future, offering a decolonial leadership framework that affirms Indigenous identity while enabling active engagement with broader societal systems.

The origins of 'Strong Like Two People' can be traced to the broader context of Indigenous resilience in Canada. The Tłı̨chǫ̀ people, like many Indigenous nations, have faced colonial disruptions, including the residential school system, systemic marginalisation and the imposition of Eurocentric governance structures. These challenges necessitated an approach that would allow Indigenous individuals to succeed within Western institutions while remaining grounded in their cultural identity. Elizabeth Mackenzie, as an elder and educator,

Mosaic Leadership: African, Asian, Middle Eastern and Indigenous Perspectives, First Edition. Edited by Jonathan Passmore, Badri Bajaj, and Mongezi C Makhalima.

Published 2026 by John Wiley & Sons Ltd.

understood the importance of ensuring that young people did not feel forced to choose between their heritage and the demands of the modern world. Instead, she advocated for an integrative approach, where individuals could develop the skills and knowledge to walk confidently in both spheres.

Central to this idea is a perspective that Indigenous knowledge and Western knowledge are not inherently oppositional but can be complementary. Traditional Tłı̨chǫ̀ teachings emphasise relational leadership, land-based knowledge, storytelling and collective decision-making. These elements contribute to a holistic understanding of leadership that prioritises community well-being, sustainability and long-term vision. In contrast, Western education and governance often emphasise formal qualifications, bureaucratic structures and economic imperatives. The challenge, then, is not to privilege one over the other but to integrate the strengths of both in ways that support individual and collective flourishing.

The essential ingredients of the approach can be understood through its emphasis on cultural continuity, adaptability and ethical responsibility. Cultural continuity ensures that Tłı̨chǫ̀ traditions, language and values remain central to leadership practices. This includes the role of elders in transmitting knowledge, the importance of land-based learning and the ethical responsibilities leaders hold towards future generations. Adaptability is equally crucial, as it acknowledges the dynamic nature of leadership in an evolving world. This does not mean assimilating into Western norms but rather strategically engaging with them while maintaining cultural integrity. Ethical responsibility underpins the entire framework, requiring leaders to act in ways that honour both their cultural heritage and their obligations to the broader society in which they operate.

One of the most compelling aspects of 'Strong Like Two People' is its emphasis on intergenerational learning. Leadership development within this framework does not occur in isolation but is nurtured through relationships between elders and younger generations. Storytelling is a fundamental method through which leadership lessons are imparted, as narratives carry the collective wisdom of the community. Unlike Western models that often emphasise individual ambition and competition, Tłı̨chǫ̀ leadership is inherently communal, reinforcing the idea that a leader's success is measured by the well-being of their people.

This approach has been increasingly recognised as a viable model for leadership beyond Indigenous contexts. The ability to hold multiple perspectives and integrate diverse knowledge systems is a valuable skill in an era of globalisation, environmental crises and complex social challenges. As researchers such as Battiste (2013) have noted, Indigenous epistemologies offer insights that can enhance our thinking by prioritising relational accountability and holistic thinking. 'Strong Like Two People' aligns with these broader movements towards decolonial and inclusive leadership models, providing a pathway for Indigenous and non-Indigenous leaders alike to engage with complexity in meaningful ways.

The implementation of this philosophy within governance structures, particularly through the Tłı̨chǫ Agreement, further illustrates its practical relevance. The Tłı̨chǫ Nation's self-government framework embodies the principles of 'Strong Like Two People' by ensuring that traditional laws and governance practices inform decision-making while also engaging with Canadian legal and political institutions. This has created a governance model that is both culturally affirming and functionally effective, demonstrating that Indigenous leadership rooted in tradition can operate successfully within contemporary political landscapes.

In educational settings, 'Strong Like Two People' has shaped curriculum development, ensuring that Indigenous students do not experience an epistemic disconnect between their schooling and their cultural identity. Programmes that incorporate land-based learning, Indigenous languages and elders' teachings exemplify how this framework can be operationalised. The goal is not merely to teach Indigenous content but to foster an approach to learning that respects and integrates Indigenous ways of knowing.

How to Apply It

Applying the principles of 'Strong Like Two People' to contemporary leadership development requires intentionality, structural support and a commitment to decolonial practice. In practical terms, this means creating spaces where Indigenous knowledge systems are valued and integrated into leadership training, whether in Indigenous governance, educational institutions or broader professional contexts. Leadership programmes must move beyond tokenistic inclusion of Indigenous perspectives and instead embed them as foundational elements of learning and practice.

One of the most effective ways to apply this approach is through mentorship and intergenerational knowledge sharing. Leadership development programmes should facilitate relationships between elders and emerging leaders, ensuring that learning occurs within the context of cultural transmission. This can be formalised through mentorship initiatives, but it should also be recognised as a community responsibility rather than merely an institutional function. By embedding storytelling and relational leadership into training programmes, future leaders develop not only technical skills but also the ethical and cultural grounding necessary for meaningful leadership.

Education remains a crucial area for applying this approach. Schools and universities can adopt policies that affirm Indigenous knowledge systems, including land-based education initiatives and curriculum co-designed with Indigenous communities. For non-Indigenous learners, engaging with this model provides an opportunity to cultivate cultural humility and a more nuanced understanding of leadership that transcends individualistic and hierarchical paradigms.

Organisational and institutional leadership can also benefit from this approach by fostering environments where multiple ways of knowing are valued. This might involve creating governance structures that incorporate Indigenous decision-making processes, ensuring that Indigenous voices are present at leadership tables and developing policies that prioritise relational accountability over purely transactional leadership models. Businesses, for example, can apply these principles by integrating Indigenous ethical frameworks into corporate governance, particularly in sectors such as environmental stewardship, resource management and social entrepreneurship.

The relevance of this approach extends beyond Indigenous contexts, offering insights into how leadership can be reimagined in a world facing ecological, social and political crises. By embracing the strengths of multiple knowledge systems, leaders can cultivate a more holistic, inclusive and sustainable approach to decision-making. This framework is not simply about Indigenous leadership; it is about the future of leadership itself, demonstrating that resilience, adaptability and ethical responsibility are crucial for addressing contemporary challenges.

Applying approaches such as this can be acts of decolonisation, challenging the dominance of Western paradigms and affirming the legitimacy and value of Indigenous knowledge. As more institutions and individuals recognise the importance of this approach, there is potential for transformative change that benefits both Indigenous communities and the wider world.

Conclusion

'Strong Like Two People' provides a transformative model of leadership that integrates Indigenous and Western knowledge systems, fostering adaptability and ethical responsibility. By embedding this framework in education, governance and organisations, leaders can create inclusive, resilient communities that honour cultural heritage while effectively engaging with contemporary challenges.

References

Battiste, M. (2013). *Decolonizing education: Nourishing the learning spirit.* Vancouver: UBC Press.

Bruneau, J. (2018) *Strong like two people.* Cited in Recognition and Implementation of Rights Framework. Retrieved on 20th January 2024 from https://tlicho.ca/news/recognition-and-implementation-indigenous-rights-framework

Mackenzie, E (2019). *Strong like two people.* Cited in Community Services Agency Report. Retrieved on 20th December 2024 from https://tlichocommunityservicesagency.ca/wp-content/uploads/2019/09/1.1-Vision-Statement.pdf

36

Indigenous Leadership, Partnerships and Other Ships in the Night

Mark Rose

Indigenous Strategy and Innovation, Deakin University, Victoria, Australia

The Big Idea—The Ancestral Mandate

The sphere of leadership and leadership development has become a veritable pop industry. Glitzy-styled programmes, literature and pop stars litter the landscape and pervade our lives in every single way. All of us are caught up in the vortex of leadership development in some way, but for those of us of Indigenous heritage, sons and daughters of the Dreaming, there is trepidation that leadership development is an extension of the colonial heel.

Colonialism is by its insidious nature a 'shape-shifting virus' with its virulence reflected in its ability to morph and disguise itself with a hegemonic pull. European colonial endeavour of the 18th century and the 19th century was far from an exacting science and was predicated upon a simple formula. These were to ***disrupt*** social and family structures, ***dismantle*** language and cultural constructs, ***disturb*** life and being and ***diminish*** enterprise. As one born under the Aborigines Protection Act, the impact of disruption, disturbance, diminishment and dismantlement crosses generations to this day. In fulfilment of my Ancestral mandate, I deal with leadership development across Indigenous communities in Australia and across the globe. My work is predicated on three Aboriginal principles: 'Respect', 'Proper Way' and 'Both Ways'.

Calling young Indigenous people to their Ancestral mandate requires strategic and nuanced leadership principles that have evolved from centralised neo-colonial propositions. In the most unequivocal

Mosaic Leadership: African, Asian, Middle Eastern and Indigenous Perspectives, First Edition. Edited by Jonathan Passmore, Badri Bajaj, and Mongezi C Makhalima.

Published 2026 by John Wiley & Sons Ltd.

of terms, a graduate with a world-class MBA looks and sounds nothing like an Aboriginal and Torres Strait Islander leader. Indigenous leadership comes from within and is predicated on an ancient ancestral lineage. Simply put, we as First Peoples are humankind's oldest living continuous culture and consequently are also the oldest living intellectual tradition in which leadership continues as a central plank. Why would we ever want to surrender that tradition for the pop trade in Western leadership? Within many Western leadership constructs, be they Eurocentric or Turtle Island-centric, their vestiges are often disguised. Their programmatic architecture and methodology often focus more on the choreography of leadership rather than the igniting of the cultural leadership gene that catalyses the leader from within. Modern forms of leadership philosophy, be they authentic or adaptive, are edging towards these Indigenous principles, but fall short of nailing it.

The Aboriginal principle of 'Respect' is the basis of any Indigenous exchange across the lands. 'Respect' revolves around the inherent value and dignity of all people and knowledge. The notion of 'Proper Way' relates to Aboriginal knowledge and education philosophy. In the Aboriginal lore of knowledge exchange, the teacher becomes the learner and the learner becomes the teacher. It is a seamless egalitarian exchange based on relationship not transaction, removing hierarchy and power from the interaction. The third foundation is the notion of 'Both Ways' education, developed at Batchelor Institute of Indigenous Education in Darwin in the 1970s. It has subsequently and heavily informed the rise of the Blak Academy across the nation.

'Both Ways' education is perhaps the most complex of the three because it does send warning flares of potential assimilation, particularly for those who don't fully understand it. 'Both Ways' does not surrender our constructs, nor does it reconcile and forgive the past, but what it does do is equip Aboriginal and Torres Strait Islander peoples with tools to progress the cause as 'Warriors in the Boardroom'. The participants come to know that data and narrative are their new spear and shield. The architects of 'Both Ways' were fully cognisant that education can be both an oppressor and a liberator. What they essentially espoused was what Noel Pearson refers to as 'bi-cultural competency'. While we will never cede sovereignty as people, in the vein of guerrilla warriors, we need to understand the working mechanisms of the occupiers in whatever form they take. This leaves an enduring question of how much and in what way do we acquire the skill set and acumen of the other.

For our young Indigenous people today in Australia, the future is bright but fraught with contradictions, hidden traps and a subliminal fear that we could complete the colonisers' work, if we are not careful. Our work constantly reminds participants that while they may be on the Main Street, the majority of our people in this country reside on the Struggle Street, with social indicators of third-world standards. They are constantly reminded that the ways of the West are seductive. We recognise the privileged positions we hold and our place in them as part of the long war and not a short war.

The best example of this comes from my own teaching career. For over two decades, much of my work was delivering leadership as part of MBA programmes in Southeast Asia for an Australian university. My epiphany came one day when I realised that I was teaching business to the best businesspeople in the world, the Chinese. While my colleagues would start their lessons with this is 'the way you do it', I would acknowledge that if you can do something in a Chinese way, then do it, but if you want to know how the West thinks in business, then listen to this. This shifted the paradigm and ensured I was not yet another educational coloniser. It is this concept that sits at the base of the Executive Indigenous Leaders Program (EILP). This paradigmatic nuance elevates the cultural compass for Aboriginal and Torres Strait Islander leadership development.

How to Apply It

The EILP at the Australian Graduate School of Management, like many great initiatives, had its genesis in a coffee shop in Sydney. An invitation from the University of New South Wales (UNSW) was initially met by me with 'Not another bloody leadership program!' From this starting point, I met with a dynamic educator and consummate professional, Eva Friedman. Eva listened attentively, and we found ourselves espousing many of the principles of leadership development that we did not like. We then dreamed of what one could look like. The principle of 'Both Ways' was easily translatable into a concept of 'walking in two worlds', which can be best explained as delivering the best of Indigenous and the best of Western knowledge.

Part of walking in two worlds means that we need to expunge the deficit notion often inherent in equity programmes. We simply argue that the participants are here for a reason, an Ancestral mandate that they carry, and as Indigenous people, they bring more to the workplace than what they take. The role they occupy is not an accident or coincidence because it is their Ancestors that have called them to leadership. The EILP aims to ground the participants culturally while also developing professional skills.

It was through the leadership and imagination of Eva Friedman that the University of New South Wales went to a courageous place professionally. The challenge was for the nation's leading management school to allow Indigenous culture to sit side by side with Western knowledge, with probity and integrity for both. Many institutions across the nation claim they do this; however, the EILP really does. In 2025, they will deliver the programme to the ninth intake of participants.

Our delivery architecture includes five modules, with one online over 12 months, earning two MBA subjects. The five modules included leadership from both a Western and Indigenous perspective, strategy, open mindset and creativity, resulting in an applicable strategic challenge with workplace and community implications. The point of differentiation is that the programme has been imbued with the principles of 'Respect', 'Proper Way' and 'Both Ways'. Programme participants are Aboriginal and Torres Strait Islander corporate executives from elite corporate, sporting, mining, government and community organisations. All participants are at various points on their cultural and professional journeys. We go to great lengths to reinforce the deep Indigenous inherent values in the learning contexts of the classroom, online or on country. One transformational piece of the delivery is by reflecting through 'Deep Listening' complex managerial and leadership principles and then deconstructing them 'on Country as blakfullas' in the way of their elders and ancestors.

A phenomenon that we were particularly proud of, after the first intake returned to their workplaces, was that their direct managers were so impressed with the transformation they saw that they themselves signed up and became the second cohort. One of the principles that we insisted on was that, unlike a cookie cutter model that spits their participants out at the end of the programme, our participants become part of an ongoing community of practice called 'New Tracks'. Every year, 'New Tracks' convenes around a particular theme, a think tank, Black Shark Tank or as a business or enterprise incubator.

The EILP has come to be regarded as the nation's elite programme and has been recognised with a global teaching award from the

European Foundation for Management Development (EFMD). We never lose focus on why we work in this way. We work to liberate our people by igniting each participant's Ancestral mandate.

Conclusion

As the first generation of Aboriginal and Torres Strait Islander peoples afforded a full education beyond Grade 6, much has been given and much is expected. The principles of 'Respect', 'Proper Way' and 'Both Ways' are our guiding star. We will not rest until our people are fully emancipated, as part of our ancestral mandate.

37

Yup'ik

Rose Domnick

Nuyalnguq Training & Consulting, Bethel, Alaska, USA

The Big Idea

To be Yup'ik means to be a real human being. It is what we called ourselves prior to Western contact. It is such a huge word loaded with such deep meaning that you can only internalise when you are raised to be a human being in the way of our ancestors. The word Yua is a base for Yup'ik, it translates to spirit, spiritual essence. I recall as a child how my grandmother or my parents would tell me 'Yuunrituten'—they reminded me that I was not behaving as a human being. I heard this when I misbehaved, being mean to my siblings or others, not properly caring for others in the community or not living up to the teachings that our ancestors have followed for generations upon generations. These teachings were gifted to us by the creator to teach us how to be a good human being.

The first learnings of how to be a good human being are taught from birth. I use the phrase 'first learnings' because it is the closest translation from our Yup'ik language. They include Unconditional Love, as in expressive, selfless acts of caring for other human beings without any condition. This was followed by Service. Lessons nurtured our obligation to serve others. Service means to help and care for another human being in a way that is fulfilling to both the person receiving help and the helper. Being of service, we are taught, is the right way to treat others. The next learning is Generosity. Being generous is to have the ability to share without the expectation of gaining anything in return. The lesson nurtures the ability to give to and share with the less fortunate so that everyone is cared for.

Mosaic Leadership: African, Asian, Middle Eastern and Indigenous Perspectives, First Edition. Edited by Jonathan Passmore, Badri Bajaj, and Mongezi C Makhalima.

Published 2026 by John Wiley & Sons Ltd.

The first learnings included Humility. To be humble is the ability to see yourself as someone who is no better than another who may not be as fortunate as you are. A humble person is able to value the elders, widows and orphans, or others who are unable to care for themselves. These learnings teach us to focus on others' needs above our own, to be committed and willing to give of ourselves so that we are capable of taking care of our family and our community as well as the world around us. These virtues can be difficult for human beings to live by but are foundational to the well-being of the community. For this reason, the learnings were, by design, taught effectively as a way of life.

Another important learning included in the teachings of skill of Awareness. This is the learning of how to be mindful and purposeful. It includes how to take care of our body, mind, heart and spirit. Our word for this is Calricaraq, in essence, it is a way we achieve a healthy, balanced life physically, mentally, emotionally and spiritually. It encompasses our beliefs, values, teachings, traditions, rituals, ceremonies and our way of life which together result in producing a good human being.

When we are taught Calricaraq, we come to understand several things. These include understanding that:

- All aspects of life are interconnected.
- The whole of creation has a purpose.
- Our way of life is guided by knowledge and wisdom to help us to live a healthy life taking care of ourselves, others and the world around us.
- Self-awareness of our whole being enables us to seek and maintain balance for health, well-being and more.
- Self-control allows us to influence the balance and well-being around us.
- Calricaraq was designed for us to be fully internalised for us to live by and more importantly to pass on to each successive generation.

How to Apply It

We are taught that our elders are highly respected. We spend time and listen to them as we serve and care for them. They are the ones who teach us from the perspective of deep wisdom and knowledge. They teach us from a place that fully understands the outcome of experience and lessons learned. When they teach and talk to us, it is from a place of unconditional love. They fully understand that a young or youthful mind will be open and hungry and will internalise these teachings when done in an approach using love, generosity, kindness, patience, respect and empathy. We learn that our elders are our best teachers.

We are taught that we should not question why we learn the teachings of our way of life. This instills faith and fosters a belief in following the teachings regardless of why these ways are taught. We begin to see the positive outcomes of following the teachings in ourselves and all around us.

When we follow the teachings, we see that it results in balance and well-being for ourselves and others around us. It results in good relationships, happiness, peace and a long fruitful life. When we follow our own personal way, we are often selfish, thoughtless and mindless. Our elders tell us that when we ignore Calricaraq, we are forging a path that is made of hardship, grief, stress and ultimately death.

Making our choices in everyday life, whether it is following the ancient teachings or direction set by our own mind, we inevitably begin to see the outcome of each choice. Awareness of these outcomes results in gaining wisdom, knowledge and understanding to help guide us in being a good human being.

Conclusion

We are taught that our way of life was gifted to us by our Creator. These ways are inclusive of all the attributes of the Creator: love, generosity, kindness, respect, patience, non-judgement and empathy. Our ways teach us how to be as balanced and well as the natural laws of life allow. We are taught that the teachings in our culture are not made by human beings. As such, it is the right way to be, a good way to be. The way of our ancestors is complete. It is everything we need to guide us to live a good, fulfilling life and to be a good human being.

Our elders have taught us that a person who is taught our way of life, who knows our values, rituals and ceremonies will grow up to be knowledgeable, smart, aware, mindful, purposeful, intuitive and capable of dreaming. The person that lives in this way is visionary. They are capable of guiding others.

Our way of life intentionally produces good leaders. We believe that the attributes, knowledge and skills gained in the first learnings and living in balance are fundamental for strong leadership. Leadership, like other things, is shared, carefully considered, compassionate and supports the balance in the community. The teachings described here support the skills and knowledge required of everyone whether you are an elder, a parent/grandparent, a skilled hunter and provider, a shaman or healer. Those that diligently pursue the path of being a good human being rise to leadership because they engender the confidence and respect that others want to follow. Our ways teach us and empower us all to be good leaders. We do this by being a good human being and practising our teachings in every aspect of living every day of our lives.

Further Reading

https://unpblog.com/2018/04/18/a-language-of-love-new-editions-of-yupik-wisdom/

https://www.yupikscience.org/index.html

http://www.calistaeducation.org/featured-books.html

https://learninglab.si.edu/collections/the-yupik-people-and-their-culture/xod4NAt5dGj7uNPy

https://alaskapublic.org/news/2016-10-04/ykhcs-calricaraq-gains-national-recognition-and-is-invited-to-receive-honoring-nations-award

Section 3

Looking Forward

38

The Relational Worldview

Terry L. Cross

National Indian Child Welfare Association, Portland, Oregon, USA

Introduction

This chapter describes the relational worldview of Indigenous peoples, as well as how the indigenous ways of knowing inherent in this worldview can and are being employed in the Relational Worldview Model™ (Cross & Kastelic, 2021), developed by the National Indian Child Welfare Association (NICWA) to guide its work in supporting and developing Native programs. This work is an example of decolonisation.

The colonisation of Indigenous nations has been ongoing since Christopher Columbus sailed into the Western Hemisphere. For the first three and a half centuries of contact, the balance of military power, the strength of political alliances, a rich economic capacity and deep Indigenous knowledge of the environment kept colonialism at bay. Popular colonial settler myth holds that Europeans dominated from the start. In reality, it was not until early in the 19th century that colonialism began to overwhelm the Indigenous population (Blackhawk, 2023). To achieve their colonial mission, government, business and settler forces employed five intentional strategies (Cross, 2021). Land was taken by trickery, fraud or force. Natural resources were appropriated and used to build the colonial economy. Native nations' governing structures were dismantled and sovereignty subjugated to colonial oversight. Indigenous ways of knowing culture and spirituality were suppressed, labelled as primitive, marginalised and, in many cases, criminalised. Most

Mosaic Leadership: African, Asian, Middle Eastern and Indigenous Perspectives, First Edition. Edited by Jonathan Passmore, Badri Bajaj, and Mongezi C Makhalima.

Published 2026 by John Wiley & Sons Ltd.

devastatingly, the children were taken to residential schools designed to 'kill the Indian, save the man' (Churchill, 2004).

The second colonial settler myth is that this process ended sometime in the early 20th century. The truth is that it is still going on. Colonial settler societies continue to take land and natural resources, limit sovereignty, and take children. The colonisation formula, and the myths that emerged from it, proved devastating but not decisive. Despite the colonisers best efforts, Native nations and peoples in the USA and First Nations in Canada continue to exist and are not only recovering but also thriving. They are thriving, but not as assimilated subjects as planned by colonial societies, but rather, as distinct Indigenous peoples and nations rebuilding their capacities through revitalising their cultures.

If colonisation is a process of taking territory, appropriating natural resources, limiting sovereignty, delegitimising culture and taking children, then decolonising can be described as any process that undoes the wrongful taking, restores that which was taken, or affirms and asserts the pre-colonial integrity of Indigenous territory, resources, governance, ways of knowing or the family. NICWA's work focuses on three of them: strengthening Native governance for self-determined decision-making regarding children; reclaiming Indigenous ways of parenting, keeping children safe and preventing the unwarranted removal of Native children; and using an Indigenous worldview and associated values to help Native organisations and programs thrive.

The Relational Worldview

The relational worldview, as described by Cross et al. (2019), is inherent in Indigenous culture. This worldview understands the human experience as a balance between mind, body, spirit and context (Cross, 1998). The relational worldview contrasts starkly with the linear worldview of European and settler colonial societies. Where the linear worldview has rigid ideas of cause and effect, past, present and future, and analyses through compartmentalising to reduce complexity, the relational worldview is holistic, embraces complexity and understands the world through the synthesis of cycles and patterns. It is fluid and in constant flux. Well-being is dependent on balance among the four aspects of life.

The relational worldview is often illustrated (across various Native nations) as a four-quadrant circle. The relationships between these quadrants are determined by principles. For example, nothing in any single quadrant can change without every other quadrant being affected. Everything matters (Blackstock, 2009). This worldview fosters values that are also in stark contrast to those of the linear worldview. Where the linear worldview values knowledge, the relational values wisdom. Where the linear worldview values individuality, the relational values collective well-being. Where the linear worldview values acquiring wealth, the relational values sharing and generosity. In linear society, time is money. To Indigenous peoples, time is a connection. The most important values within the relational worldview are gratitude, respect, integrity and connection to the natural world.

The description of Indigenous worldview here is intended as a high-level, overarching concept. Each Native or First Nation has a unique culture that is an expression of their worldview. Each has its own rich customs, practices and ceremonial cycles that affirm and celebrate their values. Each has associated teachings that provide guidance on how to live, in health through balance, and a satisfying life through pursuing harmony. This discussion is not intended, and should not be taken, to represent any single Indigenous group. Rather, it presents an amalgamation of different ways of knowing that shares a common underlying worldview.

The relational worldview has historically been applied to individual well-being as a balance between context (relationships and environment), mind (intellect and emotions), body (physical health) and spirit (the spiritual nature of the human experience). For an individual, health or wellness is achieved by maintaining balance among the four quadrants of the circle. The interrelating factors are constantly balancing and rebalancing. The biological concept of homeostasis illustrates the point. However, in the relational worldview, every event or circumstance relates to all other events influencing everything continuously. Health depends on balance. It happens naturally but is enhanced by awareness and intention. As humans, we have the capacity to be aware and to make choices. Thriving is intentional. Harmony is achieved through following cultural teachings and adhering to the highest standards of conduct as laid out by the Nation's customs.

This relational manner of understanding the world, particularly in health care, social service or leadership, is very different from the linear worldview. The linear is dependent on a diagnosis to understand the disease, dysfunction or problem, so that a treatment, intervention or solution can be offered. The relational doesn't ask what's wrong. It asks how balance can be restored. In solving social problems, the linear compartmentalises problem-solving into silos. Relational-oriented societies build collaborative circles of care that address issues holistically (Cross et al., 2000). In leadership, the linear debates what style of leadership is most effective while the relational approach structures leadership to fit the demands of the circumstances (see *Cross*, Chapter 5).

Cause and effect exist in both worldviews. The linear view attempts to isolate a cause on a timeline and conducts experiments to observe the relationships. It uses statistics (i.e. the mathematics of probability) to describe causal relationships. That approach is valuable for testing medicines or developing new technologies, but it has challenges. It tends to create side effects. It results in technologies that may harm as much or more than they help in the long term. Our current climate crisis is a case in point. The relational worldview is valuable in promoting wellness, harmony among people and for carefully weighing future consequences of current action. Many Native cultures teach the value of considering the needs of the seventh generation in the future in every decision today. The challenge of the relational approach is that it is hard to measure and hard for linear societies to understand.

How NICWA Applies the Relational Worldview

During 1990s, NICWA developed its own culturally based approach to community and organisational development, the Relational Worldview (RWV) Model™. NICWA was one of only a few Native-led, self-determined and culturally based organisations engaged in community development at the time. NICWA developed its model in response to witnessing a pattern over decades of linear approaches to child welfare harming Indigenous families, worsening historical trauma and disrupting whole communities. For example, by 1976, one in four Native children was in out-of-home care and 85% were in non-Native homes and institutions (Byler, 1977). Western colonial linear problem-solving approaches brought to Indigenous communities often made matters worse. No solution brought from outside had ever left these communities stronger. NICWA set out to create a holistic model based on their

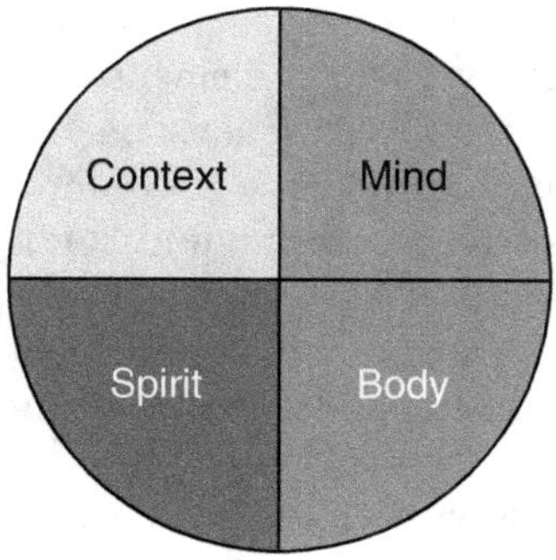

Figure 38.1 The Relational Worldview.

worldview. This decolonised approach has guided NICWA's successful community development work for almost 30 years (Cross, 1998, Cross et al., 2000; Cross & Kastelic, 2021).

NICWA's RWV Model™ uses the four-quadrant relational circle in its organisational model: the body quadrant becomes the resources of the organisation, the mind becomes the infrastructure, the spirit becomes the mission and the context becomes the environment. These four factors represent forces that shape organisational wellness (Figure 38.1).

By the late 1990s, NICWA was using its model to provide community development services to help tribal Nations develop a system of care approaches to children's mental health (Cross et al., 2000). NICWA has since served over 100 Native nations and Native non-profit organisations using its culturally based approach.

Using the relational worldview, NICWA community development staff focus on understanding the organisational balance of those we serve. The helper becomes part of the environment and in so doing begins to impact the balance across the quadrants. The role of the staff is that of the helper, consultant and coach. The work is to assist the community to identify the strengths and challenges that contribute to balance or threaten equilibrium. Approaches do not have to be linear. Relational approaches only need to shift the balance. Interventions can truly be strengths based. Building strengths in any quadrant will change the dynamics in the organisation.

NICWA's community development work begins with conducting a RWV Model™ assessment which helps reveal the elements of environment, infrastructure, resources and mission that lend themselves to critical actions that will promote a desired change.

In conducting scores of such assessments for over more than 25 years, NICWA has identified consistently critical elements. For example, in reviews of Native nation's child welfare departments, alignment of cultural values (mission) with policies, procedures and program design (infrastructure) is critical to community confidence (environment). An RWV Model™ assessment reveals strengths and challenges impacting balance. Staff development needs or stakeholder engagement are also among many factors that influence balance.

NICWA staff illustrate for leaders, service providers and consumers how their own cultural teachings can help strengthen the quality of services. The staff facilitate an organisational development plan that builds on strengths and reduces challenges. Working with leaders, managers, consumers, board and partners, the consultant can influence the organisation environmentally, structurally, through access to resources, and through clarifying mission, vision and values. As a coach, an NICWA staff helps key players identify strategies that are feasible and which are most closely aligned with the cultural values of the community. Organisations begin to thrive by intentionally building strengths and vital habits that promote balance and harmony (Cross and Kastelic, 2021).

Conclusion

One of the most critical aspects of decolonisation is restoring the legitimacy of Indigenous thought. NICWA's Relational Worldview Model™ uses ancient Indigenous wisdom regarding balance and harmony to help Native Nations develop strong programs. Strong Native programs decolonise by helping families reclaim health and safety through balance. This work exemplifies the notion that cultural ways of understanding the world are interdependent with solving challenges. In the relational view of the world, everything matters (Blackstock, 2009).

References

Blackhawk, N. (2023). *The rediscovery of America: Native peoples and the unmaking of U.S. history* (pp. 206). New Haven, CT: Yale University Press.

Blackstock, C. (2009). *When everything matters: Comparing the experiences of First Nations and non-Aboriginal children removed from their families in Nova Scotia from 2003 to 2005* (pp. 35). University of Toronto.

Byler, W. (1977). *The destruction of American Indian families* (pp. 1–11). Association on American Indian Affairs.

Churchill, W. (2004). *Kill the Indian, save the man. The genocidal impact of American Indian residential schools by Ward Churchill* (pp. 14). City Lights Books.

Cross, T. (2021). *Working with substance abusing families in tribal/first nations child welfare* (pp. 190). National Indian Child Welfare Association.

Cross, T., & Kastelic, S. (2021). *The case for strong institutions of governance and cultural match in tribal child welfare.* NICWA.

Cross, T. L. (1998). Understanding family resiliency from a relational world view. In *Resiliency in Native American and immigrant families* (Vol. 2, pp. 143–157).

Cross, T. L. (1997). *Understanding the relational worldview in Indian families.* Pathways Practice Digest 12.4. National Indian Child Welfare Association.

Cross, T. L., Earle, K., Solie, H. E. H., & Manness, K. (2000). *Cultural strengths and challenges in implementing a system of care model in American Indian communities. systems of care: promising practices in children's mental health, 2000 Series* (pp. 62). ERIC.

Cross, T. L., Pewewardy, C., & Smith, A. T. (2019). Restorative education, reconciliation, and healing: Indigenous perspectives on decolonizing leadership education. *New Directions for Student Leadership, 2019*(163), 101–115.

39

The Future of Leadership

Jummy Okoya[1], Dumi Magadlela[2,3], & Jonathan Passmore[4]

[1] *Leadership & Inclusive practices, University of East London, London, UK*
[2] *Founder and CEO: Afrika Coaching, Johannesburg, South Africa*
[3] *Vice Principal: The Coaching Centre (TCC), Cape Town, South Africa*
[4] *Department of Leadership, Organisation and Behaviour, Henley Business School Greenlands Campus, University of Reading, Henley-on-Thames, UK*

Introduction

In the closing chapter of the book, we seek to discuss the emergence of models and frameworks from African, Asian, Middle Eastern and Indigenous people. In truth, these frameworks have existed for thousands or possibly tens of thousands of years. These ideas often pre-date the rise of the US-European hegemony, the 400-year rise and fall of European colonialism and the 100 years of post-colonial dominance of management ideas by North American and European writers.

What this book has set out to explore, in its own way through a multiplicity of voices, ideas and style of presentation, is the belief that emerging and developing leaders should look more broadly to ideas, concepts and frameworks beyond their immediate experience and frames of reference. While many of these ideas were not written down in academic journal papers, books or shared on the conference circuit of North American business school, this does not deny their value as a way of making sense of what leadership is, how it can be developed and how it should be applied.

Mosaic Leadership: African, Asian, Middle Eastern and Indigenous Perspectives, First Edition. Edited by Jonathan Passmore, Badri Bajaj, and Mongezi C Makhalima.

Published 2026 by John Wiley & Sons Ltd.

Where Have We Come From?

To understand the current dominance of Western voices in leadership and management development, we must first consider the historical evolution of leadership theories and frameworks. Leadership development has a long history, but the Western-centric approach largely took hold during the industrial revolution, when Western European nations began formalising organisational leadership to manage factories, armies and colonial enterprises. During this time, the leadership models that emerged were primarily hierarchical, with a top-down approach reflective of military-style leadership. Power and authority rested in the hands of a few, and leaders were viewed as individuals who commanded obedience and executed strategic control.

The works of Frederick Taylor in the early 20th century marked a pivotal moment in the study of leadership and management (Taylor, 1911). Taylor's 'scientific management' approach advocated for increased efficiency through standardisation, task specialisation and command-driven authority. This management model fits well into the capitalist and industrialist context of North America and Europe. Similarly, Henry Ford's administrative theory (Ford, 1926) and Max Weber's bureaucratic theory (Weber, 1904) further entrenched a Western view of leadership as systematic, organised and driven by formal authority.

Throughout the 20th century, the voices of North American and European scholars have continued to dominate the discourse on leadership development. The theories of leadership that emerged during this period—such as trait theory (Allport, 1927), behavioural theory (Lewin, 1935; MacGregor, 1960), contingency theory (Fiedler, 1964) and transformational leadership (Bass, 1990)—were based largely on Western assumptions of individualism, competition and hierarchical control. Trait theory, for instance, suggested that certain individuals possess innate qualities that make them more effective leaders. In contrast, behavioural theories emphasised leadership styles, such as authoritarian, democratic or laissez-faire, focusing on how leaders could influence their followers by adapting their styles to suit.

These early models and approaches reflected the values of the societies in which they were created. Individualism, self-reliance and competition were seen as key traits for successful leadership in the capitalist economies of the West. The 'great man' theory of leadership, which posited that leaders are born with natural abilities to lead, further cemented the idea of exceptional individuals at the top driving organisational success. In this context, leadership was viewed through a lens of power dynamics and competitive advantage, which aligned with the goals of Western imperialism and economic dominance.

As globalisation has accelerated in the post-World War II era, North American and European multinational corporations have become the primary exporters of management practices. The development of business schools, particularly in the USA, institutionalised these Western-centric models of leadership. Harvard, Yale and others have over past decades promoted leadership theories and frameworks that reflected the interests and values of Western, specifically US, capitalism. Some overtly so, others in more subtle ways, such as servant leadership, pioneered by Greenleaf (2003), which emphasised the role of leaders in serving their followers, yet still operated within the philosophical framework of a Western mindset.

With the rise of global capitalism, Western leadership frameworks spread across the world, often displacing local or Indigenous approaches to leadership. This process of intellectual colonisation mirrored the economic and political colonisation that had taken place in previous centuries. In African, Asian and Indigenous communities, local leadership traditions that emphasised community, collective decision-making and the spiritual or cultural dimensions of leadership were often marginalised or dismissed as irrelevant to the modern world of business and management.

This dominance of Western leadership ideas is particularly evident in the widespread use of leadership development programs, corporate training modules and executive coaching models that rely on Western-based theories and frameworks as adopted by global consulting firms from McKinsey to Boston Consulting Group. The standardisation of leadership training programs, which are often exported to countries in the Global South, perpetuates these ideas and the principles of North American and European societies.

However, the growing critique of Western hegemony in leadership studies has led to calls for decolonising leadership development. Scholars argue that the imposition of Western leadership models often overlooks the rich and diverse leadership traditions that exist in non-Western cultures. For instance, African leadership models like Ubuntu, which emphasises community, interconnectedness and mutual care, offer an alternative to the competitive, individualistic models of leadership that dominate Western business schools.

The Colonial Legacy in Leadership

To understand the need for decolonising leadership, it is essential to examine the colonial legacy that has shaped modern leadership theories. Colonialism was not merely a political and economic system; it was also a cultural and ideological project that sought to impose Western values, knowledge systems and ways of being on colonised people. Leadership models emerging from this context were designed to serve the interests of colonial powers, emphasising control, authority and the centralisation of power.

For example, the 'great man' theory of leadership, which emerged in the 19th century, celebrated individualistic, charismatic, and often male leaders who were seen as inherently superior. This theory reflected the values of its time—values that were deeply intertwined with colonialism, patriarchy and capitalism. Similarly, transactional and transformational leadership models, which dominate contemporary leadership discourse, often prioritise efficiency, productivity and goal attainment, reflecting the neoliberal values of the Global North.

These models have been critiqued for their lack of cultural sensitivity and their failure to account for the diverse ways in which leadership is understood and practised in different contexts. By universalising Western notions of leadership, they have marginalised Indigenous and non-Western perspectives, silencing alternative ways of knowing and leading.

In the context of leadership development, decolonisation involves recognising that leadership is not a universal concept and that different cultures have developed their own ways of leading, organising and making decisions. It also means challenging the assumption that Western models of leadership are superior or more effective in all contexts. Instead, it encourages leaders and scholars to engage with alternative leadership models that may be more appropriate for different cultural, social and economic environments.

While Western leadership models have contributed valuable insights into organisational management, they are not the only way to understand leadership. As we look towards the future of leadership development, there is now more than ever a need to acknowledge and engage with non-Western and Indigenous approaches to leadership. These models can offer important lessons that can enrich and expand our understanding of what it means to lead. The process of decolonising leadership development requires a commitment to listening to diverse voices, embracing multiple perspectives, realigning, revitalisation of Indigenous leadership paradigms to more challenges and fostering a more inclusive and equitable approach to leadership.

In the following sections, we will explore where we are now and where the future of leadership development may be headed, with a focus on how models from African, Asian and Indigenous traditions are gaining recognition and being integrated into the global discourse on leadership.

What Does It Mean to Decolonise Leadership?

Decolonising leadership involves challenging the dominance of Western leadership models and creating space for alternative approaches that are rooted in diverse cultural, historical and social contexts. It is a process of unlearning and relearning—of questioning the assumptions, values and practices that underpin traditional leadership theories and of embracing more inclusive, equitable and culturally relevant ways of leading.

At its core, decolonising leadership is about recognising the interconnectedness of all beings and the importance of relationships, community and collective well-being. Many of these models provide an alternative to the individualism and hierarchy that characterise many Western leadership models and instead emphasises collaboration, reciprocity and mutual respect. In effect, many of these models move our thinking from the individual to the system. Decolonising leadership also involves centring the voices and experiences of those who have been marginalised by colonial systems, including Indigenous peoples, women, and communities of colour.

Why Decolonising Leadership Matters

Decolonising leadership is not just about adding diversity but about fundamentally shifting the ways in which leadership is understood and practised. It involves recognising and dismantling oppressive structures, amplifying historically excluded voices and valuing leadership styles that prioritise collective empowerment over individual dominance.

Key Reasons for Decolonisation

1. **Inclusion and Representation:** Traditional leadership structures often exclude women, Indigenous peoples and other historically marginalised groups. Decolonisation fosters inclusivity.
2. **Cultural Relevance:** Leadership models must be contextually appropriate and responsive to diverse cultural values and needs.
3. **Collective Empowerment:** Decolonised leadership values collaboration and shared decision-making over individualistic power dynamics.
4. **Ethical and Sustainable Change:** A leadership approach grounded in decolonisation supports justice, equity and long-term societal well-being.
5. **Enhanced Innovation and Creativity:** Embracing diverse leadership approaches encourages fresh perspectives and solutions to global challenges.

Principles of Decolonised Leadership

1. **Relationality and Interconnectedness:** Many Indigenous and non-Western cultures understand leadership as a relational practice that is deeply embedded in community and context. Decolonised leadership models emphasise the importance of relationships, recognising that leaders are not separated from their communities but are deeply interconnected with them. This perspective challenges the individualism of Western leadership models and instead focuses on collective well-being and mutual support.
2. **Collective Decision-Making:** Decolonised leadership often involves collective decision-making processes that prioritise consensus and inclusivity. Rather than relying on a single leader to make decisions, these models distribute leadership across the community, ensuring that diverse perspectives are heard and valued. This approach challenges the hierarchical nature of traditional leadership models and creates space for more democratic and participatory forms of leadership.
3. **Cultural Relevance and Contextual Sensitivity:** Decolonised leadership models are rooted in the cultural and historical contexts in which they emerge. They recognise that there is no

one-size-fits-all approach to leadership and that effective leadership must be responsive to the specific needs, values and traditions of a given community. This principle challenges the universalising tendencies of Western leadership models and instead emphasises the importance of cultural relevance and contextual sensitivity.

4. **Sustainability and Stewardship:** Many Indigenous leadership models emphasise the importance of sustainability and stewardship, recognising that leaders have a responsibility to care for the future generations and other species, through stewardship of land and resources. This perspective challenges the extractive and exploitative practices that are often associated with Western leadership models and instead promotes a more holistic and long-term approach to leadership.
5. **Healing and Restoration:** Decolonised leadership models often incorporate practices of healing and restoration, recognising the trauma and harm caused by colonial systems. These models prioritise the well-being of individuals and communities, creating space for healing and transformation. This principle challenges the focus on productivity and efficiency that characterises many Western leadership models and instead emphasises the importance of care, compassion and restoration.
6. **Embracing Cultural Humility:** Cultural humility is the practice of recognising and respecting cultural differences without imposing one's own cultural values. Decolonised leadership development emphasises the importance of cultural humility, encouraging leaders to approach cultural differences with curiosity, openness and respect.
7. **Challenging Power Dynamics:** Decolonised leadership development seeks to manage hierarchical power structures through a balance of power distributed among different individuals and groups, creating greater equitable forms of leadership. This involves embracing collaborative, participatory and community-centred approaches to leadership.
8. **Integrating Indigenous Knowledge:** Indigenous knowledge systems offer valuable insights into leadership, sustainability and community-building. Decolonised leadership development integrates Indigenous knowledge into leadership frameworks, recognising the wisdom and practices of Indigenous cultures.
9. **Promoting Social Justice and Addressing Systemic Inequities:** Decolonised leadership development is deeply rooted in the principles of social justice, equipping leaders with

the tools to identify, challenge and dismantle systemic inequities. This approach fosters a commitment to equity, inclusion and justice, ensuring that leadership practices actively work to uplift marginalised communities and create fairer systems. Leaders trained in decolonised frameworks are empowered to recognise and confront discriminatory practices, whether they occur within their organisations or broader societal structures. This might involve advocating for policy changes that promote fairness, implementing inclusive hiring and promotion practices and creating environments where diversity is not only welcomed but celebrated. By addressing systemic inequities, decolonised leadership development ensures that leaders are not only just effective in their roles but also transformative in their impact, driving a meaningful change towards a more just and equitable world.

Practical Steps Towards Decolonising Leadership

To create meaningful change in leadership practices, individuals and organisations must take deliberate and actionable steps towards decolonising leadership. This process requires a commitment to dismantling colonial ideologies and fostering inclusive, equitable and culturally responsive systems. Below are practical steps that can guide this transformative journey:

1. **Critically Examine Existing Leadership Structures:** The first step towards decolonising leadership is to critically assess how colonial ideologies have shaped current leadership practices and decision-making processes. This involves questioning the assumptions, values and norms that underpin traditional leadership models, many of which are rooted in Western, individualistic and hierarchical paradigms. Organisations can conduct audits of their leadership frameworks to identify areas where colonial influences persist, such as in power dynamics, communication styles or performance evaluation criteria. By understanding how these structures perpetuate inequities, leaders can begin to challenge and reimagine them.
2. **Promote Collective Leadership:** Decolonised leadership emphasises collaboration and shared responsibility over

hierarchical control. Organisations can encourage team-based leadership models that prioritise collective decision-making and distribute power more equitably. This might involve creating cross-functional teams, fostering participatory governance structures or implementing consensus-building practices. Collective leadership not only challenges the dominance of individualistic leadership but also creates space for diverse perspectives and voices to contribute to organisational success. By shifting away from top-down approaches, leaders can build more inclusive and resilient systems.

3. **Integrate Indigenous and Marginalised Perspectives:** A key aspect of decolonising leadership is ensuring that leadership training and development programs include non-Western frameworks and voices. This involves actively seeking out and integrating Indigenous knowledge systems, cultural practices, and perspectives from historically marginalised communities. For example, leadership programs might incorporate teachings from Indigenous elders, explore non-Western philosophies such as Ubuntu or Buen Vivir, or highlight case studies of leaders from diverse cultural backgrounds. By centring these perspectives, organisations can create leadership frameworks that are more inclusive, culturally relevant and globally informed.
4. **Adopt Anti-Racist and Anti-Oppressive Policies:** Decolonising leadership requires addressing systemic discrimination and inequities within organisations. This involves adopting anti-racist and anti-oppressive policies that actively challenge biases and barriers in leadership development and hiring practices. Organisations can implement measures such as bias training, equitable recruitment processes and transparent promotion criteria to ensure that underrepresented groups have equal opportunities to lead. Additionally, leaders must be equipped to recognise and address microaggressions, discrimination and other forms of oppression within their teams and organisations. By embedding these principles into policies and practices, organisations can create more just and inclusive leadership environments.
5. **Redefine Leadership Success:** Traditional leadership models often measure success through individual performance metrics, such as profit margins or personal achievements. Decolonised leadership, however, shifts the focus to community and organisational well-being. Leaders should be evaluated based on their ability to foster collaboration, promote equity and contribute to

the collective good. This might involve redefining key performance indicators (KPIs) to include metrics such as team satisfaction, diversity and inclusion outcomes, or social impact. By prioritising collective well-being over individual success, organisations can align their leadership practices with decolonised values.

6. **Create Inclusive Leadership Pipelines:** To ensure that leadership reflects the diversity of the communities it serves, organisations must create inclusive leadership pipelines. This involves providing mentorship, sponsorship and development opportunities for individuals from underrepresented groups. For example, organisations can establish mentorship programs that pair emerging leaders from marginalised backgrounds with experienced mentors or create leadership development initiatives specifically designed to address the unique challenges faced by these groups. Additionally, organisations should actively work to remove barriers to leadership, such as unconscious bias in hiring or lack of access to professional networks. By investing in diverse leadership pipelines, organisations can cultivate a new generation of leaders who bring fresh perspectives and innovative solutions.
7. **Foster Continuous Learning and Unlearning:** Decolonising leadership is an ongoing process that requires continuous learning and unlearning. Leaders must be willing to reflect on their own biases, privileges and assumptions and challenge the colonial ideologies that have shaped their worldview. Organisations can support this process by providing opportunities for leaders to engage in critical dialogue, attend workshops on decolonisation or participate in cultural immersion experiences. Additionally, leaders should be encouraged to seek feedback from their teams and communities, and to use this feedback to inform their growth and development. By fostering a culture of continuous learning, organisations can ensure that their leadership practices remain dynamic, responsive, and inclusive.
8. **Build Partnerships with Marginalised Communities:** Decolonising leadership cannot be achieved in isolation; it requires building meaningful partnerships with marginalised communities. Organisations should collaborate with Indigenous groups, grassroots organisations and other community stakeholders to co-create leadership frameworks that reflect their values and priorities. This might involve consulting with community leaders, inviting them to participate in leadership

training programs or supporting community-led initiatives. By building these partnerships, organisations can ensure that their leadership practices are grounded in the lived experiences and knowledge of the communities they serve.

9. **Advocate for Systemic Change:** Finally, decolonising leadership requires advocating for systemic change at both the organisational and societal levels. Leaders must use their influence to challenge inequitable systems and policies, and to promote more inclusive and just practices. This might involve lobbying for policy changes, supporting social justice movements or using organisational platforms to amplify marginalised voices. By taking a stand against systemic oppression, leaders can contribute to broader efforts to decolonise society and create a more equitable future.

Strategies for Decolonised Leadership Development

1. **Redefining Leadership Competencies:** Traditional leadership competencies often reflect Western values such as individualism, assertiveness and competition. Decolonised leadership development redefines these competencies to include values such as collaboration, empathy and cultural awareness. For example, future leaders might be assessed on their ability to build inclusive teams, navigate cultural differences, and identify and manage across the system in the interests of all stakeholders.
2. **Incorporating Diverse Pedagogies:** Decolonised leadership development incorporates diverse pedagogies that reflect the cultural contexts of participants. This might include storytelling, oral traditions, experiential learning and community-based practices. By using diverse teaching methods, leadership programs can create more inclusive and engaging learning experiences.
3. **Creating Inclusive Learning Environments:** Inclusive learning environments are essential for decolonised leadership development. This involves creating spaces where participants feel safe to share their experiences and perspectives. It also means addressing power dynamics within the learning environment, ensuring that all voices are heard and valued.

4. **Partnering with Indigenous and Marginalised Communities:** Decolonised leadership development involves partnering with Indigenous and marginalised communities to co-create leadership programs. This ensures that leadership frameworks are grounded in the lived experiences and knowledge of these communities. Partnerships might involve collaborating with Indigenous elders, community leaders and cultural practitioners.
5. **Emphasising Reflective Practice:** Reflective practice is a key component of decolonised leadership development. Leaders are encouraged to reflect on their own cultural biases, assumptions and privileges and to consider how this impacts their leadership practices. Reflective practice helps leaders develop greater self-awareness and cultural humility.

The question arises: Could Indigenous leadership models be the missing link in leadership transformation for a world which requires a systemic and collaborative approach. By tapping into the timeless wisdom of Indigenous cultures, these models offer a way to harness collective awareness and translate it into tangible progress. Examples from across the world illustrate the potential of such approaches:

Case Studies in Decolonised Leadership Development

Case Study 1: Banff Centre's Indigenous Leadership Program

In Canada, Indigenous leadership programs have emerged as a powerful example of decolonised leadership development. These programs are designed and led by Indigenous communities, incorporating traditional knowledge, values and practices. For example, the Banff Centre's Indigenous Leadership and Management Development Program focuses on building leadership capacity within Indigenous communities, emphasising cultural identity, community building and sustainability.

Participants in these programs learn to lead in ways that are grounded in Indigenous values, such as reciprocity, respect and interconnectedness. They also gain practical skills in areas such as governance, strategic planning and community development. By centring Indigenous knowledge and practices, these programs challenge colonial leadership paradigms and create more inclusive and culturally relevant frameworks.

The Banff Centre's Indigenous Leadership Programs have empowered numerous leaders who have subsequently applied their enhanced skills and knowledge within various organisations and communities. While specific organisations practicing the Banff Centre's Indigenous Leadership Program are not publicly listed, the Centre's programs are designed to equip Indigenous leaders with the tools necessary to drive positive change in their respective communities and organisations.

Case Study 2: Ubuntu Leadership in South Africa (Desmond & Leah Tutu Legacy Foundation)

Ubuntu, a Nguni Bantu term meaning 'I am because we are', is a philosophy that emphasises interconnectedness, community and mutual respect. In South Africa, Ubuntu has been integrated into leadership development programs as a way to decolonise leadership practices.

Ubuntu leadership programs focus on building relational leadership skills, such as empathy, collaboration and collective decision-making. Leaders are encouraged to prioritise the well-being of their communities and to lead in ways that promote social justice and equity. By incorporating Ubuntu principles, these programs challenge individualistic and hierarchical leadership models and promote more inclusive and community-centred approaches.

One example of an organisation that practices Ubuntu Leadership in South Africa is the Desmond & Leah Tutu Legacy Foundation.

This foundation, inspired by the late Archbishop Desmond Tutu, embraces the philosophy of Ubuntu. It promotes ethical leadership, social justice and reconciliation by fostering a sense of shared humanity and responsibility. Through various programs, the foundation works to uplift marginalised communities, encourage dialogue and empower young leaders with values of compassion, respect and interconnectedness.

Case Study 3: University of Auckland, New Zealand

In higher education, there is a growing movement to decolonise leadership development programs. For example, the University of Auckland in New Zealand has developed a decolonised leadership program for academic leaders. The program incorporates Māori knowledge and practices, emphasising values such as whanaungatanga (relationships), manaakitanga (hospitality) and kaitiakitanga (stewardship).

Participants in the program learn to lead in ways that are culturally responsive and inclusive, recognising the unique cultural context of New Zealand. They also gain skills in areas such as cross-cultural communication, collaborative decision-making and community engagement. By integrating Māori knowledge and practices, the program challenges Western leadership paradigms and creates more inclusive and culturally relevant frameworks.

Case Study 4: Feminist and LGBTQ+ Leadership Models

Feminist and LGBTQ+ leadership models also offer important insights into decolonised leadership. These models challenge the patriarchal and heteronormative values that underpin many traditional leadership theories and instead emphasise collaboration, inclusivity and care. Feminist and queer leaders often prioritise the voices and experiences of marginalised groups, creating space for more diverse and equitable forms of leadership, and are exemplified by initiatives such as AWID (Association for Women's Rights in Development), FRIDA, OUT & EQUAL, and The Astraea Lesbian Foundation for Justice.

Case Study 5: Examples From the African Continent

In Nigeria, the 'Igbo Council of Elders' plays a vital role in conflict resolution and decision-making, drawing on traditional values and wisdom to promote unity and community well-being. Their leadership, based on age, experience and moral authority, makes them highly respected mediators and decision-makers within their communities. They act as neutral arbitrators in disputes, using Igbo proverbs, folklore and ancestral wisdom to facilitate peaceful resolutions through consensus-building and traditional ethics. Upholding and enforcing Igbo customs, they ensure that decisions align with 'Omenala' while addressing modern challenges in a way that honours Igbo heritage.

In governance, the Council advises local leaders such as the 'Igwe', 'Eze' or 'Obi', collectively making decisions on land disputes, marriages and chieftaincy matters, reinforcing democratic principles in traditional leadership. They also promote unity by organising reconciliation ceremonies like the breaking of the kola nut, symbolising peace and hospitality. Their emphasis on restorative justice ensures offenders make amends rather than face harsh punishments, fostering long-term social harmony. As custodians of Igbo spirituality, they consult diviners and priests in critical decisions, ensuring leadership guided by truth (*Eziokwu*), fairness (*Ogu*) and justice (*Ofo*).

The Council embodies the philosophy of communalism—'onye aghana nwanne ya' (let no one be left behind)—ensuring that peace, order and cultural continuity are maintained in Igbo society.

Challenges and Opportunities

While decolonising leadership is essential, several challenges hinder its implementation. One of the primary obstacles is the pervasive influence of Western leadership models, which continue to dominate global discourse and practice. Many organisations and institutions are deeply entrenched in these models, making it difficult to create space for alternative approaches. Additionally, decolonising leadership requires a willingness to confront and unlearn deeply ingrained assumptions and biases, which can be a difficult and uncomfortable process. Resistance to change is a significant barrier, as traditional power structures often resist shifts towards shared leadership. Decolonised leadership development challenges established power structures and paradigms, which can lead to resistance from those who benefit from the status quo. Another challenge is the lack of resources required to develop and implement decolonised leadership programs, including funding, expertise and time. Many organisations may struggle to allocate these resources, limiting their ability to adopt decolonised practices.

Cultural sensitivity is another critical challenge in decolonised leadership development. It requires a deep understanding of diverse cultural contexts, and without proper cultural sensitivity, programs risk perpetuating cultural appropriation or tokenism. Furthermore, many leadership spaces still lack diversity, making it difficult to drive meaningful change. Institutionalised Eurocentrism remains a significant barrier, as leadership education and training continue to be dominated by Western ideologies. Tokenism is another issue, where some institutions adopt superficial diversity initiatives without addressing deeper structural inequalities. Structural inequities within societal and organisational systems also reinforce exclusionary leadership practices, further complicating efforts to decolonise leadership.

Despite these challenges, there are significant opportunities associated with decolonising leadership. By embracing diverse and culturally rooted approaches to leadership, organisations and communities can create more inclusive, equitable and sustainable systems. Decolonised leadership models have the potential to foster greater collaboration, creativity and resilience, as they prioritise relationships, collective well-being and contextual sensitivity. These models challenge the individualism, hierarchy and exploitation that characterise many traditional leadership theories, offering a powerful alternative that aligns with the values of interconnectedness and social justice.

Decolonising leadership is a vital and transformative process that challenges the dominance of Western leadership models and creates space for diverse, inclusive and culturally rooted approaches to leading. By embracing principles such as relationality, collective decision-making, cultural relevance, sustainability and healing, decolonised leadership models offer a pathway to more equitable and inclusive systems. While the process is not without its challenges, it also offers significant opportunities for creating systems that prioritise collaboration, creativity and resilience. As we move forward, it is essential to continue questioning and challenging the assumptions and values that underpin traditional leadership models and to embrace the rich diversity of leadership practices that exist around the world. By doing so, we can cultivate leaders who are not only effective but also culturally aware, socially just and globally inclusive, paving the way for a more equitable and sustainable future.

Decolonised Corporate and Organisational Leadership

Businesses and organisations can integrate decolonised leadership models by:

- **Shifting from Hierarchy to Horizontal Leadership:** Encouraging shared governance, team-led decision-making and participatory leadership structures.
- **Valuing Diverse Knowledge Systems:** Integrating Indigenous and non-Western knowledge into leadership development.
- **Implementing Equity-Based Leadership Policies:** Ensuring leadership pathways are accessible to historically marginalised groups.
- **Redefining Success Metrics:** Moving beyond profit to measure success through community impact and sustainability.

Where Are We Now?

The Importance of Incorporating Indigenous Leadership Development into MBA Programmes

As globalisation continues to shape business practices, there is a growing recognition of the value of diverse leadership models. Indigenous leadership, grounded in communal decision-making, sustainability and ethical governance, offers invaluable insights for modern management. Incorporating Indigenous leadership development into MBA programmes is essential for fostering inclusive, ethical and culturally aware business leaders who can navigate today's complex and interconnected world.

Enhancing Ethical and Sustainable Leadership

Indigenous leadership principles emphasise stewardship, long-term thinking and responsibility to the community rather than short-term profit maximisation. Many Indigenous communities practice leadership models that prioritise balance between economic, social and environmental well-being. For example, the Māori principle of kaitiakitanga (guardianship) in New Zealand and the Native American concept of seventh-generation decision-making stress sustainable resource management for future generations. Integrating these perspectives into MBA curricula can help develop business leaders who are more attuned to ethical responsibility, corporate social responsibility (CSR) and environmental, social, and governance (ESG) principles.

Fostering Inclusive and Collaborative Leadership

Traditional Western leadership models often emphasise hierarchical structures and individual decision-making, while Indigenous leadership focuses on collective governance and consensus-building. Indigenous approaches, such as the African Ubuntu philosophy—'I am because we are'—underscore the importance of relationships, shared success and community-oriented decision-making. By embedding Indigenous leadership frameworks in MBA programmes, business schools can cultivate inclusive leaders who value diversity, collaboration and social impact—essential qualities in an increasingly interconnected and multicultural corporate landscape.

Bridging the Gap Between Indigenous and Corporate Sectors

Many Indigenous communities face economic marginalisation due to historical injustices, limited access to financial resources and exclusion from mainstream business networks. MBA programmes that incorporate Indigenous leadership can play a crucial role in bridging the gap between Indigenous enterprises and the corporate world. By educating future leaders on Indigenous economic models, cooperative businesses and Indigenous-led entrepreneurship, business schools can foster cross-sector partnerships that create equitable economic opportunities. Moreover, business graduates who understand Indigenous governance structures are better equipped to engage respectfully and effectively with Indigenous stakeholders, whether in policy-making, resource management or corporate partnerships.

Strengthening Global and Cross-Cultural Business Competencies

The modern business environment requires leaders who can operate across cultural boundaries. Indigenous leadership teachings encourage a holistic worldview, adaptability and resilience—all crucial traits in international business. Many Indigenous communities emphasise oral traditions, storytelling and intergenerational knowledge transfer, offering unique approaches to problem-solving and strategic thinking. MBA students who learn from these perspectives can develop stronger cross-cultural communication skills, emotional intelligence and a more nuanced understanding of global business dynamics.

Incorporating Indigenous leadership development into MBA programmes is a critical step towards creating ethical, inclusive and globally competent business leaders. By embracing Indigenous values of sustainability, collective leadership and cultural awareness, MBA graduates can navigate the complexities of today's business world with greater responsibility and wisdom. Business schools that integrate these principles will not only enrich their curricula but also contribute to a more just and sustainable global economy.

The Future of Leadership Development: A Global Endeavour

The coming decade requires a different approach. Decolonising methodology requires a shift in thinking from 'individualistic' towards 'collaborative' relationships, from 'transactional' to 'transformational' and 'quarterly performance' time horizons to 'generational' time horizon: a shift in thinking which values one world view over and above others and a shift in thinking and in educational curriculum and education practice from Western to one which includes non-Western knowledge systems, treating all as equally valid and legitimate on their own terms. This involves not only acknowledging the contributions of these systems but also creating space for them to shape research questions, methods and outcomes. In the context of leadership development, this means allowing African, Asian and Indigenous knowledge systems to inform not just the content but also the processes of leadership training, mentoring and assessment.

Some might see this as a rejection of Western models. But this is not our view. It's not a rejection of one set of models in preference for another, but an opening up of a space for alternative histories, perspectives and ways of being and leading. In a globally connected world, we see this is essential for both modern leaders to understand and recognise different ways of leading and more importantly for the next generation of leaders to actively engage with multiple alternative ways of being which extend beyond their personal experience.

Such a step seems radical but is one which we believe starts with every MBA programme in the Global North reflecting, reviewing and adapting its content—not to replace models from the Eurocentric perspective but to present alongside them alternative frameworks and ways of thinking.

To ensure that these alternative perspectives join the curriculum, leadership development programmes must move beyond tokenism and actively engage with the philosophies and practices of non-Western cultures. This could involve redesigning curricula to include case studies and frameworks from African, Asian, Middle Eastern and Indigenous contexts, inviting leaders from these communities to share their experiences and fostering partnerships with organisations that are already practising decolonised leadership. For example, leadership development programmes could incorporate the principles of participatory leadership often found in African and Indigenous governance structures, where decision-making is inclusive, transparent and consensus-driven.

The growing decolonisation movement has important implications for the future of leadership development, not only in terms of the content being taught but also the values that underpin leadership practices. By centring the ideas of African, Asian, Middle

Eastern and Indigenous peoples, leadership development can become more inclusive, socially responsible and responsive to the challenges of the coming decades. These knowledge systems offer rich insights into leadership that are often neglected in Western frameworks, including a focus on collective well-being, relationality and sustainability. As the world faces increasing social, environmental and political challenges, these alternative perspectives can help shape leaders who are better equipped to navigate complex, interconnected global realities.

As leadership development continues to evolve, there is a growing recognition that Western-centric models are insufficient for addressing the diverse needs and challenges of today's globalised world. We need an epistemic shift, advocating for the recognition of multiple ways of knowing and being in the world. This shift is particularly important in leadership development, where the dominance of Western paradigms has often excluded valuable perspectives from the Global South. By embracing the ideas of African, Asian and Indigenous peoples, leadership development can move towards a more pluralistic, inclusive and equitable future.

Conclusion

The decolonisation of leadership development offers a transformative framework for rethinking how leaders are cultivated in an increasingly interconnected and diverse world. By moving away from one-size-fits-all approaches rooted in Western paradigms, this process embraces the richness of global knowledge systems, particularly those of African, Asian, Middle Eastern, Indigenous, and other marginalised communities. Decolonised leadership development fosters inclusive, socially responsible and sustainable practices that are essential for addressing the complex challenges of the 21st century. It equips leaders to navigate multicultural environments, challenge systemic inequities and create spaces where diverse voices are valued and empowered.

At its core, decolonising leadership is about more than just who leads—it is about how leadership is exercised. It requires a shift from hierarchical, exclusionary models to approaches that prioritise collaboration, equity and cultural responsiveness. This transformation demands critical self-reflection, institutional commitment and a willingness to dismantle entrenched systems of power. Leaders must be prepared to confront their own biases, challenge discriminatory practices and advocate for policies that promote fairness and inclusion. By doing so, they can create environments where all members of a community feel seen, heard and valued.

Institutions play a crucial role in this process. By institutionalising transparency, accountability and inclusivity, organisations can create the structures necessary to sustain long-term, equitable development. This includes fostering participatory decision-making, equitable resource distribution and ethical governance. When institutions prioritise these values, they lay the groundwork for leadership that thrives at all levels and reflects the diversity of the communities they serve.

Leadership, however, is not confined to individuals or institutions alone—it is a collective endeavour. From government officials to community leaders and entrepreneurs to educators, everyone has a role to play in guiding societal progress. Meaningful change requires collaboration, with everyone contributing their unique skills, perspectives and efforts. By working together, communities can address complex challenges such as poverty, inequality and environmental degradation, drawing on the wisdom of Indigenous and culturally rooted leadership models. These models, which emphasise interconnectedness, sustainability and collective well-being, offer valuable alternatives to the individualism and hierarchy that dominate traditional frameworks.

To fully realise the potential of decolonised leadership, it is essential to integrate Indigenous knowledge and practices into leadership development programs. This requires a deep understanding of local contexts, traditions and values, as well as a commitment to honouring the wisdom embedded in these systems. Solutions must be tailored to resonate with the specific needs of communities, ensuring that development is both culturally relevant and sustainable. Overcoming institutional resistance to these approaches will require collaboration between traditional leadership structures and modern governance systems, creating hybrid models that blend the strengths of both.

Fostering cross-sectoral partnerships—both within regions and globally—is another critical step. By bringing together governments, businesses, civil society organisations and local communities, these partnerships can leverage resources, expertise and networks to address shared challenges. Global collaborations on issues such as climate change, public health and economic development can benefit from the inclusion of Indigenous perspectives, ensuring that solutions are equitable and sustainable. Similarly, regional partnerships can promote knowledge exchange and solidarity, enabling communities to learn from one another and build on shared experiences.

Ultimately, decolonising leadership development is about creating a future where leadership is inclusive, collaborative and grounded in the values of justice, equity and respect for all. It challenges the dominance of Western paradigms and creates space for diverse ways of knowing, leading and organising. By prioritising inclusivity, equity and cultural relevance, this approach addresses the root causes of inequality and injustice, fostering a more just and sustainable world.

While the journey towards decolonised leadership is not without its challenges, the opportunities for creating more inclusive, equitable and sustainable systems are immense. By critically examining existing structures, promoting collective leadership, integrating diverse perspectives and advocating for systemic change, individuals and organisations can cultivate leaders who are not only effective but also socially just, culturally aware and globally inclusive. Decolonising leadership is not just a necessity—it is a pathway to building a future where all members of society can thrive.

References

Allport, G. W. (1927). Concepts of trait and personality. *Psychological Bulletin 24*(5), 284.

Bass, B. M. (1990). From transactional to transformational leadership: Learning to share the vision. *Organizational Dynamics* 18(3), 19–31.

Fiedler, F. E. (1964). A contingency model of leadership effectiveness. In *Advances in Experimental Social Psychology* (Vol. 1, pp. 149–190). New York: Academic Press.

Ford, H. (1926). Mass production. In: *Encyclopaedia Britannica*, vol. *13*, 821–823.

Greenleaf, R. K. (2003). *The servant-leader within: A transformative path*. Paulist press.

Lewin, K. (1935). *A dynamic theory of personality*. New York, NY: McGraw Hill.

MacGregor, D. (1960). *The human side of enterprise*. New York, NY: McGraw-Hill Book Company, Inc.

Taylor, F. W. (1911). Principles and methods of scientific management. *Journal of Accountancy 12*(3), 3.

Weber, M. (1904). *Die protestantische Ethik und der Geist des Kapitalismus*. Germany.

www.ingramcontent.com/pod-product-compliance
Lightning Source LLC
LaVergne TN
LVHW052250200926
848481LV00002B/323